The Bible Like You Have Never Seen It Before!
(It's been there all along but never realized.)

REINCARNATION
as revealed by the BIBLE

plus...

THE
SEVEN
INCARNATIONS
OF JESUS

Pauline E. Petsel

REINCARNATION

***NEWLY ADDED HELP TO FIND "JUST" THE SEVEN INCARNATIONS OF JESUS.

Read these pages in the exact order listed:

Pages 250-251: "Raised many sons"
Pages 252-260: **MELCHIZEDEK** is God's
 "ONLY BEGOTTEN SON!"
Pages 261-267: Bible verses which "tells" of
 HIM being the
 only begotten son
Pages 247-250: The different incarnations of
 Jesus, **who failed and why**
Pages 231-240: Solomon- good...bad
Pages 242-246: Solomon
Pages 240-241: **RAISING MANY SONS**

copyright © 2024 Pauline E. Petsel
ISBN: 978-1-959700-35-7

Pauline E. Petsel

Reason for this book on Bible Reincarnation

The reason for this book to even come about was something that happened during a Bible study at church. As Jesus spoke, he revealed something I 'picked up on', but yet the rest of the class went on with the rest of the passages. It was such a profound statement that I had to do some Bible searching on my own and what I found was unbelievable. It didn't stop there but went on and continued leading me on even farther, until 'this' book was formed. I was finding out things that were incredible and unbelievable, yet…there it was…right there in my own ' King James version' of the Bible! What I found, is what the Bible is 'supposed to be' about, and it points to many ministers not including the Old Testament in their sermons so are 'missing the whole different ballgame', so to speak! I will reveal a topic most ministers refuse to talk about and are quick to use a certain Bible verse to **prove** 'they' are right! ('I' will use many **more Bible verses** to **'prove' they are WRONG** and will reveal a subject they don't cover. Intrigued? Well, you will have to wait until the last part of the book to see the 'entire story' being revealed. I 'will' say, that 'one' Bible verse with **words 'directly from Jesus own mouth'** mushroomed into a multitude of incarnations of him before he became Jesus!

I have decided to give some 'vocabulary words' that are in both the UNGERS BIBLE DICTIONARY and the WEBSTER'S NEW WORLD COLLEGE DICTIONARY fourth edition. I don't know about you, but I grew up with the thoughts of the Devil being out to get us and doing certain things or believing certain things was 'devil' or 'evil' getting into our mind.

Believing in 'fairies', ghosts, or the like, fell into doing the 'occult things' the BIBLE warned against, and churches preached and embedded the message even more. Talking to 'familiar spirits', 'having anything to do with witches,' 'following false prophets who claimed to do miraculous things' were all things the churches warned against.

I decided to go through each word of the occult type of subject mentioned within the Bible and spell out for us all to have as a reference. THIS BOOK TOOK ON AN ENTIRE NEW DIRECTION than I planned, and now you will be awakened to much more than even I had knowledge of. As I worked on 'one subject', another seemed to

pop up within my mind and I went to that. If it weren't that, when I looked the things up, I got true information FROM MY TWO SOURCES. I would think it was the 'evil side' acting as a false teacher and only 'appearing' on the 'good side'. After all, that is what we've been told.
(Keep in mind of 'one thing': **If it is 'of <u>God</u>', it will make you closer to God.** ...**However, If** <u>it isn't of 'God' but is</u> instead of the 'evil' side, it will lead you <u>'away from'</u> **GOD-like things**. It may <u>seem</u> 'kind' and 'something' <u>you want</u>, but what is the 'end product'? Is it 'for' <u>self</u> or self-satisfaction, or is it the way **GOD 'wants you to be', or 'do' for everyone involved??**(...God-like)

Definitions

When I started looking up words, I chose the ones <u>we have all been</u> **warned against**. '<u>Supposedly</u>', in the Bible, and <u>definitely</u>, 'within the church', where 'masses of fellow people 'get their messages', right or wrong, but believe.
I felt myself trying to be sucked into those words we've been warned about so often... "the Satan and dark side will only be <u>'acting'</u> to be 'telling you' the good but <u>is as a wolf in sheep's clothing</u>." Was <u>I</u> being led astray? However, <u>what I was finding</u> made me '<u>closer</u>' to

God and our creator. What **IF,** all these years, it was the **'messages the churches' gave out and then used wrongly to interpret Bible verses as** <u>warnings</u> **to us to stay away, were the very things** that actually **'kept us back' from being closer to God?'**
With the Unger's Bible dictionary and Websters dictionary as the sources, there will be things to 'boggle your mind' from what YOU thought before!
The 'source' for all things...GOD THE CREATOR! Known by many names with top ones being **Elohim (Divine Power), Jehovah (fullness in power), and Yahweh (As WHO IS / Divine Self Existence).**
Think of it. **The Creator of all things has no background to trace, can't be seen, not usually physically 'heard', hard to believe even exists, yet without 'belief', which is also with no tangible assets, people** <u>have to 'trust'</u> **it exists.**
<u>'Physically' we cannot understand</u>, yet for <u>some reason,</u> there is a <u>'spiritual level'</u> that <u>exists</u>, with a powerful <u>'invisible knowing' of</u> the <u>creator's reality</u>. (Some people go even farther saying that <u>'if' there is a GOD, then</u> there 'must be' a <u>lot of unseen ones too, with</u> each

creating <u>'their own' subjects</u>. People can't seem to believe **ONE creator** could do it all. **Again, we have to depend on the 'unseen messenger' who reveals in the Bible THAT ALL THINGS, SEEN AND UNSEEN, WERE CREATED BY THE ONE GOD! One description of a meaning of God is, "GOD is LOVE!" Isn't it funny, but even that definition can't be seen! You can 'see' what love 'can do', physically,** and you can also 'see' what <u>GOD does 'for' us'</u> in 'our' lives, with physical things taking place but we can't see the tangible 'love'. WE can see the 'outcome from love' when we see the SKY, CLOUDS, STARS, RAIN, SNOW, SEASONS, PLANETS, EARTH, MOUNTAINS, LAKES, STREAMS, OCEANS, PONDS, ROCKS, TREES, and ANIMALS of all kinds on land, sky, and in water. Everywhere you look, you see GOD'S invisible LOVE!

One of the <u>biggest gifts</u> the creator gave us is also one that can't be <u>seen and that is 'free will'.</u> With all the wonderful things created for us to enjoy and use, to provide for our needs, is the **<u>freedom to use each as we wish and develop our own creation from inner thoughts, feelings, emotions, and talents provided within us.</u> WE ARE FREE TO BELIEVE OR NOT TO BELIEVE,** to do good or evil, to live for self, or with or for others. Human beings were created to help us, but it is our choice which direction to go. IT IS OUR 'FREE WILL' WHETHER TO EVEN BELIEVE **IN THE CREATOR OR NOT.**

Angels were created to help us in many ways but even they have free will and whether to stay with the creative force or succumb to self 'Wants' and create a different type of world for themselves 'without the creator's influence'. Those who go on their own for 'selfish purposes' will find others like them and they band together to influence others to try to be the powerful one.
Here is where the various words and their meanings now start, and where YOU will become as amazed as I was, at the 'wrong definitions for words which 'we' thought' were 'negative, sinful things, and to be warned against' are NOT true. "Hang on to your hats"!(Remember the two books being used as sources...**Websters New World College dictionary, fourth edition and the King James 1611 Bible verses themselves will be used.**

Pauline E. Petsel

VOCABULARY WORDS AND THEIR MEANING
WIZARD-magician, conjuror, sorcerer
    -<u>person exceptionally gifted or clever at a special activity</u>
MAGIC   -<u>excellent</u>
    -producing marvelous effects by supernatural or occult powers
OCCULT-<u>Concealed; secret; esoteric; Beyond human understanding</u>
    -Designating, or of, certain arts, studies, practices as magic, alchemy, or astrology with mysterious powers that affect the way of things.
(alchemy- <u>early form of chemistry...changing one thing to another</u>)
WITCHCRAFT<u>-S</u>UPERNATURAL powers <u>by compact with EVIL SPIRIT</u>
SUPERNATURAL- Existing out of the 'normal' existence of man. NOT explainable by the known forces of laws of nature. <u>Attributed to GOD</u> or a god- attributed to ghosts, Spirits, or the occult.
GHOSTS-altered soul; spirit; demon...a disembodied spirit...appearing to the living as pale, shadowy, semblance or <u>inkling memory.</u>
MIRACLE- an event or action that contradicts known scientific laws so thought as

supernatural causes especially to an act of GOD. Remarkable account!
GIFT-<u>The act, power, or tight of giving...A natural ability...talent.</u>
ABILITY-<u>being able or power to do something.</u>
SIN- AN OFFENSE AGAINST God, religion, or good morals

You can see there are words people attribute to the 'evil side' but can 'also be' of God! Too often our churches think of only the evil side and people who are connected to them, but under the 'GOD side' they are held back from being all they could be!
<u>So what did Jesus Himself reveal</u> that brought THIS BOOK <u>'into being'?</u> **John 8: starting with 48 AND ENDING WITH 59 ((KJV) standard) Then I looked up who Abraham was to see who Jesus was referring to. Jesus had just described a life indicating as life before himself as Jesus. (Jesus reincarnated!) It was Melchizedek! (Genesis 14:17-20)**

Pauline E. Petsel

47 He that is of God heareth God's words: ye therefore hear *them* not, because ye are not of God.

48 Then answered the Jews, and said unto him, Say we not well that thou art a Samaritan, and hast a devil?

49 Jesus answered, I have not a devil; but I honour my Father, and ye do dishonour me.

50 And I seek not mine own glory: there is one that seeketh and judgeth.

51 Verily, verily, I say unto you, If a man keep my saying, he shall never see death.

52 Then said the Jews unto him, Now we know that thou hast a devil. Abraham is dead, and the prophets; and thou sayest, If a man keep my saying, he shall never taste of death.

53 Art thou greater than our father Abraham, which is dead? and the prophets are dead: whom makest thou thyself?

54 Jesus answered, If I honour myself, my honour is nothing: it is my Father that honoureth me; of whom ye say, that he is your God:

55 Yet ye have not known him; but I know him: and if I should say, I know him not, I shall be a liar like unto you: but I know him, and keep his saying.

56 Your father Abraham rejoiced to see my day: and he saw *it*, and was glad.

57 Then said the Jews unto him, Thou art not yet fifty years old, and hast thou seen Abraham?

58 Jesus said unto them, Verily, verily, I say unto you, Before Abraham was, I am.

59 Then took they up stones to cast at him: but Jesus hid himself, and went out of the temple, going through the midst of them, and so passed by.

WARNING!

THIS BOOK WILL BE VERY CONTROVERSIAL AND UNLESS YOU PLAN TO ACTUALLY 'READ IT' SO YOU WILL FIND THAT WHAT IS BEING SAID AND <u>IS</u> ACTUALLY being 'REVEALED' WITHIN THE BIBLE ITSELF, DON'T EVEN START THE BOOK!!!!

Mixed in with the Bible 'stories' will be personal examples of actual 'real life, experiences' that fit the same story of the Bible, but in a 'modern day' time. There will be some 'strange, paranormal, and funny things', but also ones with a 'tender' spot at times. By including these, it gives a 'warmer touch' to just reading Bible verses, but it might even awaken a memory of your own which would go along with it, too. The <u>'Bible verses themselves'</u> will be both 'astonishing' and at times seeming 'unbelievable'!

Super Religious church goers, most ministers, even scholars, and in fact most writers of Biblical interpretations will not read beyond a page or two, even if you get that far. (Even finding a publisher who has strong religious views may decline from wanting to edit or publish it. They will have to have an open mind enough for 'reincarnation possibilities' even though they really don't believe it themselves and then 'especially' the part of Jesus reincarnated. So, this book has a lot of 'stumbling blocks' to even get it started.

ABOUT THE AUTHOR

I was born and raised in Cedar Rapids, Iowa as Pauline Elmarie Franks. I married my high school sweetheart, Carl L. Petsel and we lived our married life with our two boys Brian and Vincent in Fairfax, Iowa, until moving to Florida where our daughter, Kristie, was born. Our sixty years of life together was far from dull or uneventful, and over the years of having one thing after another happen, I ended up taking the advice of my friend Phyllis, who was our minister's wife, who kept urging me to write a book.

I started writing about our, what 'I' considered to be 'normal life but somehow 'others' found them to be 'unusual', 'funny', 'strange', 'scary', 'weird', frustrating', 'unbelievable', and then on to a life of 'paranormal'. 'UFO experiences' even got into the 'act'.

(Little did we know that our 'wedding day' wouldn't be just a one- time experience /coincidence but would 'follow us' throughout our life. As we were walking into the church for the marriage ceremony, the weekly air- raid siren went off and we had to return to the minister's office to wait until it was over!)

There might have been another 'clue' for our 'future' life's destination for experiences when another event happened when we went to the hospital to give birth to our first baby. We got to the hospital and the doors were locked with a sign to go to the 'back' entrance. When we got there, the area was under construction, so that door was also locked! There was a wooden plank walkway leading somewhere beyond and ended up at a single doorway with a light on. Carl opened the door and yelled inside, "Is there a way to have a baby around here?!" Success at last, and our first son was born. (All 9 lbs. 8 oz. of him!)

It didn't end there. My water broke in the early seventh month of my pregnancy of our 'second son' and I was told by a 'specialist' that I was going to go into labor and the baby would be born dead! My own doctor said, "Well, there is still a chance," but the specialist said, "No there isn't 'UNLESS' ... 'I' could' hold off with labor for two and a half more weeks." Believe it or not, I stayed in the hospital for 'that time ' plus I stayed another week for 'good measure'. Our son was born and 'he' himself was in the hospital for a month in a special 'isolation' unit where everything for him was done through 'plastic windows' and he <u>couldn't be held</u> until he was able come out.

After that, I guess when things happened, I just took it as part of life and that 'everyone' goes through this stuff. I never saw it as anything except 'just something else that happens in life.' Later when such things as me finding someone who committed suicide, or <u>almost</u> 'getting hit by lightning' '<u>SEVERAL</u>' times, (with one time having it come through our back door and bounced passed me sitting at the table) or 'words typed out on the movie screen' at a theater and apparently 'I' was the only one to see them, I 'started 'wondering' IF my life was 'normal' after all.

I was a lifeguard/swim Instructor, and I developed a course to 'teach babies to swim'. I wrote a book of instructions for doing it, and it went all over the United States, Canada, and beyond. Soon 'Swim instructors' all over the world developed their own classes from the use of my book.

I was a Sunday School teacher, church youth director, private school bus driver, first aid instructor, active in my daughter's baton twirling marching group and my sons' football endeavors, plus was a den mother for their cub scout's troop. With this, also came making

floats for parades. I was an amateur photographer, and even became a hypnotherapist and an ordained 'spiritual' minister.
I had those 'typical embarrassing moments with my kids' as parents everywhere will be able to add their own. When my younger son stopped and treaded water DURING A SWIM <u>'RACE',</u> to inform me, "Hey mom, there's a dime down here," and wasn't about to move until "I", a now embarrassed mother sitting in the stand, had to say ,"Leave it there …SWIM"!
During all these endeavors is when 'my normal life' became 'NOT SO NORMAL' in the 'eyes of those others around me'. Again it wasn't until my minister's wife said that I needed to write a book because <u>NO ONE WOULD BELIEVE ALL THIS STUFF I GET INTO,</u> that I even gave my life a second thought as to writing about it! I couldn't see why she even said that at first, until I started jotting down the different things THAT HAD HAPPENED, and after filling both sides of a page with one list of single topics and THEN ONE…page after page did I realize that I guessed my life WAS 'different' after all.
MY LIFE IS STILL …<u>'NOT'</u> NORMAL! All my books are about those 'unusual, strange, and even 'paranormal' times'. THIS BOOK you will read

REINCARNATION

'TODAY' (or some of you will)...IS NOT THE KIND I USUALLY DO, and, IF IT WEREN'T FOR the ONE BIBLE VERSE DURING A SUNDAY SCHOOL CLASS, <u>IT WOULD NOT BE A kind of BOOK I WOULD HAVE EVER DONE.</u>

Pauline E. Petsel

"WHAT ARE FRIENDS FOR?" Dedication

When I first wrote this book, many years ago, my dedication would have been a little different. It would have been to my husband Carl and my three children Brian, Vincent, and Kristie. While the three children really know nothing about what is in this book, my husband Carl did, and with him being very religious, he was aware of everything going into it. Unfortunately, he would never see the book get published and be ready to defend it,(or 'me') because, after sixty years of marriage, he unexpectedly passed away. He is deeply missed but may he witness the finished book from afar! (OR CLOSE BY, SHOULD HE CHOOSE!)
As usual, it also STILL goes to my three children, Brian, Vincent, and Kristie who have shown me through their 'living the way God wishes people to basically live,' that their pattern is definitely one to follow, (...and, naturally to my 'late husband', Carl.) Over the years I have included all my friends clumped together under 'thanking my friends' in the dedication. THIS TIME I Have THREE 'SPECIAL' PEOPLE I am dedicating THIS book to . I've used two, Phyllis and Poppy, at times, before , but this time along with POPPY I add her husband, Bryne Warrick.

Poppy has been with me through about every one of the 'strange phases' in my life. After marrying Bryne, he too has witnessed my weird unusual, and paranormal experiences and backed me with all my book endeavors. We were with each other in very 'spiritual times and through many religious and spiritual experiences,' so this kind of book is perfect to be dedicated to the TWO of them with thanks for them being who they are.

These dedications for this book in particular have two things connected. Bryne knows the Bible way better than I and almost went into a ministry by becoming a monk. He may not agree with what I'm saying in the book but I 'will be' using verses from the Bible. HOWEVER, HE has access to biblical information I only have part of, so he may be giving us 'more' interesting 'tidbits' by adding information unknown to me. (I will mention those times.)

The other person to dedicate by name this time, rather than just using 'my minister's wife', is Phyllis Rabb, who was the one who talked me into writing books to begin with. Because she too saw all the kinds of experiences I was having in my life and said, "You need to write a book! No one would ever believe all the stuff that happens to you". Well, friends, this is my 'sixteenth' book! Phyllis may not even believe in reincarnation and

Pauline E. Petsel

with 'this book' filled with it, 'she' might be a little sorry she was the reason for me writing books AND then to have 'this particular topic' 'dedicated with her name." (So, don't blame 'her' with its connection).

Letter to the Readers

Every day is a new page of your life. Like throwing dice, you never know what will come up and what fortune you could win. However, like in the movie Forest Gump, "Life is like a box of chocolates, and you don't know what you will get." There are some days you don't like, and in fact may even hate. However, there are funny, happy, and beautiful days, too, which are 'treasures' to hold within the mind.

A lot of times you aren't even aware there is anything different going on in your life, yet when you look back 'many years later', you realize all those days were the 'makings for a book'. Your book! Your 'own' special book. An 'entirely yours book' because <u>you are</u> 'special' and there is 'no one' like you, or ... 'your' book of life.

My life didn't seem that far out of the ordinary but then episodes started popping like popcorn and became like a small snowball rolling down hill and gathering speed, weight, and size. At that point, just as looking through a kaleidoscope, the chips roll around bringing beauty with every twist and turn, and opening a world of change and beauty, IF you allow yourself to notice the changes.

You can 'fight life' or 'embrace it'. Be aware that the 'not so great times' may be the best times because they are trying to teach you some kind of lesson or trying to give you guidance. My life had many phases and this book was in a lifetime of making.

The topic of this book has intrigued you for some reason so there is a thread being woven within you in some way or a 'seed' that is starting to grow for information, experiences, guidance, or to find some way to a kind of 'peace' within. Whatever the reason you have been drawn to it, may you receive a 'positive connection' for your life.

As you make your way through the book, you will see 'misspelled words' everywhere. This is 'not' because I had a bad 'proofreader' but that a lot of the book was 'directly copied' things from the Bible. Sometimes it was the way the language was spoken back in time or how it came out when the people doing the Bible along the way 'just happened' to put it in. (Maybe 'they' had no proofreader or the people didn't know how to spell!) If you want 'perfection' don't read this book...or...the Bible! I even did 'one place' where the words were from the '1611' Bible edition, and boy is 'that' <u>one</u> difficult to have to try to decipher. I found

REINCARNATION

mistakes 'with information' I looked up, with different places having a slightly different definition for things. There are probably 'newer Bibles' or different type Bibles that have had scholars go through and find the mistakes and 'change the words around' to be 'correct ways to say the things, or in 'their eyes and thoughts' anyway.
BUT there 'ARE PLACES WITHIN THE BIBLE ITSELF' which state ...'NOTHING IS TO BE ADDED NOR ANYTHING TAKEN OUT. 'I' can understand this 'firsthand'. I wrote a book called 'Spiritually Yours' but ACTUALLY it was WRITTEN BY THE 'SPIRIT WORLD'. I had my pencil on a paper one day when the darn pen started moving by itself and doing one page after another. I didn't have any time to even think about words being written. There was no punctuation and had many misspelled words, plus probably not with correct grammar. At the end of the book, I had a phenomenal book with a profound message. I put the book out 'exactly with the words the way it was written, (also included an example of what it looked like in the 'handwriting' itself.) People who have read the book are amazed and I get e-mails or phone calls every week or sometimes every day, wanting to 'take over and redo the book and

cover, so it could get the 'publicity it needs'. Some are just merely wanting to have 'me' pay 'them' to do it. The 'point is...YOU DON'T CHANGE WHAT SPIRIT (OR GOD) HAS WRITTEN OR 'SAID'. If these people wanting to 'redo' the book really understood the book, they would not be wanting to 'change' it.
I stay with my King James 'standard' version of the Bible throughout the book, rather than switching different Bibles where 'each' may have different wording.
IN FACT, THERE ARE SO MANY BIBLES CLAIMING THEY ARE STATING THE 'KING JAMES' VERSION BUT ARE ACTUALLY THEIR 'OWN' RENDITION AND INTERPRETATION OF IT, THAT 'PEOPLE' MAY BE SUCCUMBING TO 'FALSE INFORMATION', IN THE 'NAME OF' RELIGION, AND THEY HIDE BEHIND SAYING THEY ARE STATING THE 'KING JAMES SCRITURES'. THE ORIGINAL KING JAMES HAS ACTUALLY HAD TO GO ON THE COMPUTER WITH 'AUTHORIZED' KING JAMES Bible and this is the only source I use.
So with all that being said, 'you the reader' will have to do 'your part' and 'accept it as is, to glean the 'unbelievable at times' information that is directing my way to tell.

      Sincerely, Pauline. E. Petsel

REINCARNATION

TABLE OF CONTENTS

1-Reason for book	3
"WARNING"	12
2-About the author	14
3-What are friends for? ...Dedication	19
4-Letter to the readers	22
5-Table of contents	26
6-Reincarnation removed from the Bible	28
7-Reincarnation makes sense	36
8-Sunday is the Holy Day!	82
9 -World before the world- dinosaurs	89
Dinosaurs	89
Leviathan	94
Titans	103
10—Togetherness	104
Double sexed	104
Hermaphrodite	109
'Made in our image.'	110
TWO Pictures -Coins and	125
Giraffe without spots	127
11-Abraham	135
**PICTURE- blood work	152
12-I AM	154
13-ADAM	187
14-ISAAC	195
15-REBEKAH	202
16-JACOB	206
17-Jacob and Esau- Reincarnation of Cain and Abel?	222
18-JOSHUA	226
19-SOLOMON	231
20-SONS...**IF Y**OU!	247
21-MELCHIZEDEK	252
22-Tie These Together	261
23-Book of ENOCH	270

24-John the Baptist	286
25-John the Baptist a Nazarite	294
26-Seven Facets of Jesus	303
27-Jesus (Miscellaneous)	305
28-Regeneration and BORN AGAIN	315
29-Timeline for death of John the Baptist and Jesus death	350
30-From 'my' own collected thoughts	354
"GOOD 'FER NOTHING!"	368
31-I SHOW YOU A MYSTERY: ANSWER REVEALED!	377
32-God is Love!	406
**PICTURE of 'Love makes the world go 'round'	414
33-Golden Age and Ages	415
34-It's time to put the book to bed	433
35- **PICTURE –"Be Aware of God around US."**	435
36- Thank you/Acknowledgments	437

REINCARNATION REMOVED FROM THE BIBLE

At least forty years ago I had read an article where reincarnation had been removed from the Bible way back in history. I also read there were something **like 27 different Bibles which were used to <u>choose from</u> for the 'final' pick.** I thought that was strange that **one man** chose what 'you and I' would be using to live 'our' lives by. Yes, the part of the Bible we have now is true, **but there were <u>more 'truths'</u>** which were <u>chosen, even in them,</u> **to be blocked** from us. Even though the <u>obvious,</u> **'WHOLE VERSES OF REINCARNATION WERE REMOVED FROM THE BIBLE,** <u>there are still many 'bits and pieces' left in the Bible they didn't realize were there, and 'those' traces reveal a lot.</u>
In 553, the second council of Constantinople, Emperor Justinian and Empress Theodora were chosen to decide what was to be acceptable Christian 'practices' as well as what they were to 'believe', and here became the 'seed of death' for the idea of reincarnation.
Anyone who even 'believed' in this was damned and anyone who tried 'pushing the idea' were

excommunicated from the church. (Boy, am I going to be in trouble!)

The Catholics <u>didn't believe it was a true council</u> and 'refused to remove the existence of the soul'. **THEY became the ROMAN CATHOLIC CHURCH, but the East became the ORTHODOX church with the dividing thoughts continuing to today. (It reminds me of a current disagreement between churches today and even the division between the UNITED METHODIST CHURCH and the now, plain, Methodist church. The 'UMC' has now opened the church to allowing homosexuals and same sex marriage including that they can even become clergy. The 'now' plain Methodists say it is against the Bible and refuse to allow it.**

These thoughts and practices laid also on the minds of 'famous' people of the past. Most of you won't know of them so this is merely 'information' to pass on. St. Justin Martyr during 100-165 A.D. stated his belief that the soul lives through more than one human body, and 'Origen', during 185-254 A.D. was considered being the churches greatest teacher to the apostles by St. Jerome. Moving forward in time, the bishop of Nyssa, St. George Bishop in 257-332 said each soul needs to be purified and if they can't do it during the lifetime they

are in, then they must come back again until it is accomplished. In 350-430, St. Augustine who was one of the Christian churches greatest theologians even believed that the philosopher Plotinus Pilot was the reincarnation of Plato. **Let's move further up in time to 'many other famous people'** <u>**who believed in reincarnation,**</u> **but these will have names many of you 'can' recognize.**
Benjamin Franklin, Voltaire, George Eliot, Goethe, Leo Tolstoy, Henry Ford, Carl Jung, Richard Wagner, Walt Whitman, Mark Twain, David Lloyd George, William Wordsworth, Rudyard Kipling, John Masefield, Thomas Edison, Kahlil Gibran, William Butler Yeats, Gandhi, Edgar Cayce.
To bring you even more famous people who believe in reincarnation and would cause a laugh, look up 'Recent people who believe in reincarnation' (on the internet). Click on the page after page of 'current people' **with 'look alike' of person from back in time. (supposed reincarnation theory). Michael Jackson and President Barac Obama are in the pictures.**
So, it's clear that believing in reincarnation and karma puts us with good company. They seem to touch on things that well-known

people have done in the past including JESUS! They were 'gifts' of the spirit.
The King James Bible has **'hints'** of reincarnation but also has many verses indicating it, showing reincarnation or <u>Karma.</u> I guess I shouldn't worry about 'this' book being 'controversial' as people have argued this for generations and the people will believe what they want to believe.
Hopefully, I might be able to find some small 'truth' (always will be backed by Bible verses and shown in just the right way to bring the 'truth' out for the readers to latch on to.) **I feel I am 'being led' <u>to 'say this or that'</u> and then also 'led' to find the verse to use. (Remember, 'I am keeping my own thoughts out of it' and when I myself find a question that doesn't seem right, somehow the 'Bible verse pops up' with the answer.)**
(I wrote one other 'Spiritual' type BOOK: "Spiritually Yours"... but that one HAD 'SPIRIT WORLD DOING ALL THE WORK WITH 'COMPOSING' AND ALL I DID WAS HOLD A PENCIL!
After the 'Automatic movement' took place ... 'Voila' a book was done and was filled with 'profound' messages. I sure would not have

come up with this kind of a profound message myself.
HOWEVER, 'THIS BOOK' is driving me nuts. I still seems to be given 'messages' and directed, but by 'thoughts' to the Bible verses to use. I never know if that 'thought' was mine or <u>from somewhere else.</u> Then, too, I had questions as to where to put it in the book, as the way it seemed to be made me try to switch locations. THAT really screwed me up and now I'm lost half the time. **SOMEHOW 'THEY' (the powers that be... are painstakingly trying to put me on the right track again. I'm learning the lesson to "LISTEN"... and "OBEY"! (If I would have done it sooner, I would have saved time and much frustration. Maybe I could have even been done already.)**
TWO THINGS... The book will have no indentation for paragraphs because of the type of book it is. Also, the same Bible verses will be repeated at times and so will the 'same' information 'with knowledge' but because people think differently, one way of saying the 'same' thing might finally be 'picked up ' and realized by someone else. **Jesus spoke in parables to the crowds, but the people heard only what 'they' were supposed to hear.**

Pauline E. Petsel

'Some' remembered while **some 'heard it' but then** <u>forgot.</u> Yet, **others got nothing from what he was saying.** REPETITION IS A KEY. So, there will be times when you may feel you read a passage used before, but it is because it also fits with a different angle.

I'm going to put in something of my own here which has nothing to do with reincarnation but does show that 'repetition' is useful. By slipping in an example of a 'real-life experience' from time to time, which sort of goes along with the 'biblical' story, it might help 'some' people to relate easier with the 'spiritual' account.

I devised a swim program to teach 'babies' to swim and my daughter was on the cover swimming to an underwater camera at three months old. I wrote a book with instructions which went over the United States, Canada, and beyond. (Now just 'republished' fifty years later) Swim instructors all over the world used my book to develop swimming classes of their own. The thing is that if a child falls into water they will drown right where they fell in. Although they wouldn't understand 'big people's words' at that age, the **'repetition' of the sound of 'words with the action caused the infant or child to understand. Using this 'repetition method'** I would throw the child up in the air

but instead of catching her, allowed her to go underwater. (The 'falling' caused her to take a breath'. I then turned her around to the wall with the verbal words saying, "GET THE WALL"..., "GET THE WALL". Over and over the 'same words and actions' caused her to do what the 'action' was doing. Soon you could just throw the child in as if falling into the water, "Get the wall...get the wall", and they responded. **Well, when my daughter was three years old, she was carrying around a teddy bear that stunk to high heaven. I couldn't stand it anymore so threw it into the washing machine. Shortly afterward I couldn't find Kristie anywhere and looked all over for her. I listened carefully and got the sound of her small voice and followed it. There she was standing at the washing machine yelling to her teddy bear..."Get the wall Teddy, get the wall!"** If you don't get anything from the whole book, maybe at least you just got a chuckle to make your day!!) Anyway, 'repetition' does serve a purpose. So it may help with this book and when you are aware of me 'having said it before' know that maybe you understood it before but 'this time' it just 'hit home' for someone else.

By 'reading the Bible and paying close attention to what is being revealed' rather than what 'people' are trying to put forward with their 'own beliefs' or even, their own 'religion' wanting to control 'our thoughts and beliefs', may we **all find** the 'truth'!

Yes, I myself believe in reincarnation, but it's 'not' from my church (which I don't know the beliefs in it. If I get 'tarred and feathered when this comes out, I may find 'that' answer!)

My belief came from Bible verses themselves that reveal it. By now, knowing the history of what 'had been' believed from back in history and what is being taught now, one might read the Bible and will look for the verses differently to that place which will point to the truth. Not 'just a verse here and there', **but ones that have a trail to follow**.

YES, "reincarnation "with its advancement from Adam to Jesus....maybe 'that' is the reason for Jesus to want people to pay attention to what is being revealed. 'He' says that it talks about **HIM.** (Everyone takes that to mean 'him', ... as the coming of Jesus)... **But that isn't true! IF you follow the things being revealed**, you will find so much more. **Yes, it IS about** HIM...(many stories)....but...it is **ALSO about** 'other' **INCARNATIONS 'OF' ...' HIM'.**

REINCARNATION MAKES SENSE

Think of you as a parent, or of yourself being raised 'BY <u>your</u>' parents. How many times over your lifetime growing up did you do things you shouldn't have done, or things that were either naughty, distasteful, cruel, wrong, or immoral?

How many times did you lie, cheat, or maybe even steal? Were you 'mean, hurtful' to someone, or did you do any 'other' kinds of things that weren't the right thing to do?

Did your parents give up on you at the earliest age you showed these things, or did they consider your age and teach you a better way to live?

Each age has its 'trials and temptations' and 'an atmosphere for doing wrong.' Do parents give up and get rid of you? No, they work with you to guide you through your wrong doings in various ways, for corrections, to be able to become the best you can be.

GOD IS LOVE. If HE is a loving Father too, wouldn't HE also give you the opportunity to become better so to end up where HE wants everyone to be... with HIM?

Reincarnation/regeneration is that capability

and it is 'up to you' and 'your ability' to change and become better yourself.
(Here is where the BIBLE thumpers grab the verse of the Bible which says, "YOU DIE ONCE AND THEN THE FINAL JUDGEMENT." REVELATION 20:12)
And I saw the dead, the great and the small, standing before the throne, and books were opened; and another book was opened, which is the book of life; AND THE DEAD WERE JUDGED FROM THE THINGS WHICH WERE WRITTEN IN THE 'BOOKS', ACCORDING TO THEIR DEEDS.
So. Here again is the very first thing a lot of people will say is: "THE BIBLE SAYS YOU LIVE ONCE AND THEN YOU DIE. 'THEREFORE', THERE IS NO SUCH THING AS REINCARNATION! ...So, BEFORE THIS BOOK EVEN BEGINS, WE WILL ADDRESS that STATEMENT AND GIVE YOU BACKGROUND ABOUT REINCARNATION.
First of all, the definition of 'reincarnation' in the WEBSTER'S NEW WORLD COLLEGE DICTIONARY (FOURTH EDITION) is, "rebirth of the soul in a different body...a new incarnation or embodiment... a doctrine that the soul reappears after death in another and

different bodily form. (If you notice, it says the word, 'soul'.)

In the UNGER'S BIBLE DICTIONARY, ELEVENTH EDITION BY MOODY BIBLE INSTITUTE OF CHICAGO, the 'SOUL' has many places in the Bible with verses where it can be found. It HAS THE MEANING OF THE SEAT OF FEELINGS, DESIRES, AFFECTIONS, AVERSIONS (HEART, SOUL, ETC.) DESIGNED FOR EVERLASTING LIFE. 3 JOHN 2; HEB 13:17, JAMES 1:2, 15:2-21, PETER 1:9. It says IT IS DIFFERENT FROM THE BODY AND <u>CANNOT BE DISSOLVED BY DEATH.</u> MATT. 10, ACTS 2:27,31.

SPIRIT AND THE SOUL ARE BASICALLY THE SAME THING BUT THERE IS ONE DIFFERENCE, because the SOUL can get 'lost', yet the SPIRIT is of God and is 'always' there. The way a 'soul' gets lost is by going off course for the way a person 'should' be living, and away from what God wishes us to be. In other words, 'allowing one's own wants for things' to take over walking as God would like.

(This brings in that Bible verse about 'living once and then you die' and are judged. You see... THAT 'IS' TRUE! The person you are 'right now' 'WILL' die... and 'YOU' <u>WILL BE</u>

JUDGED as TO HOW 'YOU' LIVED 'that' LIFE... AS 'THAT' PERSON. 'YOU', AS WHO YOU ARE 'right now', will 'NEVER' LIVE AGAIN, but "whatever you did" in this life, YOU WILL PAY FOR IT in some way ...**BUT**... **DURING** a '**DIFFERENT**' incarnation. The 'soul' never dies so it comes again with a 'different body' to learn to do better in the new life. **SAME SOUL** but a different body. So, understand...The SOUL is then given a chance to correct itself and learn and change from what you did wrong before.

THOSE WHO USE THE QUOTE 'LIVE ONCE' will also be 'slightly aware' of one other statement, but they tend to 'pass it by' for they don't understand what it is showing. There is something mentioned called 'FINAL' JUDGEMENT. (If you were already judged at your death, WHY would there be a 'FINAL judgement'? FINAL means you would be judged again...but why would you get judged again for the same thing done so many years before after you die!? (I don't 'think' so.) This is simply one of those 'CLUES' pointing to **LIVING 'ANOTHER' LIFETIME, (or...LIFETIMES!) THIS MAKES SENSE BECAUSE OUR LOVING FATHER IS TRYING TO HELP US BECOME**

REINCARNATION

BETTER PEOPLE, SO WE WOULD BE GIVEN ANOTHER CHANCE BY BEING GIVEN A KIND OF LIFE NEEDED WHERE YOU CAN LEARN, EXPERIENCE, OR GROW AND CORRECT WHAT YOU NEED TO CHANGE: A 'NEW INCARNATION'. This wouldn't just happen once, but AS MANY TIMES AS NEEDED, **until** you might finally get it right. In time for… **THAT … 'FINAL'… JUDGEMENT!**)

Like with our children where you give them chances to learn and grow and so it is with friendships or relatives. No one is perfect, and we need to give some leeway to life's situations, so we don't sit back and punish them or never speak to them again the first time they do something.

THIS FIRST SECTION of the book is going to be used for the MANY EXAMPLES in the BIBLE TO PROVE TO YOU THAT REINCARNATION EXISTS! It's a shame that our 'churches' have led us astray and given us 'false information' to benefit themselves. Because of this, many people have gone astray and many a soul has gotten 'lost'.

You can look up **reincarnation and the Bible** and find **many authors (and even some Bible scholars)** telling you

there is **no such thing as reincarnation because otherwise the Bible would say so**. <u>The 'sum total' of 'what all these people are saying' is that the Bible says that everyone is mortal and our spirits live forever in heaven or hell, and</u> **they stop there.**
THEY WILL NOT MENTION (or don't know) THE FACT **that REINCARNATION 'USED TO BE' IN THE BIBLE** <u>but was **REMOVED FROM CHRISTIAN DOCTRINE DURING THE FIFTH ECUMENICAL COUNCIL IN THE YEAR 553 (ALSO KNOWN AS THE SECOND COUNCIL OF CONSTANTINOPLE.)**</u> THE council released a list of decrees to put an end to the idea of reincarnation, and although there were all kinds of 'reasons' passed around as to why this happened, which ones are true and what's not is unknown for sure. The 'answers' range from 'suggestions' that **Empress Theodora** wanted reincarnation removed from Christianity because she wanted to be deified. Other theories suggest that the **'Church' intentionally removed** all mentions of **reincarnation** from the **Bible and** scrapped all traces during many rewritings and updating of the **Bible. Even some 'stories'** were

intentionally lost. No matter what the reason, the idea of **reincarnation WAS 'REMOVED'**. There was also **Martin Luther** who was **a German monk and theologian, who instigated the protestant movement for change**. Mostly known for **his** released 1522 and 1534 **translation of the Bible into German**, he did make some **changes to the text of the Bible**, but he mainly was trying to make it more available to the Germans. **He believed that this life was simply a series of journeys toward our final destination ,with a 'final outcome' being heaven or hell**. (*Sounds like many lives to me!*) Martin Luther, was born November 10, 1483, in Germany. He was a religious reformer with a big part in the 16th-century **Protestant Reformation. His words and actions gave way to basic various Christian beliefs that ended up dividing Roman Catholicism and the new Protestant traditions** like Calvinism, the Anglican, etc. and **continued to revise his translations until he died in 1546.** (www. Deseret news William Hamblin and Daniel Peterson, Columnists. Aug 18, 2017, 9:00pm EST)

During his time he had 'removed' SEVEN BOOKS from the Bible.

MANY PEOPLE SEEM TO THINK CATHOLICS "ADDED" BOOKS TO THE BIBLE, BUT THEY MERELY PUT BOOKS 'BACK IN' THAT LUTHER TOOK OUT. (Luther *removed* seven entire books plus 'parts' of THREE others and '<u>all</u>' because '<u>they' didn't fit 'HIS IDEA' of</u> "what God really wanted". HE FELT they celebrated Judaism and 'HE wanted a reason to prove 'his own' authority of the 'Catholic Church'. So he just 'threw them out'. In fact, HIS first 'German translation was' missing 25 books! (i.e., Genesis, Exodus, Leviticus, Numbers, Deuteronomy, Esther, Job, Ecclesiastes, Jonah, Tobias, Judith, Wisdom, Sirach (i.e., Ecclesiasticus), Baruch, 1 and 2 Maccabees, Matthew, Luke, John, Acts, Romans, Hebrews, James, Jude, and Revelation)
(***<u>You Bible readers</u>, what do YOU think about these books being gone? WHAT do YOU <u>read</u>?) Protestants, deciding that Luther wasn't *really* inspired by the Holy Spirit, <u>replaced most of the books he had removed.</u>

Remember, ALL these changes to the Bible are BY 'PEOPLE' and are keeping YOU AND I from knowing the truths.
It seems, that like with 'everything' there are many views, and while THIS BOOK of mine will **NOT BE a Bible study, it will instead** show you that by using BIBLE VERSES themselves, there **IS REINCARNATION. WE HAVE** lived and **WILL** live, other lives.
IF it would be just a 'concept' of what each person 'believes', it really wouldn't matter. HOWEVER, **REINCARNATION is MORE THAN THAT! How a person lives and what they do, as well as how they treat others 'determines' the life you will be given to live with the next time around.** If you did something 'really' bad...LOOK OUT! You pay for it in some way, at 'some' time.
Crimes always deserve punishments. (I wonder what lives all those people who have taken things from our Bibles and thrown 'us' astray, will be, coming back as?)
(I will insert here that there were other books taken out of the Bible too but at

least got listed close by through something known as the Apocrypha. Some of those books have high importance and do reveal things such as 'other lives', and other important information. **Enoch** is mentioned **in the Bible** itself and who, because of his 'great character' was 'taken up' instead of dying. **Yet the BOOK of 'Enoch' is one of those in the 'Apocrypha' and 'not'** within the Bible. **ENOCH IS A BOOK THAT SHOULD HAVE HIGH PRIORITY. LATER IN HISTORY, THE IMPORTANCE OF ENOCH WAS REALIZED AFTER THE DEAD SEA SCROLLS WERE DISCOVERED.** SO, AGAIN, just CERTAIN 'PEOPLE' (HUMANS)...**made a decision to remove them** FOR their <u>OWN REASONS</u>. (No wonder we have problems reading and understanding the Bible.)

You can see with 'just what has been revealed', that what we read in the Bible is what **we are '<u>ALLOWED</u> to see'**, as **determined '<u>BY A FEW</u>'** who are going by '<u>their</u> own' views!
LUCKILY, THERE ARE SCRIPTURES THAT HAVE 'SLIPPED THROUGH'

REVEALING THE FACT OF REINCARNATION. (?God provided?)

(As you read the Bible, start thinking about what and 'who' **you** are using as the reference for **your** BIBLE study. Are you simply using one person's **'own interpretation' of what the Bible is saying BECAUSE** their view matches what YOU THINK or was a 'recommendation for a source to be used by your denomination BECAUSE it is what 'THEY' think. Depending on the personal reference used, it **can** sway the **'real message', to...or away from...** the Actual TRUTH!

THIS BOOK will be using only **THE 'BIBLE VERSES' themselves** to 'PROVE' THE POINTS I MAKE. (**MY 'OWN' THOUGHTS AND IDEAS ARE 'NOT' USED... unless being stated as such by '***'**)

I use the King James 1611 or standard edition of the Bible as my source. This has been the most recognized Bible used and considered a top in its field. I found something interesting while doing this book. If I 'looked up' something I would state 'KING JAMES VERSION'. I was finding 'OTHER Bibles' were placing ...'THEIR' VIEWS FOR those KING JAMES SCRIPTUIRE VERSES but placed them on the computer 'implying'

it 'WAS' the King James version. You've probably heard about persons paying for some advertisement in order to get placed 'first', so 'seen' first. Well, it's almost that way with all the other Bibles and articles using that "King James version as a 'tie-in' logo to have 'their place' seen.

In fact, there are so many using this feature that at times in order to find the 'AUTHORIZED' King James version, I've had to use second, third, fifth or even more clicks to the 'next computer page' lists, before finding the AUTHORIZED King James version. If all these other Bibles are latching on to the words KING JAMES VERSION to get 'their site' read, it sort of shows how important the King James Bible really IS! Too bad other people take advantage and use it, close at times, like scams just to 'be first' with THEIR 'interpretations' and 'NOT 'what the Bible itself is saying.

The King James Version ((KJV)), also the King James Bible (KJB) and the Authorized Version, is an Early Modern English translation of the Christian Bible for the Church of England, which was commissioned in 1604 and published in 1611 by sponsorship of King James VI and I. The 80

books of the King James Version include 39 books of the Old Testament, 14 books of Apocrypha, and the 27 books of the New Testament.

There have been a lot of famous people over the years who believed in reincarnation and the prestige of most of them makes a 'lot of points' toward the plus side <u>FOR</u> reincarnation.

A belief in rebirth was held by Greek historical figures, as well as in various modern religions... Pythagoras, Socrates, and Plato, Jack London, Napoleon.

Many more famous people's names of believers in reincarnation can be added to make an even longer list than just others having been mentioned. You even may recognize many of them yourself. Gandhi, Friedrich Nietzsche, Albert Schweitzer, Ben Franklin, William Butler Yeats, Voltaire, Kahlil Gibran, John Masefield, Goethe, Leo Tolstoy , Goethe, Mark Twain, Edgar Cayce, Ralph Waldo Emerson, Henry David Thoreau, George Patton, Rudyard Kipling, Thomas Edison, George Elliot, David Lloyd George, Henry Ford, Carl Jung, Richard Wagner, Walt Whitman, William Wordsworth (plus many more). There are other famous people and celebrities who not only believe in reincarnation but believe they knew who they were before, as once mentioned before the internet.

Remember, Reincarnation is a belief that when someone dies, they will be reborn and live a new life as a new living person. Several religions that accept that idea include, Hinduism, Jainism, and Buddhism, so you can see, it shows its belief has been around a long time.

Remember, there have been a lot of famous people over the years who believed in reincarnation and the prestige of most of them makes a 'lot of points' <u>toward</u> the plus side 'FOR' reincarnation.

LET'S LOOK AT THE BIBLE ITSELF. After all, **that is where many of the 'church going' non- believers of reincarnation will be. (Remember… "you die once and ye are judged!" …THEN again, why is there a verse that says "<u>final</u>" judgement !?**

John 5:28-29 (KJV) is a Bible verse that says that **all who are in the graves will hear the voice of Jesus and come forth, either to the resurrection of life or the resurrection of damnation. This makes it seem like when you die you lay in the ground forever until the end**

of time and Final judgement. What a waste of time that could be when 'reincarnations' would be serving a 'positive purpose'. Look at this verse from the BIBLE ITSELF.
(JOHN 3:5 (KJV) "**Jesus answered**, Verily, verily, I say unto thee, <u>Except a man be born of water and of the Spirit, he cannot enter into the kingdom of God.)</u>
<u>**There are Bible places which speak of people coming out of the grave at final judgement**</u>. The word 'grave' in Unger Bible dictionary tells all the ways persons put their people into graves. Depending on the culture, that process was very different. Some even killed their loved pets and placed them with the dead and many put elaborate table settings with food. One culture even buried the persons horses and other favored animals ALIVE so to be used with the deceased. Others built huge coverings and even pyramids and I only covered a few.(***Is this 'revealing' that at final judgement time all the people coming out of the grave are simply 'figuratively speaking' of the 'combination' of all the 'makeups' each person had been and judged for at the time but now at the FINAL JUDGEMENT will be viewed to see what each person did and the accomplishments that have taken place to

see if people were really trying to become better?

Revelation 20:11-13
Then I saw a great white throne and Him who sat upon it from whose presence earth and heaven fled away, and no place was found for them. **And I saw the dead, the great and the small, STANDING BEFORE THE THRONE, AND BOOKS WERE OPENED**; and **ANOTHER BOOK WAS OPENED,** which is the BOOK OF LIFE; and the DEAD WERE JUDGED FROM THE **THINGS WHICH WERE WRITTEN IN THE BOOKS** ACCORDING **TO THEIR DEEDS**. And the SEA GAVE UP THE DEAD which were in it, and DEATH AND HADES GAVE UP THE DEAD WHICH WERE IN THEM; AND THEY WERE JUDGED, EVERY ONE OF THEM ACCORDING TO THEIR DEEDS.

This appears to 'some' to be saying the dead are dead and that is all of it. It appears to be thought that their bodies would be taken from the ground at final judgement. This also was the Bible writers' thoughts at

the time but was NOT all the Bible revealed. 'That' body had died and they, as 'that' person, was dead and to never be alive again. (***Therefore all that food or animals and luxuries buried with them would never, **ever,** be used. And how long did they think that food they buried would last?... 'til' final judgement?!...Ha!)
HOWEVER, THAT **'SOUL'/Spirit had been released at each 'incarnations' death.** The SOUL never dies. **"Then shall the dust return to the earth as it was: and the spirit shall return unto God who gave it." Ecclesiastes 12:7 (KJV)**
This means that WHEN WE DIE, OUR SPIRIT RETURNS TO GOD WHILE OUR BODY ON EARTH DECAYS OR IS DESTROYED. GOD KEEPS OUR SPIRIT WITH HIM UNTIL THE TIME WE ARE RESURRECTED.
The Bible also teaches that the spirit or soul cannot be destroyed and that it will live on after death ."And whosoever liveth and believeth in me shall never die. Believest thou this?" John 11:26 (KJV)
Think, IF REINCARNATION USED TO BE IN THE BIBLE, just taking it out doesn't mean it doesn't exist. (We could take out the

Pauline E. Petsel

GETTYSBURG WAR FROM OUR HISTORY BOOKS so there would be nothing left to say as to if it ever happened. However, it wouldn't mean it didn't.) So even though, with the subject of reincarnation itself removed, **there are plenty of scriptures remaining in the Bible that prove reincarnation exists.**

(*** I have to add something here which personally happened to me and needs to be told. This particular book is way off from what kinds of books I usually do because my usual books are about 'real life experiences' and are of 'strange or even paranormal' things. THIS addition fits both the 'soul' subject being mentioned as well as an experience concerning the same thing. Most people reading the Bible or this book have to use their 'faith' to believe there is a soul. 'I' 'experienced it' and can tell you for a fact…there IS!
One night I was in bed sleeping, when suddenly I woke up and found I was about to fall out of bed. I jerked to put myself back onto the bed **when I discovered, … I was 'already there!** You might be thinking, "Oh she was just dreaming because some dreams do seem real at times." …**But 'this lasted' too long and too much was experienced for 'that.' I saw my body on the bed next to my husband. (You never see yourself from 'behind'**

and that in itself was strange.) The 'other me' was moving toward the body on the bed but was doing so very slowly! YOU WOULD THINK IF SOMETHING 'HAD SEPARATED' THE TWO PARTS, (BODY AND SOUL) WOULD 'SNAP TOGETHER' QUICKLY. THIS WAS NOT THE CASE. THE 'BODY ON THE BED' COULD NOT MOVE UNTIL… THE 'SOUL'… CONNECTED WITH IT. WHILE THE 'SOUL' WAS SLOWLY MOVING TO THE BODY ON THE BED, I HAD THE MOST 'AWESOME FEELING I'VE EVER HAD.' THERE ARE NO WORDS IN THE ENGLISH LANGUAGE TO EVEN COME CLOSE TO THAT FEELING! As I was slowly moving I had the thought come to me "Boy, if THIS is what people who die feel like,…<u>they have got it made! When my soul finally connected to the body on the bed, I could sit up</u>! I wanted to wake up my husband to tell him about it but decided to just let him sleep and instead 'I' sat up experiencing my awesome feeling that was still there. I told my husband about it and for a week when I'd go to bed. I kept saying to Myself, "Body separate …body separate," which I could never do. The thing is, that for even as long as a year, I could strongly actually '<u>feel</u>' what that 'body separation' was like. Even to this day, though it is more vague, it remains strongly there in remembrance. Many, many years later when my husband passed away, I could not grieve for his loss. We had sixty years together, but because of that 'out of body experience', I KNEW what 'feelings' he was enjoying and I could not 'begrudge him' the experience.

Should you think 'out of body' experiences don't happen, I give a Bible verse. 2 Corinthians 12:2 (KJV)..."I knew a man in Christ above fourteen years ago, (**whether in the body, I cannot tell; or whether out of the body, I cannot tell: God knoweth**) such an one caught up to the third heaven." Hopefully by adding to my experience here, it might do 'two things': It might help those people who have lost loved ones to get through their loss, plus it will cement the fact that <u>there IS a soul separate from the body,</u> so 'that saying' of the 'souls/spirit' never dies, is proven.

When the Bible is saying the dead will be taken from the grave, it is merely acknowledging that the ACCOUNT OF what those who died did DURING EACH LIFETIME will be added together in the book of life **to be judged as a whole.**

**Those words FINAL JUDGEMENT SHOULD BE THE ONLY THING YOU NEED TO REALIZE THERE IS MORE THAN ONE LIFE.
However, I will go on a bit further using other examples from the Bible which are showing reincarnation, so it might help again, help to 'cement' the thought into your mind.**

"And as Jesus passed by, he saw a man which was blind from his birth." John 9:1 (KJV)
(In **King James version**) **Jesus and his desciples came upon a man BORN BLIND.** (His own desciples asked him if the man was **born blind** 'because' of **'HIS OWN SIN', or** was it the **sins of 'his parents'**.
https://www.kingjamesbibleonline.org/John-9-39/
Jesus answered, "**Neither hath this man sinned, nor his parents:** but that the works of God should be made manifest in him." John 9:3 (KJV)
This is revealing 'many things'. First, it was the **disciples** who were asking Jesus the question, **so there must have been a 'belief'** that **either of these things could be true**. THEN...if it was from the **man's OWN SIN**, there has to be reincarnation, or how could "**HE**" HAVE **SINNED** to cause it? (*** my

guess about the 'parent sinning and causing it' would be that 'they' had perhaps caused someone to lose their sight at some time so must now experience what type of thing they caused by having to have a life repaying through caring for someone day and night. Perhaps both were paying by being blind, one could be paying for a sin they caused, and was coupled with another who had to pay a different way. Remember 'this' is merely 'my' 'maybe' thoughts.)

Then the scripture says, "Jesus says it was neither of these" but for another purpose, (and explains it), notice that when HE said it wasn't neither,<u>'that' in itself was indicating</u> that it **'could have been' one or the other**, but **'not this time' or he would** surely **have set them straight**...if these weren't possible,

So then, **if this is true, and a person WILL PAY for some sin they did in a <u>previous life,</u> MAYBE WE NEED TO PAY ATTENTION as to HOW we LIVE our lives NOW!)**

People go to cemeteries and place flowers on graves of loved ones, but it is more for their own remembrance of who they had been with 'that body' they knew. Their SPIRIT/'SOUL' <u>LIVES ON</u> and each is given a chance to become a better

person and go toward the way and goal God wishes us to reach.

SO...
Jesus answered, "Neither hath this man sinned, **nor** his parents: but that the works of God should be made manifest in him." John 9:3 (KJV)
"I must work the works of him that sent me, while it is day: the night will come when no man can work." John 9:4 (KJV)
"As long as I am in the world, I am the light of the world." John 9:5 (KJV)
(***Is day speaking of 'light being GOD time ..."light of the world" and a time when people will no longer have the opportunity to 'work' to make amends when the 'dark' will come... 'Satan' is known as the 'dark side'... HELL? **Final Judgement**!? Remember Jesus spoke in parables so: "**those with eyes might see.**"***)
And said unto him, "When he had thus spoken, he spat on the ground, and made clay of the spittle, and he anointed the eyes of the blind man with the clay." John 9:6 (KJV) "**Go, wash in the pool of Siloam.**"
He went his way therefore, and washed, and came seeing." John 9:7 (KJV) Sight cometh,

The neighbours therefore, and they which before had seen him that he was blind, said, "Is not this he that sat and begged?" John 9:8 (KJV)
Some said, "This is he." Others said, "He is like him." But he said, "I am he." John 9:9 (KJV)
Therefore said they unto him, "How were thine eyes opened?" John 9:10 (KJV)
He answered and said, "A man that is called Jesus made clay, and anointed mine eyes, and said unto me, 'Go to the pool of Siloam, and wash': and I went and washed, and I received sight." John 9:11 (KJV)
Then said they unto him, "Where is he?" He said, "I know not." John 9:12 (KJV)
<u>They brought to the Pharisees him that aforetime was blind. John 9:13 (KJV)</u>
And it was the sabbath day when Jesus made the clay, and opened his eyes. John 9:14 (KJV)
Then again the Pharisees also asked him how he had received his sight. He said unto them, "He put clay upon mine eyes, and I washed, and do see." John 9:15 (KJV)
Therefore said some of the Pharisees, "This man is not of God because he keepeth not the sabbath day." Others said, "How can a man

that is a sinner do such miracles?" And there was a division among them. John 9:16 (KJV)
They say unto the blind man again, "What sayest thou of him, that he hath opened thine eyes?" He said, "He is a prophet." John 9:17 (KJV)
But the Jews did not believe concerning him, that he had been blind, and received his sight, until they called the parents of him that had received his sight. John 9:18 (KJV)
And they asked them saying, "Is this your son, who ye say was born blind? How then doth he now see?" John 9:19 (KJV)
His parents answered them and said, "We know that this is our son, and that he was born blind." John 9:20 (KJV)
"But by what means he now seeth, we know not; or who hath opened his eyes, we know not: he is of age; ask him: he shall speak for himself." John 9:21 (KJV)
These words spake his parents because they feared the Jews: for the Jews had agreed already that if any man did confess that he was Christ, he should be put out of the synagogue." John 9:22 (KJV)
Then again called they the man that was blind, and said unto him, "Give God the praise: we know that this man is a sinner." John 9:24 (KJV)

Then said they to him again, "What did he to thee? How opened he thine eyes?" John 9:26 (KJV)

He answered them, "I have told you already, and ye did not hear: wherefore would ye hear it again? Will ye also be his disciples?" John 9:27 (KJV)

Then they reviled him and said, "Thou art his disciple; but we are Moses' disciples." John 9:28 (KJV)

"We know that God spake unto Moses: as for this fellow, we know not from whence he is." John 9:29 (KJV)

He answered and said, "Whether he be a sinner or no, I know not: one thing I know, that, whereas I was blind, now I see." John 9:25 (KJV)

The man answered and said unto them, "Why herein is a marvellous thing, that ye know not from whence he is, and yet he hath opened mine eyes." John 9:30 (KJV)

"Now we know that God heareth not sinners: but if any man be a worshipper of God, and doeth his will, him he heareth." John 9:31 (KJV)

"Since the world began was it not heard that any man opened the eyes of one that was born blind." John 9:32 (KJV)

"If this man were not of God, he could do nothing." John 9:33 (KJV)
They answered and said unto him, "Thou wast altogether born in sins, and dost thou teach us? And they cast him out." John 9:34 (KJV)
Jesus heard that they had cast him out; and when he had found him, he said unto him, "Dost thou believe on the Son of God?" John 9:35 (KJV)
He answered and said, "Who is he, Lord, that I might believe on him?" John 9:36 (KJV)
And Jesus said unto him, "Thou hast both seen him, and it is he that talketh with thee." John 9:37 (KJV)
And he said, "Lord, I believe." And he worshipped him. John 9:38 (KJV)
AND JESUS SAID, "**FOR JUDGMENT I AM COME INTO THIS WORLD, THAT THEY WHICH SEE NOT MIGHT SEE**; AND **THAT THEY WHICH SEE MIGHT BE MADE BLIND.**" JOHN 9:39 (KJV)
These verses seem to be repeating the situation and seem a waste of space. However, they are 'as it is IN THE BIBLE itself!

And some of the Pharisees which were with him heard these words, and said unto him, "Are we blind also?" John 9:40 (KJV)

JESUS SAID UNTO THEM, "_**IF YE WERE BLIND, YE SHOULD HAVE NO SIN**_: **BUT NOW YE SAY, WE SEE; THEREFORE YOUR SIN REMAINETH**." JOHN 9:41 (KJV)

(***Here it is saying they are still living in 'sin'...therefore they will have to make amends for those sins...
REINCARNATION!)

Here it will be noted by many that it is saying they have to be 'born again' and receive the holy spirit through water baptism. They get that idea from Jesus having them wash in the water and they came out 'seeing', so the churches baptize with water to have people be 'born again' in the spirit. Some churches use sprinking of water and some have people dipped in water, but there are some who have the entire body immersed in water.

The problem with all of this is that it is nothing but a 'symbolic gesture' and does nothing. Think about it. How many people are 'baptized in water in some way and go out and do things that are not God like? If you notice the baptisms (so to speak) mentioned, all started with clay being placed on the eyes before going into the water. That 'clay' represented the body God made man from when ADAM was made in the garden of eden when 'sin' came into the world. **WHEN man has gotten to a point of NOT HAVING TO SEE HIS SINS COMMITED SO that they have to be again accounted for,... is he THEN able to be born again IN 'SPIRIT' OF GOD.**

John 14:2 "In my Father's house are many mansions: if *it were* not *so*, I would have told you. I go to prepare a place for you."

**The mention of heaven having many mansions indicates there are many choices as to where a departed soul might go. If they had issues with the way they lived their life, they just left and must return to make amends, learn, or better their life before that 'final judgement' so they would go to the 'mansion' level they are on, and where their chance for growth is needed. Should a person have reached the highest level and a closeness with God, they may go to a place where opportunities to serve is needed...
perhaps as a guide, protector, angel, or whatever because they were good enough not to have to reincarnate again. They would not be in heaven itself yet until Jesus dies and opens the heavenly gate. If you look up the word heaven, you will find there are different descriptions of levels.**

Matthew 25:34 In the vast home filled by my Father 'lighted' by his smile of recognition and reconciliation in the high and holy place.
(Heaven is a large place; its possibility can be only as far as your own your imagination will let you go.)
Isaiah 63:15; Deuteronomy 26:15 are "many mansions" prepared from the foundation of the world
There is a bible verse... "be not forgetful to entertain strangers: thereby some have entertained angels unawares." Hebrews 13:2 (KJV)
Most people have heard it spoken about people being 'baptized' but there are many who don't know why or what it means. They just know it is about water being put on someone's head. Actually, it can be performed in many ways, according to who is doing it. Baptism began in early Jewish culture with some thinking it was associated with priests cleansing themselves before performing their priestly ceremonies. (Leviticus 16: 4 and 23-24) Baptism is an 'outward expression' with an 'inward' way of thinking, to believing in Jesus Christ and by faith believing what he can do for us. Once one professes to believing in Jesus, no sin can ever take away the

invisible mark sealed at baptism. (Jesus died for our sins.) 'With the performance of baptism comes the 'inner feelings' of 'wanting to share and spread the word' to others of forgiveness for sins because of Jesus. There was a man named John the Baptist who went around teaching about God and baptizing people so to gather more for their sins to be forgiven. Jesus himself had John baptize him, acknowledging the fact.

Jesus spoke about John the Baptist and through 'HIS' own words, he reveals a proof of 'reincarnation'.

Matthew 11:7 (KJV) "And as they departed, Jesus began to say unto the multitudes <u>concerning John.</u> <u>BUT WHAT WENT YE OUT FOR TO SEE? A PROPHET?</u> **YEA, I SAY UNTO YOU,** AND **MORE THAN A PROPHET**."

"For this is he, of whom it is written, Behold, I send my messenger before thy face, which shall prepare thy way before thee." Matthew 11:10 (KJV)

"Verily I say unto you, Among them that are born of women there hath not risen a greater than John the Baptist: notwithstanding he

that is least in the kingdom of heaven is greater than he." Matthew 11:11 (KJV)

And from the days of **JOHN THE BAPTIST** until now the kingdom of heaven suffereth violence, and the violent take it by force.
FOR ALL THE PROPHETS AND THE LAW PROPHESIED <u>UNTIL JOHN</u>. AND <u>IF YE WILL RECEIVE *IT*, THIS 'IS' ELIAS, WHICH WAS FOR TO COME</u>.
<u>HE THAT HATH EARS TO HEAR, LET HIM HEAR.!!!!!</u>

(***Now speaking of John the Baptist··· 'I' will be going off on my OWN thoughts here but will give actual BIBLE verses as to why I have them. However it is for those who 'did not catch it' with my... 'punctuation indicator.' Jesus is saying... What I will be 'eventually' revealing··· However 'I' will be giving the <u>background</u> leading up to it, from 'back' in time.)
"Elias was a man subject to like passion as we are, and he prayed earnestly that it might not rain: and it rained not on

the earth by the space of three years and six months." James 5:17 (KJV)
And they asked him, saying, "Why say the scribes that Elias must first come?" Mark 9:11 (KJV)
And Jesus answered and said unto them, "Elias truly shall first come, and restore all things." Matthew 17:11 (KJV)
And he answered him, "I am: go, tell thy lord, behold, Elijah is here." 1 Kings 18:8 (KJV)
"And behold, there appeared unto them Moses and <u>Elias talking with him</u>." Matthew 17:3 (KJV) And <u>if ye will receive it, this is Elias, which was for to come."</u> Matthew 11:14 (KJV)
And they asked him, saying, "Why say the scribes that Elias must first come?" Mark 9:11 (KJV)
"BUT I SAY UNTO YOU, <u>THAT ELIAS IS INDEED COME, AND THEY HAVE DONE UNTO HIM WHATSOEVER THEY LISTED, AS IT IS WRITTEN OF HIM." MARK 9:13 (KJV)</u>
And he answered and told them, "Elias verily cometh first, and restoreth all things; and how it is written of the Son of man, that he must suffer many things, and be set

at nought." Mark 9:12 (KJV) (dead; and therefore mighty works do shew forth)
Herod had laid hold on John, and bound him, and put him in prison.
John 8:58 - Jesus said unto them, "Verily, verily, I say unto you, before Abraham was, I am."
And he cried against the altar in the word of the LORD, and said, "O altar, altar, **thus saith the LORD; Behold, a child shall be born unto the house of David, Josiah by name; and upon thee shall he offer the priests of the high places that burn incense upon thee, and men's bones shall be burnt upon thee.**" And he gave a sign the same day, saying, "This is the sign which the LORD hath spoken; **Behold, the altar shall be rent, and the ashes that are upon it shall be poured out." 1 Kings 13:3 (KJV) And it came to pass, when king Jeroboam heard the saying of the man of God which had cried against the altar in Bethel that he put forth his hand from the altar saying, "Lay hold on him." And his hand, which he put forth against him, dried up,**

so that he could not pull it in again to him. 1 Kings 13:4 (KJV)
"The altar also was rent, and the ashes poured out from the altar, according to the sign which the man of God had given by the word of the LORD." 1 Kings 13:5 (KJV)
And the king answered and said unto the man of God, "Intreat now the face of the LORD thy God, and pray for me, that my hand may be restored me again." And the man of God besought the LORD, and the king's hand was restored him again, and became as it was before. 1 Kings 13:6 (KJV)
<u>**And the king said unto the man of God**, Come home with me, and refresh thyself, and **I will give thee a reward.**</u>
<u>**AND THE MAN OF GOD SAID UNTO THE KING**, IF THOU WILT GIVE ME HALF THINE HOUSE, **I WILL NOT GO IN WITH THEE, NEITHER WILL I EAT BREAD NOR DRINK WATER IN THIS PLACE:**</u>

<u>**FOR SO WAS IT CHARGED ME BY THE WORD OF THE LORD, SAYING,**</u>

EAT NO BREAD, NOR DRINK WATER, NOR TURN AGAIN BY THE SAME WAY THAT THOU CAMEST.

These above passages were probably both boring to read and even so hard to understand that you simply passed them by. However, they will turn out to be VERY important and reveal something phenomenal!)

The man left and went a different way and caused people to seek him out.

And **went after the man of God,** and found him sitting under an oak: and he said unto him, "*Art* **thou the man of God that camest from Judah?" And he said, "I *AM*."**

Then he said unto him, "Come home with me, and eat bread."

And he said, "I may not return with thee, nor go in with thee: neither will I eat bread nor drink water with thee in this place:" 1 Kings 13:16 (KJV)

For it was said to me by the word of the LORD, "Thou shalt eat no bread nor drink water there, nor turn again to go by the way that thou camest." 1 Kings 13:17 (KJV)

HE SAID UNTO HIM, **"I AM A PROPHET ALSO AS THOU ART; AND AN ANGEL SPAKE UNTO ME BY THE WORD OF THE LORD SAYING, BRING HIM BACK WITH THEE INTO THINE HOUSE, THAT HE MAY EAT BREAD AND DRINK WATER.** <u>BUT HE LIED UNTO HIM</u>." 1 KINGS 13:18 (KJV)

"So he went back with him, **<u>and did eat bread in his house, and drank water. 1 Kings 13:19 (KJV)</u>**

"And it came to pass**<u>, as they sat at the table</u>**, **that THE WORD OF THE LORD <u>CAME UNTO THE PROPHET THAT BROUGHT HIM BACK</u>:"**
<u>1 KINGS 13:20 (KJV)</u>

And he cried unto the man of God that came from Judah, saying, "Thus saith the LORD, forasmuch as thou hast disobeyed the mouth of the LORD, and hast not kept the commandment which the LORD thy God commanded thee."
1 Kings 13:21 (KJV)

22. But camest back, and <u>HAST EATEN BREAD AND DRUNK WATER</u> in the place o<u>f the which *the LORD* did say to thee</u>, Eat no bread, and drink no water; <u>thy CARCASE SHALL NOT COME UNTO THE SEPULCHRE OF THY FATHERS</u>.

And it came to pass, after he had eaten bread, and after he had drunk, that he saddled for him the ass, to wit, for the prophet whom he had brought back." 1 Kings 13:23 (KJV)
"**And when he was gone, a lion met him by the way, and slew him: and his carcase was cast in the way, and the ass stood by it, the lion also stood by the carcase." 1 Kings 13:24 (KJV)**
And, behold, men passed by, and saw the carcase cast in the way, and the lion standing by the carcase: and they came and told it in the city where the old prophet dwelt. 1 Kings 13:25 (KJV) And when the prophet that brought him back from the way heard thereof, he said, "It is the man of God, who was disobedient unto the word of the LORD: therefore, the LORD hath delivered him unto the lion which hath torn him and slain him, according to the word of the LORD, which he spake unto him." And he spake to his sons, saying, "Saddle me the ass." And they saddled him. 1 Kings 13:27 (KJV)
1 Kings 13:26 (KJV) And he went and found his carcase cast in the way, and the ass and the lion standing by the carcase: THE LION HAD NOT EATEN THE CARCASE, NOR TORN THE ASS." 1 KINGS 13:28 (KJV)

And the prophet took up the carcase of the man of God, and laid it upon the ass, and brought it back: and the old prophet came to the city, to mourn and to bury him. 1 Kings 13:29 (KJV)

And he laid his carcase in his own grave; and they mourned over him, saying, "Alas, my brother!" 1 Kings 13:30 (KJV)

And it came to pass, after he had buried him, that he spake to his sons, saying, "When I am dead, THEN BURY ME IN THE SEPULCHRE WHEREIN THE MAN OF GOD IS BURIED; lay my bones beside his bones." 1 Kings 13:31 (KJV)

Did you catch the things being **similar to the person we know as John the Baptist? For John the Baptist came neither eating bread nor drinking wine. His lifestyle was spent in the desert, apart from the ordinary joys and pleasures of men, not even sharing in what are usually termed the necessities of life and drank no wine or fermented drink. IF this was an incarnation of John the Baptist, people read the Bible as pointing to being killed by a lion for going against God's Word. So then he paid in that lifetime for not following God's instructions, at his 'next lifetime' coming**

back with the same lifestyle but having to 'repent! (Now, that is if you didn't really read the passage. His body was NOT eaten by the animals and later in the book you will see why not.)

Here were Jesus' words concerning John the Baptist

Matthew 11:11
>Verily I say unto you, Among them that **are born of women** there hath not risen a greater than John the Baptist: notwithstanding he that is least in the kingdom of heaven is greater than he.

And it came to pass, as they were burying a man, that, behold, they spied a band of men; and <u>they cast the man into the sepulcher of ELISHA:</u> <u>and WHEN THE MAN was let down, and touched the bones of Elisha, HE revived, and stood up on his feet. (2 Kings 13:21).</u>

REINCARNATION

IN THE <u>NEW</u> TESTAMENT, JESUS REVEALS THAT JOHN THE BAPTIST <u>WAS THE FULFILLMENT OF MALACHI'S</u> <u>PROPHECY:</u> ALL THE PROPHETS AND THE LAW PROPHESIED <u>UNTIL JOHN.</u>

Some Christians think that Elijah will come just before Jesus' second coming, but according to the Bible, <u>JESUS</u> EXPECTED HIM <u>IN HIS 'OWN LIFETIME,' and REVEALED IT IN MALACHI</u>.

People will say that John the Baptist never 'indicated anything' about coming to reveal Jesus, so, he **wasn't 'some' incarnation'** like ones try to say.

That doesn't mean a thing. People have no idea 'why' they came into this lifetime. DO YOU know why you are here?? There is a passage which says God knew us 'before' we were born and Jesus himself revealed that John the Baptist was someone 'special' and KNEW he was to come and make way for himself.

(With 'reincarnation' as the key, John himself doesn't identify himself or know himself as Elijah who is to be the forerunner.) Persons from 'one lifetime' have no idea as to any 'other incarnations'

they've had. **JESUS KNEW who John was, and what he will do, even if John the Baptist himself is in the dark. In fact, when he hears of Jesus, he sends a messenger to ask if he is the one 'they' are <u>waiting for?</u> Then** taking from a prophecy foretelling the return of the Jewish people from exile, they had nothing to link it to the supposed mission of John as the forerunner of the Messiah. The exile of the Jewish people was not even terminated during John the Baptist's lifetime.
However, <u>because of this 'prophecy'</u>, the religious leaders of Jesus' day believed that the old testament prophet **Elijah, who had not died but had been <u>taken by God directly to heaven in a chariot of fire</u>** (<u>1 Kings 17 through 2 Kings 2</u>), **<u>would literally return to earth prior to the appearance of the Messiah whom Israel was waiting for God to send, and would turn Israel to God in preparation for the Messiah's</u> coming, just as he had worked in Old Testament times to turn Israel away from idolatry, and to return it to the worship of God.**
1 Kings 19:9-18
<u>And he came thither unto a cave, and lodged there; and behold, the word of the</u>

LORD *came* to him, and he said unto him, What doest thou here, Elijah?

10 And he said, I have been very jealous for the LORD God of hosts: for <u>the children of Israel have forsaken thy covenant, thrown down thine altars, and slain thy prophets with the sword;</u> and I, *even* **I only, am left; and they seek my life, to take it away.**

11 And he said, Go forth, and stand upon the mount before the LORD. And behold, the LORD passed by, and a great and strong wind rent the mountains, and brake in pieces the rocks before the LORD; *but* the LORD *was* not in the wind: and after the wind an earthquake; *but* the LORD *was* not in the earthquake:
12 And after the earthquake a fire; *but* the LORD *was* not in the fire: and after the fire a still small voice.

And Jehu the son of Nimshi shalt thou anoint *to be* king over Israel: and **Elisha the son of Shaphat of** Abelmeholah shalt **thou anoint *to be* prophet in thy room**.

1 Kings 19:17 (KJV) **17**And it shall come to pass, *that* him that escapeth the sword of Hazael shall Jehu slay: and him that escapeth from the sword of Jehu shall Elisha slay.
18 Yet I have left *me* seven thousand in Israel, all the knees which have not bowed unto Baal, and every mouth which hath not kissed him.
19 So he departed thence, and found Elisha the son of Shaphat, *oxen* before him, and he with the twelfth: and Elijah passed by him and cast his mantle upon him.
20 And he left the oxen, **and ran after Elijah**, and said, Let me, I pray thee, kiss my father and my mother,
and *then* I will follow thee. And he said unto him, Go back again: for what have I done to thee?

He has made everything beautiful in its time; also he has put eternity into man's mind, yet so that he cannot find out what God has done from the beginning to the end…..That which is already has been; that which is to be already has been; and God seeks what has been driven away.

("<u>Nothing new</u> under the sun"...(<u>11</u>)-There is <u>no remembrance</u> of <u>former things, nor will there</u> be remembrance of later things to happen among those who come after.") Ecclesiastes (1-12)
The **sting of death is sin** and the <u>power of sin</u> **is the law.** <u>But thanks be to God, who gives us the victory through our Lord Jesus Christ.</u>
1 Corinthians 15-56

<u>BORN AGAIN</u> is believed to be the PERSONAL CONVERSION EXPERIENCE OF A PERSON IN THE CHRISTIAN FAITH. THE <u>ORIGINAL MEANING WAS</u>... THE <u>CHANGE FROM HEATHENISM</u> TO THE JEWISH FAITH.
The wording was THEN <u>**IMPROPERLY USED by the Christian faith and 'sprinkling of water' became the mode used by the church for those who claimed they want to be converted or 'born again'.**</u>
BORN AGAIN MEANS TO BE 'COMPLETELY CHANGED' <u>WITH THEIR WAY OF LIFE AND THINKING INTO A BETTER LEVEL WITH GOD.</u>
(King James Bible) John 3:3 Jesus answered him "Truly, truly I say to you, <u>**UNLESS ONE IS BORN 'OF THE SPIRIT', HE CANNOT SEE THE KINGDOM OF GOD."**</u>

3:5 "TRULY, TRULY I SAY TO YOU, UNLESS ONE IS BORN OF WATER <u>AND SPIRIT</u>, HE CANNOT ENTER THE KINGDOM OF GOD.
3:6 THAT WHICH IS BORN OF THE FLESH IS FLESH AND THAT WHICH IS BORN OF THE SPRIT IS SPIRIT.
This statement will be repeated many times, so you will grasp it in your mind.
(YOU WILL SEE SHORTLY THE REASON FOR REINCARNATION OF ALL OF US AND YOU WILL VIEW THE EXAMPLES OF THE INCARNATIONS OF JESUS HIMSELF AS TO HOW A SOUL NEVER DIES, BUT 'CAN BE'... LOST. YET WE ARE ALL GIVEN A CHANCE TO BE RENEWED... AND... 'REGAINED' THROUGH THE 'NEVER DYING SPIRIT' OF GOD.)

Sunday is Holy Day!

This book is becoming far more than I ever planned it to be. Remember, the subject I 'chose' to write about was because of a statement in the Bible made by Jesus, so the last part of the book that covers that subject was easier to do and faster to accomplish. The fact is, I had originally entitled the book, "The unraveling" so to cover things that make the Bible hard to read and I thought I could 'unravel' some of those knots that stopped the 'free' flow. By using each subject and attaching the actual Bible verses, it might help people understand what was being 'said' easier. It was going pretty well until at times 'another thing' seemed to pop up causing me to have to follow 'that' thread. By now, it has so many very strange and controversial things come forward, through no cause of my own, that I find myself in a huge dilemma. If it weren't for the Bible verses being found to 'back' what I'm revealing, I would think SATAN is having a heyday with my mind.

 The only thing is that SATAN <u>does things to cause you</u> to 'question' God and turn you away from Him. These things are rather a 'strengthening' of GOD'S presence and is, as 'if' I am being 'led' <u>to reveal</u> certain things in order to get people in the world back on track. I've had Divine intervention at other times in my life, but this is almost overwhelming.

I am going to have a whole lot of people wanting to 'tar and feather' me before this is done. This next subject 'sort of' falls in with the last one of the Sabbath being on Saturday. When I mentioned a large religious denomination have been a reason for black people to be seen as slaves, I didn't mention which one, and left it to you to find, if you are interested. THIS TIME I will NOT do that as it affects us in a way that could be making US to living in sin. (ME INCLUDED.) **I go to church each SUNDAY! BUT WHY? The Bible says God created the world in six days and on the 'seventh day', he rested. That makes SATURDAY the holy day.** Why has it been **changed to the FIRST day** of the week? That's **not** what GOD said.

The Catholic tradition says the church began with Jesus Christ and his teachings, so it considers itself a continuation of the early Christian community established by the disciple of Jesus. They believe their Bishops to be the ones who follow next in line to **Saint Peter,** who went to Rome after Jesus appointed him head of the church. (First of all, it said it was the Catholic 'TRADITION'. A tradition is a belief, thought or 'story' handed down generation after generation. That <u>doesn't</u> **make it true**...just 'something' <u>passed along from generation TO GENERATION.</u>

While you 'non -believers' are still busy trying to keep from even 'coming close' to wondering if 'perhaps' there 'might be' reincarnation, I give you 'something else' to ponder..
You've heard MANY PEOPLE SAY THAT THE BIBLE IS NOTHING BUT A PLACE WHERE, 'WHATEVER' YOU THINK, YOU CAN FIND A 'PASSAGE' TO GO ALONG WITH YOUR THOUGHTS. And that is 'sort of true'. Reading a passage here and there throughout the book you can find something that agrees with you and if you find something that goes the other way, you simply 'dismiss it' until you can find another place that does agree. The thing is...I have discovered that the Bible reveals many 'slightly' CAMOUFLAGED TRUTHS, but It 'ALL' makes sense.
So comes the 'new topic' ..."<u>The Holy day!</u>"
Jesus was a Jew, and they believed the Holy day was on Saturday because that is the 'seventh' day...the day for rest! 'With our

calendar',... **SUNDAY is the' <u>FIRST day'</u>** and would only be right if the calendar 'started' on MONDAY. Then SUNDAY 'WOULD BE' correct and the last day, but it 'doesn't' and 'isn't' (but then it wouldn't be the first one on the Calendar.) Then I noticed something. NOWHERE in the Bible when mentioning the Sabbath did it 'ever' mention the '<u>name</u>' of the seventh day? I realized why. The world is on different time zones, so what is one named day in one place isn't so everywhere. The Bible is smart enough to reveal this IF 'we' would only realize what it is revealing. That is true throughout the whole BIBLE. (May those with eyes see!) So, it merely says the 'holy day' is <u>after six days of work</u>.

'GOD CAME TO THIS EARTH ACCORDING TO THE <u>PROPHECIES OF</u> <u>THE BIBLE</u>', AND 'REVEALED THE TRUTH' HIDDEN IN DARKNESS '<u>OF WORSHIP WE SHOULD OBSERVE</u>'. THE SABBATH, <u>THAT THE 'CHURCH OF GOD' KEEPS HOLY</u> ON SATURDAY, THE SEVENTH DAY, IS THE PURE TRUTH OF THE EARLY CHURCH WHICH CHRIST RESTORED AT HIS SECOND COMING.

JESUS DIED ON FRIDAY ...dying for our sins as well as the sins of the 'first'...Adam who... 'brought sins' into the world.

ON 'SATURDAY', AFTER HIS DEATH, ...SAYING," IT IS <u>'FINISHED'</u>!" He 'rested' ....(on... <u>THE SEVENTH</u> day. Saturday!?)
ROMANS 5 TEACHES US THAT ADAM WAS "A PATTERN OF THE ONE TO COME". 1 CORINTHIANS 15
DEVELOP CONTRASTS BETWEEN **"DEATH THROUGH ADAM" AND "LIFE THROUGH CHRIST".** (One brought sin into the world...the other took our sins away! ...'reincarnation!!!???)
Jesus Christ is called the 'Second Adam' because of the parallels between his and Adam's life. Romans 5, Adam was "a pattern of the one to come" (Romans 5:14). Jesus followed that same pattern. However, whereas <u>Adam disobeyed God and brought sin</u> and death into the world, <u>Jesus obeyed God</u> so that the world could receive God's free gift of righteousness and eternal life.
THE <u>**CHURCH COMMANDS US TO KEEP THE SUNDAY HOLY INSTEAD OF THE SABBATH BECAUSE ON SUNDAY CHRIST ROSE FROM THE DEAD, AND ON SUNDAY HE SENT THE HOLY GHOST UPON THE APOSTLES**</u>.
WE KEEP SUNDAY INSTEAD OF SATURDAY HOLY ALSO TO TEACH THAT

THE OLD LAW IS NOT NOW BINDING UPON US, BUT THAT WE MUST KEEP THE NEW LAW, WHICH TAKES ITS PLACE. In the period of reconstruction after the end of the Second World War, the acclaimed goal was a restoration of Western Civilization.
The Greek writer Aristotle clearly understood that the 'entire focus of man's existence' was leisure. It is he who explains that man accepts being in a state of "not-at-leisure" *in order* to be "at-leisure". That is, the "rest-from-work," which we commonly refer to as "relaxation." The dictionary's definition of leisure ranges from not a hurried time but a time for pleasure, rest, and recreation, not working for a living. The Catholics used the influence of one man's book to base their change to Sunday because 'leisure' is the key for our existence. Sorry, I can't make myself go with this. I warned elsewhere in the book about using authors' definition or views of what areas of the Bible are saying because you are getting just 'that' person's views and here is an example of this. **The change of the HOLY DAY from Saturday to Sunday** has affected Christian's everywhere and could be causing '**us**' to be sinning by not keeping GOD'S Word. Then again, we have no choice because everything

REINCARNATION

is set up for Sunday so you either go to church or don't. However, if you realize the theory behind the seventh day for rest, you are still following the rule and no name was ever given to the seventh day as such.

Pauline E. Petsel

World before the world - Dinosaurs

The more I try to reveal information to you, the more confusing it gets. **I will tell you one thing only to say something completely different one page later.** The 'culprit' in **all cases** is to use the internet to look up places for their 'expertise', so I will give you the best I can. The problem comes with the fact that while each are 'great sources' in themselves, when it deals with the Bible, a 'clash' causing an entanglement takes place. Even using supposed 'Bible deciphering versions' of various sources only pile up the weight to 'misinformation'. This example is 'loud and clear' with what I am about to use, plus goes along with the 'make man in our own image, male and female' topic.

DINOSAURS / CREATION- "DAYS" DIFF. <u>Since dinosaurs predate almost all mammals, THERE WERE NO HUMANS WHEN DINOSAURS ROAMED THIS PLANET.</u> Dinosaurs were wiped out 65 million years ago but even that probably took thousands of years. <u>(God creating the world in seven days sure gets shot to death if people think of it being 'seven' of our 'work week days'</u>. **(Remember, 'One' of 'God's days' equals a thousand years.)**

Dinosaurs existed before humans. Dinosaurs evolved around 245 million years ago, while humans evolved around 80 thousand years ago[1]. Dinosaurs became extinct around 65 million years ago[12]. Small mammals, including shrew-sized primates, were alive at the time of the dinosaurs[2]. The dinosaurs that the earliest humans lived among were not the huge lumbering lizards we most commonly think of when we see the word. Those had been extinct for almost 66 million years before the first humans began to make their mark[3].

Here starts a huge difference and controversy as to even the age of creation. Even big named resources like the various encyclopedias, dictionaries, scientific researchers, and authorities on the subject come up with different views and answers. If you don't believe me, try looking up the subject on your own, and you will come to ONE CONCLUSION....no matter what they are experts in, they only go with information found during their own field of works and yet it clashes with another's findings from 'their studies' in 'their field'. The conclusion is... No one knows!

I warned you of this being a controversial book and one for people who like to argue and prove someone wrong will have a 'hay day' because even 'I" the author, can't agree with things I find to try to use.

I can't even use Bible sources because the interpretations at those sights are the way those particular places interpret for themselves what is being said.

Therefore, the King James standard version of the Bible's actual verses will be used and to be taken for what 'THEY' say, and NOT what 'I' say they say! Just a verse or two here or there to prove a point can't be enough, but when groups of scripture are revealed from many places in the Bible which show the same thing, it will throw some light on the 'truth'.

Early 'storyteller' had no understanding of what actually took place with the 'creation' but yet, as old as the Bible is, information can be found tucked away here and there for people to act as 'discoverers' to be found.

One thought from groups of resources is that our earliest human ancestors split from the great apes about *6 million years* ago and Modern humans have only existed for around *350 thousand years*, with "Adam and Eve" being around *2,500 years* ago. Although earliest humans came into existence less than a couple of million years ago or so, *Homo Sapiens* first left Africa around 60,000 years ago ending up in Australia. **THE BIBLE STORY STARTED LESS THAN 10,000 YEARS AGO.** Now if you look up that information, you will find the numbers are different and estimates differ as to whether it is a Christian source, scientific source, geology, or researcher of fossil's sources **because there is evidence of dinosaurs roaming the earth and they have been 'recreated' from fossil bones found.**

THE ONE THING THEY ALL 'DO HAVE' IN COMMON IS THAT THIS ALL CHANGES GOD CREATING THE WORLD IN SIX DAYS (AS WE KNOW SIX DAYS TO MEAN) AND RESTED ON THE SEVENTH!
(2 PETER 3:8) BUT DO NOT FORGET THIS ONE THING, DEAR FRIENDS: **WITH THE LORD A DAY IS LIKE A THOUSAND YEARS, AND A THOUSAND YEARS ARE LIKE A DAY. PETER REMINDS THE BELIEVERS NOT TO LOSE HEART BECAUSE GOD IS WORKING ON A DIFFERENT TIMETABLE. HOWEVER, HE ISN'T LIMITED BY TIME **BECAUSE HIS 'DAY' IS 1000 YEARS. GOD WILL KEEP HIS WORD, BUT HE**

HAS PLENTY OF TIME TO PLAY WITH TO DO IT. PEOPLE WERE LIVING TO BE 700-800 YEARS SO THE PROMISE GOD MADE TO ABRAHAM COULD TAKE HUNDREDS OF YEARS. HE ALSO HAD THE LUXURY OF FULFILLING THE PROMISE BUT IN A SLIGHTLY DIFFERENT WAY THAN PEOPLE EXPECTED. (AGAIN THE EXAMPLE OF ABRAHAM.) **Because of the thousands of years in time difference, DINOSAURS WERE ON EARTH <u>WAY BEFORE MANKIND</u>. The 'actual' word 'dinosaurs' is not found in the Bible, but that doesn't mean that what 'we label' as being a dinosaur didn't exist. Dinosaurs didn't even become a word until the 1850s.** There were several names used in the Bible that had reference to what we think of as dinosaurs. **Tannin, Behemoth, and Leviathan were words mentioned in the Bible that seemed to represent what 'we' think of as the dinosaurs we know. Except for whales and cattle, the creation story doesn't mention names, or types, of sea creatures and earthly animals which God made. However,**

Later, two strange creatures **are** named. **One beast** is a mighty **sea monster called Leviathan** and the other beast is a **large land animal named Behemoth.** Though these two creatures are believed to be mythological, **there may in fact be some scientific evidence supporting their existence, or at least proves that they once existed.** Scripture uses the Hebrew word *tannin* 28 times in the Old Testament describing a **mysterious creature resembling a giant.** THE English translations referred to it most often as a **dragon, but also as a sea-monster, serpent, and whale.**

The term ALSO can be applied to both river and marine water monster as well as a land monster. Besides giant reptiles, in **Ezekiel 29:3, the Bible** also includes several references to a monstrous and mighty beast, specifically called **Behemoth.** The Behemoth, unlike the Leviathan, is found only in **Job 40:15** and is described in verses 15 to 24.

"Behold, Behemoth, which I made as I made you; he eats grass like an ox. Behold, his strength in his loins, and his power in the muscles of his belly. He makes his tail stiff like a cedar; the sinews of his thighs are knit together. His bones are tubes of bronze, his limbs like bars of iron.

"He is the first of the works of God; let him who made him bring near his sword! For the mountains yield food for him where all the wild beasts play. Under the lotus plants he lies, in the shelter of the reeds and in the marsh. For his shade, the lotus trees cover him; the willows of the brook surround him. Behold, if the river is turbulent, he is not frightened; he is confident though Jordan rushes against his mouth. Can one take him by his eyes or pierce his nose with a snare?" possibly

describing a giant, vegetation-eating sauropod.
Encyclopedia Britannica
https://www.britannica.com/animal/sauropod

So, God the Almighty, speaks of **Behemoth** as a creature that eats grass like an ox, who moves his tail like a cedar tree, and whose bones are like bars of iron (Job 40:15-18). **Leviathan** is described as a strong sea creature whose scales cannot be pierced, and whose breath is as a flame of fire proceeding from his mouth (Job 41). **The fossil records indicate that at one time in earth's history, dinosaurs did indeed walk the earth and also inhabited the sea. Behemoth could have been a brontosaurus or even a woolly mammoth, as both of which were herbivores.
Whereas Leviathan could have been a Spinosaurus, a dinosaur that lived in water.** And even though the book of Job was written around the 6th century BC, the validity of the existence of these creatures

still holds ground. **For in God's discussion with His servant Job, the Lord speaks of things which happened from the very foundation of the world (Job 38:4).**
Remember, Genisis 1:24-25 is indicating that <u>the last day of animals' creation, the dinosaur type creatures would have been made, but IT **'ALSO' SAYS** that **'MANKIND' was made!** That would mean man was</u> in the land WITH the monsters, ….except for the fact of **God's day** being worth **1000 of ours**. Man may have still lived with the remnants of the creatures, but in fact, there are questions even today of that same 'possibility' with sightings of 'monster looking things and a lot as bigfoot. For those who have a 'logical' mind, you will be saying there are no such things, and <u>people claiming there are, are nuts</u>. However, for those who've witnessed such things personally, or been involved in some 'paranormal activity,' <u>they</u> are 'true believers'.

(King James on-line standard edition)
15 Behold now, behemoth, which I made with thee; he eateth grass as an ox.
16 Lo now, his strength *is* in his loins, and his force *is* in the navel of his belly.

17 He moveth his tail like a cedar: the sinews of his stones are wrapped together.

<u>18His bones are as strong pieces of brass; his bones are like bars of iron.</u>

20Surely the mountains bring him forth food, where all the beasts of the field play.
21He lieth under the shady trees, in the covert of the reed, and fens.
22The shady trees cover him *with* their shadow; the willows of the brook compass him about.
23Behold, he drinketh up a river, *and* hasteth not: he trusteth that he can draw up Jordan into his mouth.
24He taketh it with his eyes: *his* nose pierceth through snares.

Leviathan

"A transliterated Hebrew word (leviathan), meaning "twisted," "coiled." In Job 3:8, Revised Version, and margin of Authorized Version, it denotes the dragon which, according to Eastern tradition, is an enemy of light; in 41:1 the crocodile is meant; in Ps. 104:26 it denotes any large animal that moves by writhing or wriggling the body, the whale, the monsters of the deep. This word is also used figuratively for a cruel enemy, as some think "the Egyptian host, crushed by the divine power, and cast on the shores of the Red Sea. (Ps. 74:14). As used in Isaiah 27:1, "leviathan the piercing [R.V. `swift'] serpent, "leviathan that crooked [R.V. marg. `winding'] serpent," the word may probably denote the two empires, the Assyrian and the Babylonian.

"In that day, the LORD with his sore and great and strong sword shall punish leviathan the piercing serpent, even leviathan that crooked serpent; and he shall slay the dragon that is in the sea." Isaiah 27:1 (KJV)

Look up the word 'dinosaurs' yourself and you will find different dictionaries give the same yet slightly different descriptions. This is a combination of what is told. **Their**

combination data boils down to being reptiles of 245 million years ago and lived for 180 million years. Dinosaurs were unable to make changes when the world 'went forward' with time. (*However, there were sources saying there is proof of remnants of them that did make it to live when people did, and in fact there are some species here even today.*)

(Genesis 1:20-21) Says the Lord created great whales and other aquatic life **but on the 'SIXTH and final' day, he created the 'beasts' of the earth - Genesis 1:24-25. <u>'Man' was 'also created'</u> on the 'SIXTH' DAY, but 'only after' God created the animals. (Remember, if God's day is worth 1000 of ours, there was plenty of time to have 'some distance' between the two.)**

<u>Web</u><u>sauropod-</u> any member of the dinosaur subgroup <u>Sauropoda,</u> marked by large size, a long neck and tail, a four-legged stance, and an herbivorous ...

The Leviathan appears various times in Scripture and in other ancient literature. In that day, the LORD with his hard and great and strong sword will punish **Leviathan** the **fleeing serpent**, Leviathan the **twisting serpent**, and he will slay the **dragon that is in the sea. Job 41:1–34 describes the twisting, serpent-like Leviathan in Ter** Leviathan is a sea monster mentioned in the Bible. It appears in the Old Testament in Psalms 74:14 as a multiheaded sea serpent that is killed by God and given as food to the Hebrews in the wilderness. In Isaiah 27:1, Leviathan is a serpent and a symbol of Israel's enemies, who will be slain by God. <u>In Job 41, it is a sea monster and a symbol of God's power of creation</u> .. of a fierce, fire breathing dragon: "His sneezings flash forth light ... Out of his mouth go flaming torches; sparks of fire leap forth. Out of his nostrils comes forth smoke ... His breath kindles coals, and a

flame comes forth from his mouth."
Four-Legged Fowl
The *King James Version* describes a four-legged bird:
All fowls that creep, going upon all four, shall be an abomination unto you. Yet these may ye eat of every flying creeping thing that goeth upon all four, which have legs above their feet to leap withal upon the earth. Some suppose these creatures may have been among the pterosaurs or flying reptiles.
(More Possible References to Dinosaurs in the Bible Psalm 104:26, 148:7; Isaiah 51:9; Job 7:12.)

(If you think the dinosaurs topic is bad,...wait! There will be a topic shortly that will fry your brains!)

There is a verse that describes man on earth and the angels seeing the animals of the earth were pleasing to their sight and they had sex with them. This was NOT to be done but the

makeup of mankind was such to have the ability to do so.

TITANS
(***Pay attention to this now***)

The **Titans** were very great, strong, and POWERFUL BEINGS and could do what <u>HUMANS </u>DID. BESIDES THEIR STRENGTH AND POWER, THEY ALSO HAD '<u>SPECIAL POWERS</u>', AND **BECAUSE** <u>GOD HAD CREATED THEM</u>, **PEOPLE WORSHIPPED THEM AS ANGELS OR SEMI-GODS.** SOME OF THEM FELT THE POWER SO MUCH THAT THEY ACTUALLY FELT THEMSELVES **AS IF 'BEING'** GOD.

<u>**They liked being worshipped and came to feel they could do anything God could do so acted as if they were equal with some going further and believing they didn't need** God.</u> They had sex with the earthly beings and caused great grotesque offspring to come into being.
Some animals were violent types which also caused great chaos for the earth. <u>God punished the fallen angels (Nephilim's)</u> and taking away their powers, threw them to the earth to be held captive until the final judgement. So this indicates the Titans were angels.

REINCARNATION

'Togetherness'

This is sort of a strange thing to be writing about, much less placing it in a book about 'reincarnation', but I go where I am being 'led,' so, here it is.

I happen to personally know of a person who had both sexes and I never realized it until finding, at the age of 13, or 14, that she was going to have an operation, after deciding for herself which sex she wanted to be. It was because of her, I had thoughts about 'homosexuality'.

Born 'Intersex,' studies find as an example that <u>a female</u> infant can have external sex organs that <u>resemble male genitals</u>. About 1 in 1,000 babies have this, and in a 2022 population in just the United States, that would be close to 'Three million, thirty-eight thousand babies. Is this a cause to 'SHOW UP' WITH WHAT PEOPLE 'CONSIDER' **HOMOSEXUAL ACTIVITIES**?

 Yes, there 'are' homosexuals who just want to be that, but I've wondered about 'some' who are merely 'caught' in a situation of no fault of their own. It was here I had mentioned the 'being born two sexes at once' to a friend who was a nurse. I was amazed at the answer she gave.

She said it happens more often than people realize. When it happens, the parents decide whether they want a girl or boy, and then the procedure is done to make the correction.

What IF, when the parents decided, and chose which sex 'they' wanted to have, that **the actual 'inner being, makeup'** of the baby <u>**was meant**</u> to be the 'opposite choice'? Then as the person grows up, their inner 'feelings is for the <u>**'same sex' as they 'are'**</u>, **but only 'because'** their <u>actual</u> **'real' sexual 'inner makeup' 'should have been opposite'** and the **'wrong' operation adjustment was made<u>!</u>** 'Inwardly they are relating with the correct feelings', but their physical 'sex' is wrong!

In fact, the information I have given will have places and articles of cases they have studied and their findings. There are possibly thousands more with the same condition whom they don't know about or were never included in their studies.

Also, think about 'this'. If 'twins' were born, and one of them had the double sex issue, the parents might decide they already have one 'son or daughter' so choose the other to be the opposite so they could have 'both' a son 'and' a daughter…or it they want 'two' of whichever sex the other is, that could also cause issues later

in life and one twin could have a normal way of living for the sex they are but the other could be a gay or homosexual!
Remember…There are **'TWO' creations** in the **NEW TESTAMENT.** In **'Luke'**, the creation starts with **Adam and Eve. However,** in **Mark,** the **creation** starts with **Abraham, Isaac, and Jacob.** That **should be** all there is about **any 'creations'** needed **for a new beginning,' AFTER the flood.**
However, Genesis 1:27 says, 'SO GOD CREATED MAN IN HIS <u>OWN</u> IMAGE, in the <u>image OF GOD</u> he created him; <u>MALE AND FEMALE he created</u> 'them'. And God blessed them. "BE FRUITFUL AND MULTIPLY AND FILL THE EARTH AND SUBDUE IT AND HAVE DOMINION OVER THE FISH OF THE SEA AND OVER THE BIRDS OF THE AIR AND OVER EVERY LIVING THING THAT MOVES UPON THE EARTH.
This implies that there **was a '<u>creation</u>' BEFORE ADAM AND EVE, and** where 'MANY PEOPLE WERE CREATED THEN', and by **the way the 'punctuation' is, they were BOTH** 'MALE **AND** FEMALE' **in one..** (Punctuation means a lot, and why I gave what 'my' marks are in the book for 'my' way of speaking.)

BUT what 'if' the words ... "made them in **'OUR' IMAGE**, **'MALE <u>AND</u> FEMALE'**, wasn't a 'lack of punctuation' after all? Was it an 'actual' thing? Farfetched? I'm with you, but ... **"What IF?"** ...Then, when told to MULTIPLY AND FILL THE EARTH, it 'may have been easier' to do than thinking about all the 'couples' needed to do it.' Those had to come from 'somewhere ' to have enough to do it!

That brought up questions in my mind from a 'fantasy' standpoint. I decided just for fun, to see what would come up on the internet, so I placed 'many questions' there. (It has already been established there are people born with 'both' different sexes.) With that in mind, you, yourself, are probably knowing what questions 'you' would ask. I figured one or two questions would get me my answers. Nope! It just made me ask more. The more I placed, the more answers I found with some that boggled my mind.

I even asked if people with both sexes could breed by themselves. I learned there **'are' many species** that do just that, but what 'blew my mind' was that they **also** have **documented data proving it 'has been' done 'also' <u>with humans</u>! Think of a baby being born with both sexes and the percentage of that happening.**

REINCARNATION

What if there was a small percentage for this too? (Here I ran into different opinions for that, but then I realized there were <u>two words</u> that almost 'look the same' but are different.) Naturally 'that' led to, '**WHAT IF**'... <u>that</u> was the '<u>**way it was' in the beginning**</u>,...in order to multiply the earth. Then it got out of hand with the ANGELS having sex with the **offspring of <u>earthly</u> creatures** (...or 'beings') **to a point of God finally having to send the flood to get rid of everything**. (This may get repeated more than once just to get the possible idea ingrained.)

Having '**both sexes'**, one could then have the ability to use '' one when needed, to multiply with the earth people. It wasn't meant to be that way at all, but the '<u>fallen angels</u>' would have taken advantage of their 'male and female' abilities and used 'either one' needed, to '**multiply with <u>earthly</u>' beings**. A 'male'_ could be mated with the '**female' earthling** but could also use the 'female part' to mate with the male earthling! If it would have been just between the 'people' species, it would have been one thing, but **because animals too** had 'both organs' in one body, it made it possible for 'persons to breed with <u>animals.'</u> (So back to what I found** about 'two sexed' people. The actual term (Wikipedia, the free encyclopedia)- **HERMAPHRODISM** is not to be confused with intersexuality, which is a separate and unrelated phenomenon. (*Not to be confused with **Intersex people or Intersex (biology).mating***

The **usage of hermaphrodite to describe intersex people** is considered **both offensive, and scientifically incorrect.**
A HERMAPHRODITE is a sexually reproducing organism that produces both **male** and **female sex** glands.
HERMAPHRODITISM Is a normal condition, enabling a form of sexual reproduction in which **either partner can act as the female or male. Hermaphroditism is also found in some fish** species but is rare or absent in 'most' vertebrae.
HERMAPHRODITIC SPECIES exhibit some degree of **self-fertilization. Self-fertilization** rates among animals is similar to that of plants, suggesting that similar pressures are operating to direct the evolution of 'selfing' in animals and plants.

Sequential hermaphrodites are born with one sex **but can switch to the**

opposite sex. They're also able to produce gametes from both males and females. **Simultaneous hermaphrodites** are **born with both female and male genitalia**, meaning they have an xx chromosome and xy chromosome. **During mating, they can take on the male or female role**. (In multiple cases, the animal also has the option of self-fertilization.)

Historically, the **term hermaphrodite was used in law to refer to people whose sex was in doubt**. (Depends on which sex prevails.)

Alexander ab Alexandro in **1461–1523 stated the people who bore the sexes of both man and woman were regarded by the Athenians and Romans as monsters, so were thrown in the sea and drowned.** During the Victorian period until the early 21st century, intersex individuals were termed true hermaphrodites if their gonadal tissue contained **both testicular and ovarian tissue**.

What this all shows is that there is a lot of the 'male <u>and</u> female' being known and acknowledged, so maybe the Bible is merely revealing a truth as to how it all

happened...by God formed them 'after' OUR image!

So THEN-
[Hermaphrodite - Wikipedia](https://en.wikipedia.org/wiki/Hermaphrodite)
A hermaphrodite is a **sexually reproducing organism that produces both male and female** organs at once.

So **IF, 'BEFORE ADAM'** there was a species of God with 'both sexes,' it would sort of be an explanation for populating the world faster. **However, how do we know for sure? After all, having a person having both sexes at the same time happens a lot even now. I found these statistics on the internet under ABC NEWS – (Mar.20,2011) said 1-2000 babies are born each year as intersex.**

2023 population reporting's reveal the percentage of intersex births:

UNITED STATES
Intersex is a great deal more than what people would think. Nearly two births in every 100 or up to 2% of the population.
EUROPE
Europe has one of the smallest percentages because with all their countries, there is 1 out of every 2,000 births or 0.05 are intersex.
AUSTRALIA is estimated that about 1.7 people in every 100,000 people or 1.7% of the total population is intersex.
INDIA is high with about 2% of the total population as intersex.
CHINA does not track the number of births each year identified as intersex because of Chinas "one-child" rule; babies that were born both were pushed toward a male identification. Babies were often mutilated to conform to one gender or another so doctors would perform surgeries without first testing the infant to find out its true sex. A child would sometimes grow up very obviously a man with female genitalia. (So we have a perfect reason for some 'homosexual activity.' **Their 'true gender' was lost!). (THIS goes along with what 'my' own thoughts are.)**

CANADA
It is estimated that .24% of all births in Canada with some higher to **0.36%** of all total deliveries.

Many believe surgery should be done within the first 15 months of life, while others believe these things should be put off until the child is old enough to make his or her own decision about it, which was <u>the personal case of the person I knew.</u>

(I DID FIND ONE ARTICLE SAYING THAT DOCTORS NOW DAYS ARE ABLE TO TELL THROUGH 'SPECIAL TESTING' AS TO WHAT THE CHILDS 'INNER' MAKE UP SHOULD BE AND CAN THEN DO THE PROCEEDURE NEEDED WITHOUT INVOVING A DECISION TO BE MADE BY THE PARENTS. (It doesn't stop the DNA/genes from forming the occurrence but will save the individual from living in the wrong type of body.)

So here we have covered a whole different subject away from reincarnation, but it 'does show' the need for 'punctuation' and how vital it is. (OR....THAT WE NEED TO READ WHAT IS BEING SAID MORE CLOSELY!) This is something to 'watch for' when 'reincarnation issues' appear because 'some' will try to use words to disprove reincarnation, but the Bible verses WILL prove otherwise. Yet now in 'this case', is the punctuation NOT there BECAUSE IT 'SHOULDN'T BE'? IF SO, we are being led to a whole different bit of information not realized before?

So, reverting back to the 'creation story' with God saying, "Let us make man in **OUR** image and with OUR **meaning** 'more than one' **and they are told to** 'multiply'. IF 'our image,' male and female was in their make-up, when the angels that looked down on the 'earthly creations' and decided to have sex with them, being both sexes themselves, they could take their pick.

(The outcome weren't just 'large,' giant people, but **'grotesque MONSTERS.'**)

Numbers 13:33 (KJV) **And there we saw the giants**, the sons of Anak, which come of the giants: **and we were in our own sight as grasshoppers, and so we were in their sight. The Titans were rebellious, wicked, and violent with everything imaginable within their doings continually.**
(Unger's Bible dictionary seventh printing1961, The Moody Bible)
THE TITANS WERE KNOWN AS SEMI GODS, WHICH IS BECAUSE THERE IS ONLY ONE GOD, HE CREATED ANGELS AS 'SEMI GODS' AS OBEDIENT, POWERFUL CREATURES IN HEAVEN. THESE ARE THE, "MAKE MAN IN OUR IMAGE, MALE AND FEMALE" REFERENCE. THE PROBLEM CAME WHEN THE ANGELS FELT THE STRENGTH AND POWER THEY POSSESSED AND DECIDED THEY DIDN'T HAVE TO BE LOWER THAN GOD BUT 'COULD BE' GOD THEMSELVES. BECAUSE OF THIS, GOD THREW THEM TO EARTH AND THEY COULD NO LONGER BE IN HEAVEN. THEY FELT THEIR STRENGTH AND POWER EVEN MORE WITH THE EARTHLY PEOPLE SO THEY BECAME WICKED AND FIERCE WITH THEM CAUSING THE PEOPLE TO WORSHIP THEM THROUGH FEAR. THIS IS

THE REASON FOR THE FLOOD TO HAVE TO HAPPEN.

Think about it. All this discussion we've covered about making man in 'our' image and the question about people having both sexes, along with weird grotesque offspring from angels and earthlings having sex, then grotesque Giants living in the world, to be followed only a few chapters later, with the creation of Adam and Eve is enough to blow your mind with confusion.

In the Bible, only <u>a few chapters later from 'this'</u>... 'creating man in **'OUR' IMAGE**,... was the "garden of Eden" established, and **'MAN' being <u>FORMED FROM</u> THE 'EARTH'S DUST' AND <u>BREATH WAS BLOWN INTO HIS NOSTRILS</u> AND MAN <u>BECAME A 'LIVING BEING'.</u>**

(It is as if a totally different 'creative process' began, but then, <u>'those others' are still 'out there'... somewhere</u>. But again, keep in mind... God's days are 1000 of ours!

Even though THERE WOULD still HAVE BEEN THOSE OTHERS already on the earth, a new area called Eden is created away from it all and in the NEW TESTAMENT, it is here where LUKE'S <u>CREATION STORY</u> would <u>BEGIN</u>.

ADAM AND EVE. (Remember it is just like **another** 'new' creation. Yet, again, **'One day' is as a thousand in God's eyes. How many 'thousands of years went by <u>before</u>** 'Eden' came into being?)
RIGHT NOW, WE ARE LEFT WITH THE DILEMMA OF ALL THOSE 'OTHER' 'BEINGS' AND WHY I WAS GIVEN THIS PUZZLING SUBJECT OF POSSIBLE BEINGS HAVING '<u>BOTH SEXES</u>' with THEIR BODY, (AND then wondering <u>WHY I WOULD BE LED TO SUCH A THING TO USE FOR MY 'REINCARNATION' BOOK!</u>) This book has nothing to do with that kind of topic and I could see 'no connection' where it would even have anything to do with 'reincarnation'!
 It was in my thoughts almost constantly. I would drive down the country roads taking in all the beauty of the pastures, trees, woods, and mountains. I would see the animals in the fields and be made aware of the wildlife when a turkey, deer, opossum, groundhog, turtle, and even once, a cougar would pass close to where I was. I marveled at the way God provides with the creation for keeping our world clean, as an animal that hadn't 'made it' without being killed by a car lay 'squished' on the road only to have 'vultures'

arrive almost immediately on the scene to 'clean it all up'. I would slow the car for a second to keep from hitting one of the many birds flying in front of the car.

Throughout all of this, my 'mind' kept asking myself, "What does people having ' both sexes' have to do with 'reincarnation'?" I would think of that when I woke up each morning, when I was in the shower, eating, during commercials on television, and in bed before sleeping. In fact, there were many nights I didn't go to sleep for a long time because of thinking of it. I could just 'leave it out, but it was sent my way for a reason ...a purpose...WHY?

Something just 'popped in' (there is a 'lot of that' in this book that wasn't anything I was planning to write about), but I guess it makes a lot of sense. If there are so many people with this issue OF BORN WITH BOTH SEXES, **if my book would just reach 'one' of them to let them realize it is more common than people realize, and they aren't the only one, so LET THEM KNOW THERE 'ARE' PEOPLE LIKE THEM** even around the world, 'maybe' <u>mentally and emotionally</u> it would help someone AND not 'hate' God for doing this to them! Instead, this might 'help' them realize a loving God is

using this book at 'this moment' to reach out to them. The next 'Reincarnation' will give them a different chance to 'enjoy' a life in a better way and learn lessons to help others from having had 'this experience' to help in a next incarnation. (I haven't even convinced myself... and how would that 'one' person 'just happen ...' 'just happen'... to 'GET' the book?) **Maybe such things as this is why God changed people living for 700-800 years and reduced it to 125 years. Should they have something which showed up from a DNA source through no fault of their own, people wouldn't have to suffer 'mentally' and 'emotionally' before finding relief. Then too, LIVING life for so many years of 700-800 years, it didn't give people 'more time' to better themselves, but rather more time to SIN! Instead, by dying by 125, they can be given the causes for their sins of 'that lifetime' and given an opportunity to better themselves faster with a 'new lifetime'. This would make strides toward everyone's 'goal' for being how God wishes them to be: <u>one with him,</u> in heaven'.**
We all know that as we live our lives now, <u>at any age we are,</u> we <u>do things</u> we know we shouldn't, but do it anyway. When the

REINCARNATION

person's SOUL comes back in a totally different body, it is designed for either 'reaping rewards' from the previous life or for a chastisement which has to be 'paid for' in some way because of the sins they did. (A simple example would be a man who hated women and did all they could to make women's lives miserable with rapes, disfigurations, degrading them, slavery, and just making living for them horrible. Guess what! 'That' <u>man just might have to 'come back' as... a woman!)</u> A person's sex might not change, but a 'body' with a life, depicting a 'lesson' that needs to be learned, will be given. They 'might be given' a life with rewards if they basically led a good life. (We are 'working toward' that FINAL judgement with the goal of being fit to enter heaven with GOD.)

<u>(These have been 'my own' 'comments',</u> but they will be verified with examples in the Bible which you will find from time to time, as you go through the book.)

SO...WHY IS 'a person with 'BOTH SEXES' in my 'reincarnation' book?

What does having BOTH sexes represent? Jesus spoke in Parables. Is this what we have represented here? Let's look at it with 'that' possibility with facts available.

TWO represents both male and female sides with neither being totally one over the other. (So let's do a sort of 'parable' type story, with a parable meaning to portray a spiritual or moral MEANING.)

Use the story of a tractor. The tractor gives great service if it is taken care of. No matter who drives, it will be there to accomplish many pleasing and 'profitable' needs and experiences. The tractor provides all anyone needs by giving it the capability to work hard. 'Both' have something they need to overcome, and possibly make changes in some way they live their life. By 'making a decision' to make changes to their life, lifestyle, and the way they use their tractor to live with, they will find a completely different world to live in and they should 'give thanks' for all it provides. As a oneness with their creator and a future of living in peace with LOVE . When the tractor has given its 'all' and things need to be fixed and redone, that tractor is put aside with a new one taking its place to continue on with its intended

REINCARNATION

destination! (I would <u>not</u> be a person to talk in 'parables.' I can't convince myself, so how could I reach others?)
WELL, so, WHAT IF...
GOD 'simply' CREATED THE WORLD AND EVERYTHING IN IT!
Like any of us parents, we always want our children we created to take after us.
(White people reap white offspring, black/black, yellow/yellow, Korean/Korean, Spanish/Spanish, Italian/Italian etc. It just happens that GOD'S MAKE UP IS 'ONE' BODY WITH 'BOTH' male and female makeup in one. The Bible says there is not marriage in heaven, so this might simply be a 'heavenly' form of spiritual kind.

Little did God ever think that people would use the 'free will' he also gave US to do such despicable things to his creation! (Just as we as parents are sometime appalled at what our own offspring do.) As with the dinosaurs that proved to be a mistake because they developed into fierce dangerous creatures after a while, God changed his design for people from one of 'His' own image to the design made from the earth for Adam.

The only thing is, that once God made something, the <u>DNA</u> for that 'first' creation is 'forever' formed, and while it <u>can lay dormant</u> as if not existing, it is never really 'ever gone'. ("THERE IS NOTHING NEW UNDER THE SUN. WHAT WAS, IS, AND WILL BE'. <u>Ecclesiastes 1:9</u>)

We all probably have something to do with those words on our own level of life. How many are dealing with a health issue, (or know someone who is) that 'to be coming to us through our **DNA**, from somewhere back in our family history' and through no fault of our own, disfiguration, harmful, painful, debilitating, or even life-threatening issues have made their way through, and we reap the outcome. God isn't doing something 'to us'...it is simply someone getting caught up by it. People get sick from flu , covid, colds, diseases caught in the air from others but God didn't cause them to get it but rather 'happen to'.

So it is with creation from the beginning. **DNA can slip through with something long been changed but still lies there to be able to, at times, slip through. THE 'BOTH' SEXES AT ONCE IS A BIG ONE, AS WELL AS THE GENE FOR A BODY WITH EXTRA TOES OR**

FINGERS. Even though the main design was curtailed somewhat, there is always a possibility for it to surface AS IT IS RIGHT THERE as we saw the statistics around the world earlier.)
THIS brings up THOUGHTS of another of my 'true experience' stories, I wrote about in my book on UFO's. ("Night Lights over Greeneville") That book has a 'lot' of information I received from watching UFO's in the same area by my house every night for two hours a night for weeks. To sum it up is that I was taking pictures every night in the same area with my camera on a tripod. For a connection to this book's material we are covering,... I kept getting 'one kind of picture' a lot, so went to the internet and posted it to see if other people might be getting it too. I called it a 'Roman Coin' design, but why I chose that beats me. I have no idea what a 'Roman coin' looks like. It looked like a 'coin' with a pattern. I got ONE 'hit' but it wasn't anything I expected. It was an **'ACTUAL' commemorative COIN PUT OUT BY FRANCE IN 1640 as a 'remembrance' of a 'REAL' EVENT.** One side of the coin had people trying to grow crops, but the crops were sparse and withered. Up in the air was a '<u>UFO</u>' which **MATCHED THE PICTURE OF MY 'COIN' (but**

actually a little different image of mine from what I'd posted.)

The 'flip side' of the coin showed a 'plant' growing from the bottom of the coin to the top with the words "<u>THEY HAVE COME TO HELP!</u>" (This was indicating that 'UFO's may be A PART OF GOD'S CREATION with 'built in' features to <u>help</u> mankind! Why are we seeing so many UFO's now? This sort of points to, 'NOTHING IS NEW UNDER THE SUN! WHAT 'WAS' HAS BEEN' and 'WILL BE"! Are there so many sightings now because there is a <u>need</u> for 'helpers' to come and be around? (REINCARNATION!) Is the fact we are seeing more of them, indicating we are in more need for help?

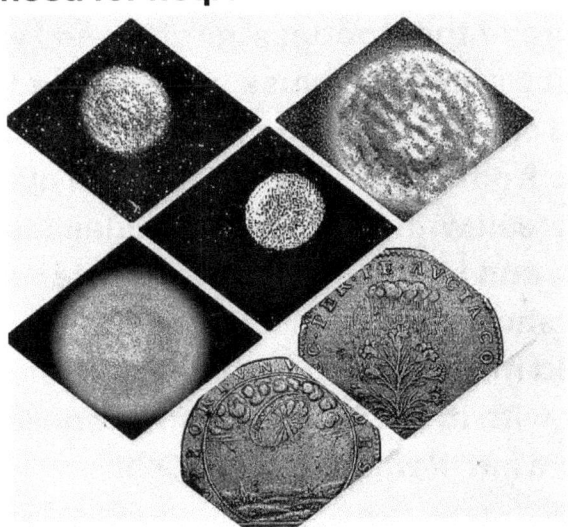

REINCARNATION

How far can this genes/DNA reach, then? Is the giraffe just born 'without spots' in Limestone, Tn., USA, a birth defect, or a species that was once on the earth back in creation and with cross breeding became giraffes with the pattern we now know? That would make the 'spotless giraffe' merely a 'once was' species. Is there some kind of cycle where the 'original' is going to show up, because since this one's birth, another giraffe like it, has just been born in another country. What's the 'odds' of it being a 'coincidence? Remember, "THERE IS NOTHING NEW UNDER THE SUN!"

I share my personal stories when they have a 'tie' or connection to the biblical topic. I have a picture of the 'spotless' giraffe and I will share it with you because in case it ends up being a species from the past and is showing up also from a lost DNA/gene. It will also give you a break with something besides Bible verses, and I happened to have gotten a 'funny shot' which caused me (and my 'warped mind') to just have to add a bit of humor with it. (BESIDES, it's MY book, and I can do what 'I' want! (ha) ENJOY!

OKAY, so we just took a break to show two instances where something from 'back in time' has been seen again', and 'perhaps' a DNA/gene slipped through 'revealing perhaps' something that existed before. SO, IS THIS 'TWO SEXES' THING **ALSO** from something 'back in creation' and 'normal' for then, and revealed the Bible

time when it was written, but people never 'picked up on' as to what was being said. (It's amazing at how many people change what it is saying to fit their own thought!) **IT 'SAYS' WHAT IT SAYS!** THE **BIBLE** IS INDICATING that **THE 'BEINGS' WERE OF THE 'SAME SEX'.**
 (especially if you didn't use 'punctuation marks').
WELL, HANG ON TO YOUR HATS'!
This has caused me many questions, many sleepless nights trying to 'figure out why the heck I was supposed to include this. At least 'you' will not have to wonder about it for weeks, as I did. In a few short pages, it will be brought to your attention and then the result found! (if right) Maybe it is still something a lot of you weren't aware of, so will have learned something new (...and is verified as true.)
*"In the early days of Amilius' rule, **the separation of the sexes had not yet begun to take place.** Though male in their outward aspect, the androgynous sons of God embodied within themselves the nature of both male and female in one person. By turning to the creative forces, they could become channels to bring into being androgynous progeny after their own kind imbued with a double soul and a*

double sexed body. *In this way,* **SEXUAL INTERCOURSE WAS UNNECESSARY AS A MEANS OF PROPAGATION."**
While life without sex doesn't seem like much fun, it points to a 'supernatural origin' for humanity; an idea shared by many ancient cultures worldwide. The "miraculous birth theme" or humans being made from clay or on a potter's wheel recurs throughout world religions and mythologies. Examples are to be found in Genesis, the Qur'an, Egyptian, Greek, Sumerian, Inca, Chinese, and some Native American mythologies.

(These have been 'my 'own 'comments', but they will be verified with examples in the Bible which you will find from time to time, as you go through the book.)
SO...WHY IS "a person with 'BOTH SEXES' in my 'reincarnation' book?
What does having two sexes in one body have to do with reincarnation? I Remember Jesus spoke in Parables. Is this what we have represented here? Let's look at it with 'that' possibility with facts available.
TWO represents both male and female sides with neither being totally one over the other. 'Both' have something they need to

overcome, and possibly make changes in some way with their life. By making a decision to make changes to their life, lifestyle, and the way they live, they will find a completely different world to live in and the life of fulfillment as a oneness with their creator and a future living in peace with LOVE. Through 'reincarnation', that goal could be reached. (I would <u>not</u> be a person to talk in 'parables. I can't convince myself, so how could I reach others!) TRY THIS.
WELL HERE IT IS! I did sort of answer it before.
GOD simply CREATED THE WORLD AND EVERYTHING IN IT! Like any of us parents, we always want our children we created to take after us. It just happens that GOD'S MAKE UP IS 'ONE' BODY WITH' BOTH' SEXES AT ONCE, so to have the ability to populate as needed. Again, white people reap white offspring, black/black, yellow/yellow, Korean/Korean Spanish/Spanish, Italian/Italian etc.)

The only thing is that once he made something, the DNA for that thing is forever formed and while it can lay dormant as if not existing, it is never really 'ever gone'.

("THERE IS NOTHING NEW UNDER THE SUN. WHAT WAS IS AND WILL BE."
Ecclesiastes 1:9)
We all probably have something to do with those words on our own level of life. How many are dealing with a health issue, (or someone we know is), that seems to be coming to us through our DNA from somewhere back in our family history. Again, through no fault of our own disfiguration, harmful, painful, debilitating, or even life-threatening issues have made their way through, and we reap the outcome. So it is with creation from the beginning. DNA can slip through with something long been changed but still lies there to be able to at times slip through. The 'both' sexes at once is a big one, as well as the gene for a body with extra toes or fingers. Even though the main design was curtailed somewhat, there is always a possibility for it to surface AS IT IS RIGHT THERE.

The **1901, Dorland's Medical Dictionary** defined **heterosexuality as an "abnormal or perverted appetite toward the opposite sex."** More than two decades later, in 1923, Merriam Webster's dictionary similarly defined it as "morbid sexual passion for one of the opposite sex." It wasn't until 1934 that heterosexuality was graced with the meaning we're familiar with today: "manifestation of sexual passion for one of the opposite sex; normal sexuality."

Quite a difference in views on sex make up. So why then does the BIBLE'S MENTION OF 'MAKE MAN IN OUR IMAGE AND THAT IS BOTH SEXES IN ONE' SURPRISE US SO? And THIS is from GOD and seems to be revealing what the Angels bodily make up is like. When they got a taste for intermingling with earthly beings, the angels fell from grace and lost their heavenly status. THAT DOESN'T MEAN THE REST WHO STAYED TRUE ARE ANY DIFFERENT SO KEEP BOTH SEXES IN ONE!

There were also Giants in the land because of the intermingling of angels and earthlings. These giants passed on some of their characteristics which HAVE ALSO SLIPPED THROUGH AND ARE SEEN EVEN TODAY.

There is one tribe where a lot of people have **six digits**: the **Waorani** in Ecuador normal-sized people that exhibit among some of them **'GIANT' CHARACTERISTICS**. They have six fingers, six toes, and double dentition (not all of them). (They are a tribe of particularly violent South American aborigines.) Fully fifty per cent of all deaths in the preceding five generations had been the result of homicide as the Waorani engaged in a continuous and deadly internal vendetta. Medically, they had no trace of cancer, cardiovascular disease, high blood pressure, allergies, or any of the known diseases familiar to us. Like the giants of past ages, they are physically very strong and violent.

Wikipedia, the free Encyclopedia- HERMAPHRODITE is a sexually <u>reproducing</u> organism that <u>PRODUCES</u> BOTH male and female organs.

HERMAPHRODITIC (Webster's dictionary)
HAVING both male and female reproductive organs

Typed a question onto the internet asking if people came from 'hermaphroditic' people and this is the answer.

According to a research from the University of Pittsburgh published in the Nov. 24, 2008, edition, research could finally provide **evidence of the first stages of the evolution of separate sexes, a theory that holds that males and females developed from hermaphroditic ancestors**. These early stages are not completely understood because the majority of animal species developed into the arguably less titillating separate-sex state too long ago for scientists to observe the transition. (**Documented early separate-sex evolution in a 'wild strawberry species'** <u>still transitioning</u> **from hermaphroditism.**)T[1][1].
Science News
from research organizations
Two From One: Evolution Of Genders From Hermaphroditic Ancestors Mapped Out

SO , WHAT I DISCOVERED AND MENTIONED about being in the Bible are that there 'were' persons CREATED <u>'BEFORE'</u> ADAM, and then with the STATEMENT, "LET 'US' MAKE MAN IN 'OUR' IMAGE", points toward a reality of God and angels being <u>both sexes.</u>

Pauline E. Petsel

Abraham
From authorized King James on-line standard edition

Romans 4:3 Context

[1]What shall we say then that Abraham our father, as pertaining to the flesh, hath found? [2]For if Abraham were justified by works, he hath *whereof* to glory; but not before God. [3] **For what saith the scripture? Abraham believed God, and it was counted unto him for righteousness.** [4]Now to him that worketh is the reward not reckoned of grace, but of debt. [5]But to him that worketh not, but believeth on him that justifieth the ungodly, his faith is counted for righteousness. [6]Even as David also describeth the blessedness of the man, unto whom God imputeth righteousness without works

Galatians 3:6 Context

[3]Are ye so foolish? having begun in the Spirit, are ye now made perfect by the flesh? [4]Have ye suffered so many things in vain? if *it be* yet in vain. [5]He therefore that ministereth to you the Spirit, and worketh miracles among you, *doeth he it* by the works of the law, or by the hearing of faith? [6]**Even as Abraham believed God, and it was accounted to him for righteousness.** [7]Know ye therefore that they which are of faith, the same are the

children of Abraham. [8]And the scripture, foreseeing that God would justify the heathen through faith, preached before the gospel unto Abraham, *saying*, In thee shall all nations be blessed. [9]So then they which be of faith are blessed with faithful Abraham [10]For as many as are of the works of the law are under the curse: for it is written, Cursed *is* every one that continueth not in all things which are written in the book of the law to do them. [11]But that no man is justified by the law in the sight of God, it is evident: for, The just shall live by faith. [12]And the law is not of faith: but The man that doeth them shall live in them. [13]Christ hath redeemed us from the curse of the law, being made a curse for us: for it is written, Cursed *is* every one that hangeth on a tree: [14]That the blessing of Abraham might come on the Gentiles through Jesus Christ; that we might receive the promise of the Spirit through faith. [15]Brethren, I speak after the manner of men; Though *it be* but a man's covenant, yet *if it be* confirmed, no man disannulleth, or addeth thereto.

Galatians 3:13 Context

[10]For as many as are of the works of the law are under the curse: for it is written, Cursed *is* everyone that continueth not in all things which are written in the book of the law to do them. [11]But that no man is justified by the law in the sight of God, *it is* evident: for,

The just shall live by faith. ¹²And the law is not of faith: but The man that doeth them shall live in them. **¹³Christ hath redeemed us from the curse of the law, being made a curse for us: for it is written, Cursed is every one that hangeth on a tree:** ¹⁴That the blessing of Abraham might come on the Gentiles through Jesus Christ; that we might receive the promise of the Spirit through faith. ¹⁵Brethren, I speak after the manner of men; Though *it be* but a man's covenant, yet *if it be* confirmed, no man disannulleth, or addeth thereto. ¹⁶Now to Abraham and his seed were the promises made. He saith not, And to seeds, as of many; but as of one, And to thy seed, which is Christ. ¹⁶Now to Abraham and his seed were the promises made. He saith not, And to seeds, as of many; but as of one, And to thy seed, which is Christ. ¹⁷And this I say, *that* the covenant, that was confirmed before of God in Christ, the law, which was four hundred and thirty years after, cannot disannul, that it should make the promise of none effect. ¹⁸For if the inheritance *be* of the law, *it is* no more of promise: but God gave *it* to Abraham by promise.

Galatians 3:16 Context

¹³Christ hath redeemed us from the curse of the law, being made a curse for us: for it is written, Cursed *is* every one that hangeth on a

tree: ¹⁴That the blessing of Abraham might come on the Gentiles through Jesus Christ; that we might receive the promise of the Spirit through faith. ¹⁵Brethren, I speak after the manner of men; Though *it be* but a man's covenant, yet *if it be* confirmed, no man disannulleth, or addeth thereto. **¹⁶Now to Abraham and his seed were the promises made. He saith not, And to seeds, as of many; but as of one, And to thy seed, which is Christ.** ¹⁷And this I say, *that* the covenant, that was confirmed before of God in Christ, the law, which was four hundred and thirty years after, cannot disannul, that it should make the promise of none effect. ¹⁸For if the inheritance *be* of the law, *it is* no more of promise: but God gave *it* to Abraham by promise. ¹⁹Wherefore then *serveth* the law? It was added because of transgressions, till the seed should come to whom the promise was made; *and it was* ordained by angels in the hand of a mediator.

Galatians 3:17 Context

¹⁴That the blessing of Abraham might come on the Gentiles through Jesus Christ; that we might receive the promise of the Spirit through faith. ¹⁵Brethren, I speak after the manner of men; Though *it be* but a man's covenant, yet *if it be* confirmed, no man disannulleth, or addeth thereto. ¹⁶Now to Abraham and his

seed were the promises made. He saith not, And to seeds, as of many; but as of one, And to thy seed, which is Christ. [17]**And this I say, that the covenant, that was confirmed before of God in Christ, the law, which was four hundred and thirty years after, cannot disannul, that it should make the promise of none effect.** [18]For if the inheritance be of the law, *it is* no more of promise: but God gave *it* to Abraham by promise. [19]Wherefore then *serveth* the law? It was added because of transgressions, till the seed should come to whom the promise was made; *and it was* ordained by angels in the hand of a mediator. [20]Now a mediator is not *a mediator* of one, but God is one law, which was four hundred and thirty years after, cannot disannul, that it should make the promise of none effect. [18]For if the inheritance *be* of the law, *it is* no more of promise: but God gave *it* to Abraham by promise. [19]Wherefore then serveth the law? It was added because of transgressions, till the seed should come to whom the promise was made; and it was ordained by angels in the hand of a mediator. [20]Now a mediator is not *a mediator* of one, but God is one. [21]*Is* the law then against the promises of God? God forbid: for if there had been a law given which could have given life, verily righteousness should have been by the law. [22]But the scripture hath concluded all under sin, that the promise by faith of Jesus Christ might be given to them that believe.

But **MY COVENANT WILL I ESTABLISH WITH** ISAAC, which 'SARAH SHALL BEAR UNTO THEE' at this set time, in the next year. **AND ABRAHAM CALLED THE NAME OF HIS SON, THAT WAS BORN UNTO HIM, WHOM SARAH BARE TO HIM,** ISAAC.

(Genesis 21:4)

And Abraham circumcised his son Isaac, being eight days old, as God had commanded him.

Genesis 21:5

And Abraham was a hundred years old when his son Isaac **was born unto him.**

Genesis 21:8

And the child grew and was weaned: and Abraham made a great feast, the same day that Isaac was weaned.

Genesis 21:10
Wherefore she said unto Abraham, "Cast out this bond woman, and her son: for the son of this bond woman shall not be heir with my son, even with Isaac."

Genesis 21:12
And God said unto Abraham, "Let it not be grievous in thy sight because of the lad and because of thy bond woman. In all that Sarah hath said unto thee, hearken unto her voice: for in Isaac shall thy seed be called."

Genesis 22:2
And he said, "Take now thy son, 'THINE ONLY SON ISAAC', WHOM THOU LOVEST, AND GET THEE INTO THE LAND OF MORIAH: AND **'OFFER HIM THERE FOR A BURNT OFFERING'** UPON ONE OF THE MOUNTAINS WHICH I WILL TELL THEE OF."

Genesis 22:3
And Abraham rose up early in the morning, and saddled his ass, and

took two of his young men with him, and **Isaac** his son, and clave the wood for the burnt offering, and rose up, and went unto the place of which God had told him.

Genesis 22:6

And Abraham took the wood of the burnt offering and laid it upon Isaac **his son: and he took the fire in his hand, and a knife: and they went both of them together**.

Genesis 22:7

And Isaac spake unto Abraham his father, and said, "My father." And he said, "Here am I, my son." And he said, "Behold the fire and wood: but where is the lamb for a burnt offering?" (***)

Genesis 22:9

AND THEY CAME TO THE PLACE WHICH GOD HAD TOLD HIM OF, AND ABRAHAM BUILT AN ALTAR THERE, AND LAID THE WOOD IN ORDER, AND BOUND ISAAC **HIS SON, AND**

LAID HIM ON THE ALTAR UPON THE WOOD.
Genesis 22:15-18

And he said, "**Lay not thine hand upon the lad, neither do thou anything unto him: for now I know that thou fearest God, seeing thou hast not withheld thy son, thine only son from me.**"

And said, "**By myself have I sworn," saith the LORD,** "for because thou hast done this thing, and hast **not withheld thy son, thine only son**, that in blessing **I will bless thee, and in multiplying, I will multiply thy seed as the stars of the heaven, and as the sand which is upon the seashore, and thy seed shall possess the gate of his enemies**.

And in thy seed shall all the nations of the earth be blessed because thou hast obeyed my voice.

*** **Genesis 17:5**
"Neither shall thy name any more be called Abram, but thy name shall be Abraham: **for a father of many nations have I made thee.**"

Genesis 17:9
And God said unto Abraham, "**Thou shalt keep my covenant therefore, thou, and thy seed after thee, in their generations.**"

Isn't this area strange in itself? Abraham is said to be father of all nations and here he is offering his 'only begotten son' as a sacrifice? Sort of matches another experience to come where an 'only begotten son' is sacrificed for the forgiveness of our sins, doesn't it?

Abraham /Isaac
And when **Abram was ninety years old and nine, the LORD appeared to** Abram, and said unto him, "I *am* the Almighty God; **WALK BEFORE ME, AND BE THOU PERFECT. AND I**

WILL make my covenant between me and thee and will **MULTIPLY THEE EXCEEDINGLY."** (Note the words being said here! These again are "Instructions" **TO BE FOLLOWED** and 'IF' it is done, 'THEN'**...**God will make his 'promise' come true. (There will be a '**pattern**' showing up **'throughout the incarnations of 'Jesus' with this 'same message'** being said. **The one word 'IF', 'begins' with ADAM, and 'most people' don't catch onto it. In the 'creation' with ADAM, HE is given 'everything anyone would ever need for life and 'would be' the 'ruler' of it all,' BUT is told there is only 'ONE' THING' he was 'NOT' TO DO..." Eat of the one tree in the garden: the tree of 'knowledge of good and evil' ... OR he would die."**
(King James Version - Genesis 11) Abraham and Sarah **were old and well stricken in age; and it ceased to be with Sarah after the manner of women. Therefore, Sarah laughed within herself, saying, "After I am waxed old shall I have pleasure, my lord being old also?"**

REINCARNATION

(King James Version - Genesis 13-14) And the Lord said unto Abraham, **"Wherefore did Sarah laugh, saying, 'Shall I of a surety bear a child, which am old?' IS ANYTHING TOO HARD FOR THE LORD? At the 'time appointed' I will return unto thee, according to the time of life, and Sarah shall have a son."** Genesis 18:18-19
Seeing that Abraham shall surely become a great and mighty nation, and all the nations of the earth shall be blessed in him?
FOR I KNOW HIM, that he will command his children and his household after him, and they shall keep the way of the LORD, to do justice and judgment; THAT THE LORD MAY BRING UPON ABRAHAM THAT WHICH HE HATH SPOKEN OF HIM.

Genesis 21:1-2
FOR SARAH CONCEIVED, AND BARE ABRAHAM A SON IN HIS OLD AGE, 'AT THE SET TIME OF WHICH GOD HAD SPOKEN TO HIM.'

And God said unto Abraham, "As for Sarai thy wife, thou shalt not call

her name Sarai, but Sarah *shall* her name *be*. ⁱ⁶ And I will bless her and give thee a son also of her: yea, I will bless her, and SHE SHALL BE *A MOTHER* OF NATIONS; KINGS OF PEOPLE SHALL BE OF HER." And God said, "Sarah thy wife shall bear thee a son indeed; and THOU SHALT CALL HIS NAME ISAAC: and I will establish my covenant with him for an everlasting covenant, *and* with his seed after him."

"My covenant will I establish with Isaac which Sarah shall bear unto thee at this set time in the next year." (Here it says Sarah will bear the child next year but in fact it was 25 years before it took place. Remember the timeline for GOD'S 'DAYS' is not the same as one of 'our days'.

ABRAHAM CALLED THE NAME OF HIS SON THAT WAS BORN UNTO HIM, WHOM SARAH BARE TO HIM, **ISAAC.**

And Abraham circumcised his son Isaac being eight days old, **as God had commanded him. And Abraham was a hundred years old when his son Isaac was born unto him.**

REINCARNATION

(THE NEXT PART OF ABRAHAM'S STORY IS SOMETHING ELSE. IN THIS DAY AND AGE, WE WOULD CALL IT A 'scam message', and any people who fell for it 'being of God' were really gullible. (However, this was NOT the internet, 'yet even then, with Bible times', there was always **Satan doing 'his' thing**. But even at that, if you 'tried to reason it out' with 'our way of thinking', **GOD** would '**not** **be wanting you to KILL someone' and especially your precious only son'. On top of 'that,' what would you be contending with by your wife when she found out what you had done! So Abraham taking his son to be sacrificed on an altar is far beyond anything I would think would ever happen!** (But then again,...those are my 'thoughts' and shows 'my' lack of faith in God, and 'why' **I** will be living a whole lot of lives until I understand! I 'do' have faith in God in many ways even now, but 'THAT" is beyond 'my' level.)

And ISAAC SPAKE: "BUT WHERE *IS* THE LAMB FOR A BURNT

OFFERING?" And Abraham said, "My son, God will provide himself a lamb for a burnt offering." So he took the fire in his hand, and a knife; and THEY WENT BOTH OF them together. ⁹**And they came to the place which God had told him of; and Abraham built an altar there, and laid the wood in order, AND BOUND ISAAC HIS SON, AND LAID HIM ON THE ALTAR UPON THE WOOD.** ⁶**And Abraham took the wood of the burnt offering, and laid** *it* **upon Isaac his son;**¹⁰**And Abraham stretched forth his hand, and took the knife to slay his son.** And the angel of the LORD called unto him out of heaven, and said, Abraham, Abraham: and he said, "Here am I." Genesis 22:11 (KJV) **He said, "Lay not thine hand upon the lad, neither do thou anything unto him: for now I know that thou fearest God, seeing thou hast not withheld thy son, thine only** *son* **me."** ¹³And Abraham lifted up his eyes, and looked, and behold, behind *him* a ram caught in a thicket by his horns: and Abraham went and took the ram and offered him up for a burnt offering **in the stead of his son.** [14]And Abraham called the name of that place Jehovah Jireh: as it is still today.

So, now, going back to 'MY' **'present way' of thinking,' mode**. WHAT DO 'YOU' THINK ISAAC HIMSELF WAS THINKING WHEN HIS DAD TIED HIM DOWN AND WAS READY TO KILL HIM WITH A KNIFE?
(Even afterwards, when he was safe, yet just knowing what had happened and how close he was for his father to have killed him,... **could he ever trust his father again?! 'Could' his father ever be trusted if he asked him if he 'wanted to go for a walk?'. That would be 'my' thoughts**, but **being who Isaac was, he possibly 'understood' and might have been pleased with Abraham! That would be far from 'my' thoughts!**

I keep inserting things from my 'own private life's story' to help you put things into a

'modern day' scenario, as an example of how something in today's world could fit with those times. Our daughter got Leukemia during her senior year of high school. I have had religious/spiritual things happen many times throughout my life and perhaps they are giving me a test like Abraham was faced with, and if so, I flunked it royally. The churches have helped with that, with their 'warning of Satan' trying to 'pretend' to be something is good and isn't.
Kristie had her blood work done at All Children's Hospital and the lab people came running in one day to announce that something very strange had happened with her blood slides. None of them had EVER seen this before, and it not only happened with 'one', but 'BOTH' her slides. They 'BOTH' came out with her blood being formed into a 'perfect' heart! I put a picture of it here even though It may not be as impressive in black and white. It was a few days later when I was awakened by a 'VOICE' saying, "There has been a healing". HERE WAS my DELEMMA! We had 'two signs' that she was healed, yet to take her off her chemo which we 'knew' would save her life, I had to make a decision as to IF what I was 'seeing and hearing' was

of GOD, or... was it of Satan pretending to be Him. If I believed the wrong way, I could be responsible for her life, or death. If it was GOD, I didn't have enough 'faith' to for sure to believe it. (A close story to the Abraham story, but HE had Faith to Believe!) I believed in my heart,... but my 'mind' ruled.

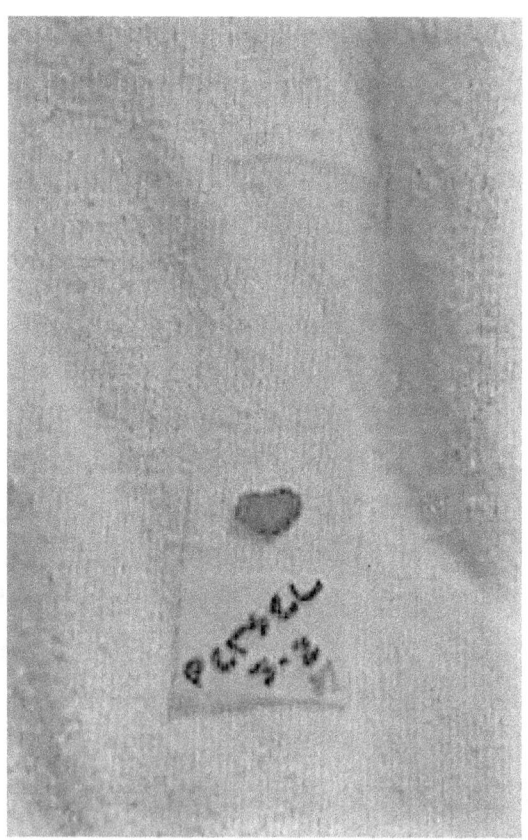

Any of you 'religious type' people reading this, that **HAVE CANCER.... Do you know what YOU would do in that same situation? (Religious people who <u>don't have cancer</u> would 'think' they know what they would do, but unless it is an actual life decision to make, it is way different!)**

Then I can add one more 'thought' and like I had wondered what Isaac was thinking about his father's actions, I know what 'my daughter' being the subject like Isaac was. I asked her years later and she said she wouldn't have let me stop her chemo that 'she' believed in.

I AM

Start off with the meaning of the words **"I AM"**! It **IS THE NAME** OF GOD! (Exodus 3:14...absolute) This is **one** which needs to be remembered . The beginning of all things. (I AM the beginning!) IN THE **IMAGE OF GOD** CREATED HE THEM.

King James Version ((KJV))
'Luke' starts the 'creation' with God's son Adam being the first created person on the earth. (Luke also mentions the **'lineage '**in Luke 3:37...son of Adam, the son of God. Genesis 5:1 — King James Version (KJV) Adam** *"IS THE 'FIGURE OF HIM' THAT 'WAS' TO COME."* Paul carries this comparison still further when he says in **1 CORINTHIANS 15:47,** *"THE FIRST MAN (ADAM) IS OF THE 'EARTH'."* THE 'SECOND MAN', (JESUS CHRIST) IS THE LORD FROM ' HEAVEN'*. (THIS IS REVEALING 'REINCARNATION' RIGHT HERE...YOU'LL SOON SEE WHY!)*

*THIS is why the **'OLD TESTAMENT'** is so vital but YET the 'biggest' part of people don't give it a thought! (They just state ... **"WHO CARES"**!?) and HE (**SETH**)WAS IN THE **'LIKENESS' OF ADAM**! (ARE WE SEEING AN EVENTUAL 'SECOND CHANCE' FOR ADAM WHO 'SCREWED UP' AND CAUSED SIN TO COME INTO THE WORLD, FOR WHICH 'WE ALL' PAY? REMEMBER too, 'ADAM HIMSELF' WAS IN THE 'LIKENESS' OF THE CREATOR GOD! SETH HAD A SON ENOSH, and AT THAT TIME MEN BEGAN TO CALL UPON THE NAME OF THE LORD!*
STORIES: EXODUS 3:6 IS THE REVEALING STATEMENT OF GOD'S MAKEUP AND 'REINCARNATIONS' OF JESUS AND STARTS 'BECAUSE OF' ABRAHAM!

I am = (Exodus)

'I AM' THE GOD OF YOUR FATHER, the 'God of Abraham', the 'God of Isaac', and the 'God of Jacob.' *(According to the Unger's Bible dictionary, 'I AM' IS 'HE WHO IS'... THE ABSOLUTE ...THE 'ONE'.)

Acts 7:32

An <u>'actual Bible verse'</u> would TAKE ON a different meaning. "I AM" (WITHOUT ANY PUNCTUATION MARK MAKES IT APPEAR AS A **SENTENCE** revealing WHO HE IS...(Thus, The Father of Abraham, Isaac, and Jacob. (showing his 'sons' names) If **I AM** had a comma afterward, it says 'I AM, the Father of Abraham, Isaac, and Jacob and **indicates <u>HIS</u> <u>name</u>**. Now all this makes a difference for who is reading this book. Non-religious people are only interested in 'proof for reincarnation'. What 'I AM' means, means nothing to them. Semi-religious people may be reading it all as I have just mentioned. RELIGIOUS PEOPLE OR SCHOLARS WOULD BE 'SEEING' THE DIFFERENCE AS TO **WHOM HE WAS SAYING HE WAS THE FATHER OF** BECAUSE THESE PEOPLE WERE ALL IN A <u>TOTALLY DIFFERENT TIME PERIOD, THUS **I AM** INDICATED THE NAME OF</u> God himself! (Jesus spoke to the crowds with parables and this is an example of how things can be heard <u>differently</u> or 'missed' altogether.)

Seeing as this book is about 'reincarnation', I'll take it a bit further. Is he saying **those are the only people he was father of and the rest of** us aren't in his 'IN' group? THEN WHY DO **WE** say, "**OUR Father** who art in heaven?" … "be present at **our table Lord**,"…"**Our heavenly Father**"…? etc.

If he said he was the <u>father of</u> Abraham, Isaac, and Jacob, THEN could that mean 'those very people' and 'offspring' were <u>the very same</u>, 'but as different' people over time? The Bible says there is only ONE GOD! Isaac's <u>son</u> was <u>Jacob and remember back then, people were living 700-800 years.</u>

So, may I refer **to John 8:58 Jesus answered**, "I tell you the truth, **before Abraham was even born, I AM!**" This is the same in all translations with very minor differences. And another quotation, **Exodus 3:14,** <u>God said</u> to Moses, **"I AM WHO I AM"**; and He said, "Thus you shall **say to the sons of Israel**, I **AM has sent me to you."** (Food for thought. If Jesus is <u>the word of God</u>, then he is a part of God, which will give him the right to say that he is **"I AM."** He has always been.)

"I am the vine, you are the branches. He who abides in Me, and I in him, bears much fruit; for without Me you can do nothing." John 15:5 (A vine branches out and then produces a 'crop' for its kind, but without the vine, it can't do anything.)

John 8:58 **Jesus answered**, "I tell you the truth, **before Abraham was** even born, **I AM!**" Exodus 3:14, "God said to Moses, **"I AM WHO I AM"**; and He said, "Thus you shall say to the sons of Israel, **'I AM'** has sent me to you." (HERE, it is showing that **I AM IS** his **NAME!**

"I AM the good shepherd. The good shepherd gives His life for the sheep." -John 10:11

Jesus said to her, "I AM the resurrection and the life. <u>He who believes in Me</u>, though he may die, he shall live. And whoever lives and believes in Me shall never die. Do you believe this?" John 11:25, 26

Jesus said to him, "I AM the way, the truth, and the life. NO ONE COMES TO THE FATHER EXCEPT THROUGH ME." JOHN 14:6

So then, with all these Bible passages in mind **CONCERNING JESUS AND 'I AM,'** let's start with Matthew's statement' concerning **ABRAHAM.**
*"**Go from your country and your kindred** and your father's house to the land that I will show you. **And I will make of you a great**

nation, and I will bless you and make your name great, so that you will be a blessing. I will bless those who bless you, and him who dishonors you, I will curse, and in you all the families of the earth. Look around from where you are, to the north and south, to the east and west. All the land that you see I will give to you and your offspring forever. I will make your offspring like the dust of the earth, so that if anyone could count the dust, then your offspring could be counted. Go, walk through the length and breadth of the land, for 'I AM' giving it to you." **(Genesis 13:14-17)**. The **original promise of land and blessings** started to come into focus as the Lord refers to Abraham's offspring for the first time. Only one problem, Abraham was now 85 years old, with no children of his own, and married to a woman who was herself unable to have children.

(Genesis 12:1-3, ESV).
I will make you a great nation;
I will bless you
And make your name great;

And you shall be a blessing.
I will bless those who bless you,
And I will curse him who curses you;
And in you all the families of the earth shall be blessed."

Genesis 17
THIRTEEN YEARS LATER, God told Abram that He would give him a son through Sarai. This son—**ISAAC**— was to BE **THE SON OF HIS COVENANT NATIONS." GOD FULFILLED HIS PROMISE TO ABRAHAM AND SARAH GAVE BIRTH TO ISAAC (GENESIS 21:1).**
(NOTE IN LUKE with the ORIGINAL 'CREATION')
GOD CREATED ADAM AND EVE UNIQUELY IN GOD'S OWN IMAGE, AND HE called them "mankind." He commanded them to " be fruitful, multiply, fill the earth and subdue it, and have dominion over... every living thing" (Genesis 1:27-28, 5:1- Genesis 17 this with Genesis 9:1-2)

I AM

Reincarnations of Jesus- I AM- FATHER OF ABRAHAM, ISAAC, JACOB

(Notice...this page is directly from the 1611 version of the Bible so misspelling will be horrible. Just thought I'd add one section of this so you can see what people dealt with back in those times. It might drive people who spell well crazy, but people who can't spell might enjoy it!)

Genesis 25:19 |
¶ And these are the generations of Isaac, **Abrahams sonne: Abraham begate** Isaac.

1 Chronicles 1:34 |
And <u>Abraham begate</u> Isaac. **The sonnes of** Isaac: **Esau, and Israel.**

Genesis 48:15 |
¶ And he blessed Ioseph and said, God **before whom my fathers Abraham and** ISAAC **DID WALKE, THE** GOD **WHICH FEDDE MEE ALL MY LIFE LONG VNTO THIS DAY,**

EXODUS 3:6 |
MOREOUER HEE SAID, I AM THE GOD OF THY FATHER, THE GOD OF ABRAHAM, THE GOD OF ISAAC, AND THE GOD **OF IACOB. AND <u>MOSES HID HIS FACE: FOR HE WAS AFRAID TO LOOKE VPON</u>** GOD<u>.</u>

And God said moreouer vnto Moses, Thus shalt thou say vnto the children of Israel; The Lord God of your fathers, the God of Abraham, the God of Isaac, and the God of Iacob hath sent me vnto you: THIS IS MY NAME FOR EUER, AND THIS IS MY MEMORIALL VNTO ALL GENERATIONS.

Exodus 4:5 | Read whole chapter(reincarnation/spirit)
That they may beleeue that the Lord God **of their fathers,**
THE GOD **OF ABRAHAM,**
THE GOD **OF** ISAAC, **AND THE GOD OF IACOB HATH APPEARED VNTO THEE.**
Acts 7:32 |
> **Saying, I am the God of thy fathers, the God of Abraham, AND THE GOD OF ISAAC, AND THE GOD OF IACOB. THEN MOSES TREMBLED, AND DURST NOT BEHOLD.**

Matthew 22:32 |
> **I AM THE GOD OF ABRAHAM, AND THE GOD OF ISAAC, AND THE GOD OF IACOB? GOD IS**

NOT THE GOD OF THE DEAD, BUT OF THE LIUING

And he said, Go forth, and stand upon the mount before the LORD. And, behold, the LORD passed by, and a great and strong wind rent the mountains, and brake in pieces the rocks before the LORD; but the LORD was not in the wind: and after the wind an earthquake; but the LORD was not in the earthquake: 12And after the earthquake a fire; but the LORD was not in the fire: and after the fire a still small voice. It is telling us right here that God is not in all those strong visual things around us but rather is invisible to the eyes but the small 'inner voice' is of God and speaks to us there. A lot of this book is coming from 'that' voice.)

- 1. John 10:30 "The Father and I are one ."
- 2. Philippians 2:5-6 "You must have the same attitude that Christ Jesus had.

- 3. John 17:21 "That they all may be one; as thou, Father, art in me, and I in thee, that they also may be one in us: that the world may believe that thou hast sent me."

And the Word became flesh and dwelt among us, and we have seen his glory, glory as of the only Son from the Father, full of grace and truth.

For unto us a child is born, unto us a son is given; and the government shall be upon his shoulder, and his name shall be called Wonderful Counselor, Mighty God, Everlasting Father, Prince of Peace.

I AM ... REINCARNATIONS OF Jesus

**I AM .... SO AM I ... SO WHAT?...
OH WOW!..................... THAT'S WHAT!**

I AM. (After reading what I am going to give Bible verses for, **it seems what he placed on the earth in his image were angels or heavenly hosts.** The creatures of every kind and sizes saw them and because everything was told to be fruitful and multiply, animals of all kinds and sizes did just that but not only amongst themselves **but also with the ones in the image of God. Those then were people known as Nephilim's, Titans, and more.** THE REASON THIS IS IMPORTANT IS BECAUSE AFTER THE EARTH HAD BEEN IN EXISTENCE 1656 YEARS, THERE WAS A NEED FOR GOD TO 'WIPE OUT EVERYTHING' **BECAUSE OF DETESTABLE ACTIONS OF THE INHABITANTS. With the angels having relations with earth animals, the outcome became detestable looking, and then with giants' actions of feeling their power because of their size and strength decided they could 'take over' God, something had to be done.** Some giants were even fourteen foot tall. WE TEND TO THINK OF ADAM AS THE FIRST PERSON BUT SURPRISINGLY THESE WERE APPARENTLY HERE BEFORE.

In **Genesis 1:26** with the unusual strengths it brought them thoughts in their mind that they didn't need God because they themselves could have the same kind of power and become rulers.

In **Genesis 2** (2 and 3), God **rests after seven days of creation**.

In **Genesis 2: 7** says and the Lord God formed **man of the dust of the ground and breathed into his nostrils the**

BREATH OF LIFE, and MAN BECAME A LIVING SOUL. And the Lord God planted a garden eastward in Eden and there he put **MAN WHOM HE HAD FORMED.** This just sounds like different stories of the same time in creation but yet there are many differences.

In **the first part,** God creates man in 'THEIR IMAGE' and **grotesque creatures come from the animals mixing with them.** ...Here... ONE MAN IS FORMED 'FROM THE EARTH' AND 'LIFE IS BLOWN INTO HIS NOSTRILS' AND HE BECOMES A LIVING <u>SOUL</u>!

THEN it follows ADAM'S LIFE ITSELF and HE goes against God's orders for the Garden of Eden, then his kids show other sins with one killing the other over jealousy and greed. This and more happens but it is closer to the time just before the flood. ADAM BROUGHT SIN INTO the world, so with everything else, God had had enough!
OFTEN PEOPLE THINK THE FLOOD WAS TO WIPE EVERYTHING AND EVERYONE OUT 'BECAUSE OF SINS' LIKE YOU AND I DO, BUT IT HAD

NOTHING TO DO WITH THAT, (although Adam's life didn't help.) BUT RATHER BECAUSE OF THE 'GROTESQUE' GIANTS and trying to take over as gods.
Remember when the flood came, it **would be 'wiping out' absolutely everything that occurred during the period of time since the beginning** and '<u>**including ties' with Adam and Eve**</u>. This was a radical movement. If it weren't for Noah and his tremendous character, the earth would be no more.

Noah asked to try to bring man to repentance and it took **one hundred twenty years** to try but failed. (Think of that, folks! That's longer than **WE live!**) Genesis 6:1-9, 1 Pet.3:20, 2nd Peter 2:5. In the meantime, the giants were still taking over everything and ruling mankind and it was causing great negativisms and harm and distress to humans everywhere. Remember that people in those years lived to be around 900 years old! It was now a long time since God's decision to wipe everything out had been made. Then it took time to build the ark and no one agrees on how long. Noah entered the ark when he was 600 years old and the flood started on the second month on the seventeenth day (Genesis 7:6,11 and kept rising for 40 days, verses 12, 15.) It didn't start to subside for 140 days. Noah kept sending a raven and finally a dove to test if the ground was sturdy enough to leave the ark. It took 150 days to go down. (Genesis 8:3) On Noah's first month and first day of his **six hundred first** year, Noah removed the cover of the ark and on the twenty seventh day of the next month, dry land returned.

So, the original plan was to wipe absolutely everything away but because of 'one man', Noah, whom God saw good, the plan was made to build an ark to house two of every animal and creature so to be able to populate the world again after the destruction of everything. When you think of that story, you really never give it a thought of how long it took for Noah to build the ark. "Stories have a tendency to have 'magic' with them and in the blink of an eye, 'voila', an ark magically appears!

However, some Bible scholars indicate it could have been as much as four years. Others have it in less time and even as few as 40 days. Think of this. All those strange creatures 'lording it over' the people of the land for that many years and now the building of the ark. I'm sure thoughts of construction ideas were already being thought of as Noah realized he was losing the battle of getting people to repent, so was preparing for the alternative.

God could have just gone ahead and done it and it would have been over, but he was trying to save His creation.

It is here where the **BIBLE ITSELF CARRIES A 'GLITCH'. HOWEVER, WHAT WE SEE AS A GLITCH MAY BE A 'HIDDEN' MESSAGE, TO 'PICK UP' ON. (Remember the quote, "May those with eyes see and with ears hear?" There is a reason for that**.) Jesus himself spoke in parables, where those very words meant something. **THIS GLITCH is where the BOOK OF MATTHEW AND LUKE IN THE NEW TESTAMENT DIFFER and by doing so, is REVEALING AN AWESOME, UNBELIEVABLE MESSAGE TO 'REVEAL SOMETHING' TO US**. Remember!

LUKE'S START covers THE CREATION OF MAN FROM ADAM AND EVE, through the eyes of Mary. **HOWEVER, 'MATTHEW' ONLY STARTS THE 'CREATION ACCOUNT' 'FROM** JUST **'AFTER THE FLOOD' AND STARTS WITH ABRAHAM and as if seen through the eyes of JOSEPH.** People who don't even read the Old Testament really don't know this important part of God's creation. The **New Testament writers give snippets here and there BUT A WHOLE**

REINCARNATION

'DETAILED STORY' LIES WITHIN THE PAGES OF GENESIS.
Think of it this way. **In the first five chapters of the entire book of the Bible, Genesis, the world is created**, the **first murder** takes place, and by **chapter six, God is fed up with what he created and wants to wipe it out**. (It was my first awakening to the fact the Bible verses are not in order. It says one thing in one verse, and you realize the verse should have come two verses later. It's no wonder people have trouble reading the Bible. When you realize this is going on, you can see the same thing recurring at other places within the Bible chapter verses. Sometimes it became the whole 'set of verses' in a chapter that are out of order. (Could be with 'creation of man' but there are too many differences to neglect.)

Once you catch on to that fact, you begin to unravel what is happening. **By only verse 'EIGHT' of the book of Genesis, man who is living to be as much as 900 years old are seen as having 'been a big mistake' and are at this time. God is ready to end everything with the flood.** After the flood, God makes a promise and puts the <u>rainbow in the sky to</u> <u>**announce his promise that he won't ever wipe out man again and that man will now be allowed to**</u>

live only 125 years! That's quite a difference from 900!
The idea with man living so long was to give them plenty of time to learn to do things the way God wanted them to live their lives. The only thing was, it just gave them more time to get worse and worse and to 'never learn' anything.
The Bible says man lives once and then dies.

Hebrews 9:27
"And as it is appointed unto men once to die, but after this the judgment:" (KJV)

Luke starts the 'creation' with God's 'son' Adam being the first person on the earth. (Luke also mentions the **'lineage' in Luke 3:37...son of Adam, the son of God.**
Genesis 5:1 — **(KJV 1900)** This *is* the book of the **generations of Adam**. In the day that God created man, **in the likeness of God made he him.** Verse 26, God says,
"Let *US* make man in **OUR** image,
in **OUR** Likeness ...("This is the only instance in the 'creation account' where God uses the **plural** form to refer to himself and **just so happens**, as he **begins to create man**. Many scholars believe this is the Bible's first reference to the **Trinity. Father** the creator, **Son** the offspring, **or carnations, and Ghost**

REINCARNATION

being the spiritual form having achieved the capability to be in spirit at home with God.

('THAT FOLKS' spells reincarnation!) **Romans 5:14, Paul says** in the BIBLE, that **'Adam' *'IS'* THE FIGURE OF <u>HIM THAT ' WAS' TO COME</u>."** Paul carries this comparison still further when he says in **1 CORINTHIANS 15:47,** "<u>THE FIRST MAN</u> (ADAM) *IS OF THE EARTH. THE SECOND MAN, (JESUS CHRIST)<u>, IS THE LORD FROM HEAVEN.</u> THIS IS REVEALING 'REINCARNATION' RIGHT HERE, AND THE* **TWO BOOKS OF THE BIBLE'S DIFFERENCES,** *MATTHEW AND LUKE,* **ARE SHOWING IT** *BUT IS YET* **BEING MISSED.** *Jesus talked in parables, and this is a perfect example of how what things are being said in the open (yet within the Bible) are missed by the people. These two books are both correct but in* **a total difference in time and who they used to relay their account through.**

At this point of (my) book, the FLOOD has just happened. GOD was fed up with everything he made, and HE sent a flood to wipe everything out.

So, we are at the point where **the flood has happened, and everything that ever existed in life from the beginning of time has been wiped out! <u>Everything is gone</u>!** No ancestors, relatives, offspring! ~ EVERTHING IS GONE. **So, where Luke started with Genesis and the start of creation at the beginning, none of that** remained after the flood. It has been written that the earth's land surface is mostly sedimentary rock that got washed away and ended up in areas that had massive grave type areas of grotesque, weird **or not worth anything. All those Bible passages concerning Adam and creation are now null and void. It is merely a 'history' to study. Genesis 2:15 ...3:17-19 ...Romans 5:12, When Adam sinned, sin entered the world. <u>Adam's sin brought death, so death spread to everyone, for everyone sinned.</u>**
There are always skeptics or non-believers who say that there never 'was' a flood. Many consider it as just another story. While Anthropologists have accounts of the many FLOOD legends from all over the world: Ancient Babylonians, Australian Aboriginals, Mayans,, Aztecs, Romans, Chinese, Greeks, and Native Americans also have recorded accounts of the looking fossils of mangled bones. There were

also minerals way off from where they should have been.

So, then there is Matthew, the 'other' book of the Bible that is a whole different time period away and BEGINS 'WITH THE GENEALOGY OF JESUS! (HE HASN'T EVEN BEEN BORN YET AND WOULDN'T BE FOR SOME TIME.) Why would they do that? It doesn't tell ABOUT CREATION OR ADAM AND EVE but instead starts WITH ABRAHAM, Isaac ,and Jacob!!! It covers fourteen years of Abraham, then fourteen years of David and his generations. **From David to the deportation of Babylonian was also fourteen years. Then it was fourteen years from the deportation to Christ. So WHY would they 'start with all that other history stuff but just lock in on Jesus himself?**

WELL, THIS is why the OLD TESTAMENT is so vital and yet with the 'biggest' part of people not giving it a thought! (Like just stated… "WHO CARES"!?) For the most part, even most 'ministers' stick with the NEW TESTAMENT, as well as do most of the Bible scholars interpreters.
In that OLD TESTAMENT, <u>we learn of the first murder:</u> (story of Cain and Able and then a

*'gift' from God to replace the death of ABEL and <u>HE</u> (SETH) WAS IN THE 'LIKENESS' OF ADAM! ARE WE SEEING AN EVENTUAL 'SECOND CHANCE' FOR ADAM WHO 'SCREWED UP' AND <u>CAUSED SIN</u> TO <u>COME</u> INTO THE WORLD <u>FOR WHICH 'WE ALL' PAY</u>? REMEMBER too, <u>ADAM HIMSELF</u> WAS IN THE 'LIKENESS' OF THE <u>CREATOR</u> GOD! (Second chances could be years away. It was thirteen years between God telling Abraham they would have their own child and when he actually gave it to him.) *** Genesis 5:26 <u>SETH HAD A SON ENOSH, and AT THAT TIME MEN BEGAN TO CALL UPON THE NAME OF THE LORD!</u>
Enosh (was Enoch). Enoch is mentioned many times in the Bible yet important details of him and his life were removed by different people for different issues. The book of Enoch was completely removed and is found in the Apocrypha only. TO SHOW YOU HOW IMPORTANT HE WAS, HE WAS ONLY THE OTHER PERSON (OTHER THAN ELIJAH) TO BE 'TAKEN UP' TO HEAVEN AFTER 365 (OF THEIR) YEARS. If he was so important, why did 'people' remove his information? I will mention more on him later. (One small tidbit of my own. Adam had been God's first son on*

earth. He screwed up and brought sin into the world. His son was murdered by his brother, God replaced him with another son, Seth, who happened to resemble Adam himself. (Who had been God's son.) SETH has a son by the name of Enoch. (Enoch was so close with God that he didn't die but was one of only two people ever 'TAKEN UP!' REINCARNATION!..?) The genealogy continues to someone who was called LAMECH who was the FATHER OF A SON whose name was NOAH, saying, "OUT OF THE GROUND WHICH THE LORD HAS CURSED 'THIS ONE' SHALL BRING US THE RELIEF FROM OUR WORK AND FROM OUR TOIL OF OUR HANDS! NOAH, who in turn became the father of Shem, Ham, and Japheth. Eventually man became so corrupt that God was going to send the flood and wipe everyone away, but then the Noah and his ark story happened. Genesis tells of the 'rainbow' put in the sky as a promise to us that he will never ever cause another flood to cover the earth. DURING THESE HUNDREDS OF YEAR TIME PERIOD, LANGUAGE WAS CHANGED SO THAT PEOPLE IN ONE AREA OF CREATION COULD NO LONGER UNDERSTAND THOSE ELSEWHERE, WHICH WAS TO KEEP MANKIND FROM BANDING

TOGETHER TO TRY TO OVERTHROW THE ESTABLISHED PLANS AND EVOLUTION OF CREATIVE WAYS. *WHILE GENESIS COVERS THE LONG YEARS BEHIND ABRAHAM'S LIFE WITH MANY OTHER STORIES. EXODUS 3:6 IS THE REVEALING STATEMENT OF GOD'S MAKEUP AND 'REINCARNATIONS' OF JESUS , plus STARTS BECAUSE OF ABRAHAM!*

I AM =(Exodus 3:14)

I AM THE GOD OF YOUR FATHER, the God of Abraham, the God of Isaac, and **the God of Jacob.** *(according to the Unger's Bible dictionary, '<u>I AM</u>' <u>IS</u> 'HE WHO <u>IS</u>,' <u>THE ABSOLUTE</u> ...THE SELF-EXISTENT ONE. EXODUS 15.16)**

I AM THE GOD OF YOUR ANCESTORS, the God of Abraham, Isaac, and Jacob. Moses began to tremble and did not dare to look. **(This proves that GOD used his voice that could be heard.)**

[27] He is not the God of the dead, but the God of the living. Mark 12:26-27

But concerning the dead, that they rise, have you not read in the book of Moses, in the *burning* bush *passage*, how God spoke to him, saying, '**I AM** the God of Abraham, the God of Isaac, and the **GOD OF JACOB**'? ²⁷ **HE IS NOT THE GOD OF THE DEAD, BUT THE GOD OF THE LIVING.**
Luke 20:37-38 Now that the dead are raised, even Moses shewed at the bush, when he calleth the Lord the God of Abraham, and the God of Isaac, and the God of Jacob.
(**These <u>same</u> VERY TWO WORDS** are also seen later in the Bible, <u>**concerning JESUS**</u>!)
John 8:58, he answered the religious leaders, saying, "Truly, Truly, I say to you, <u>**BEFORE ABRAHAM WAS, I AM**</u>." This was a clear reference to **Exodus 3:14, where God revealed His name to Moses as "I AM." The reason the religious leaders wanted to kill Him was BECAUSE JESUS CLAIMED TO BE GOD.**
Keeping **'that thought'** in mind, **should it be that people are reading it wrong,** <u>it would change what they think is being said</u>. Without punctuation, a different meaning takes place.(That is why 'I' am using so many different ways of trying to get 'MY' ideas across. Even if you don't pick up 'exactly what I'm saying, it is

enough that you can see I'm trying to convey something important...What's funny is that I 'just' started this explanation, with the word, 'I am" (...and no, I AM not!...Ha!)
So, the 'actual Bible verse' being read differently, would have a different meaning. "I AM", (merely telling us **WHO IS speaking**). **OR,** <u>Without</u> any <u>punctuation</u> and stating "I AM" **the father of Abraham, Isaac, and Jacob. Would be telling who he was the Father of (or his kids!)**
Seeing as this book is about reincarnation, I'll take it a bit further. Is he saying **those are the only people he was father of and the rest of us aren't in his 'IN' group?** THEN WHY DO **WE** say, "**OUR Father** who art in heaven? ... "be present at **our table Lord,**"..."**Our heavenly Father**"...? etc.
If he said he was the father of Abraham, Isaac, and Jacob, THEN could that mean, 'those very people' and 'offspring' from were <u>the very same</u>, 'but different' people, over time? (Reincarnation!...some would be worthy to be mentioned and needed to be told about for us to grow from. Others would also reincarnate to improve themselves as the Bible indicates with the one goal of perfection in mind.) **The Bible says there is only ONE GOD!**

(Ya, I know. By now you are thinking I not only have a screw loose, but I am demented! ...Try **'writing** this. This is no way from' **MY' thoughts but** is coming directly **through SPIRIT!** One thing 'pops in' and then swirls around making 'no sense'...**UNTIL ... all of a sudden**, IT DOES!) For anyone who likes to tell people they are wrong, or likes a challenge, you will do well to continue through this book. You will have many a shocking things come forth, yet with verses **FROM THE BIBLE** being revealed. It will not be from MY thoughts and piecing. If nothing else, you may discover why the Bible is so hard to read with my revealing several of 'those' findings.

So, may I refer to John 8:58 **Jesus answered, "I tell you the truth, before Abraham was even born, I AM!"** This is the same in all translations with very minor differences. And another quotation, Exodus 3:14, "God said to Moses, **"I AM WHO I AM"**; and He said, "Thus you shall **say to the sons of Israel**, 'I **AM** has sent me to you.'" (Food for thought. If Jesus is the word of God, then he is a part of God which will give him the right to say that he is **"I AM."** He has always been.)

If we believe what is written in Genesis 2:7, "And the Lord God formed man of the dust of

the ground and breathed into his nostrils the breath of life; **and man became a living SOUL."** The 'soul' never dies, even if the body does. You will see the connection of this shortly. Son of man is the earthly body being lived but has a **CONTINUOUS LIVING SOUL given by the Father**. The **breath of life is the 'Spirit' of God which goes away at death. The spirit dies but not the soul**. Thus, we have three in one. God the Father, Breath of Life, Son, (the earthly body), and the Holy Ghost, soul or spirit. All are the makeup of everyone with one goal of becoming perfect and fit for Gods heavenly home.
If anyone enters by Me, he will be saved, and will go in and out and find pasture." John 10:9

Jesus said to her, "I am the resurrection and the life. He who believes in Me, though he may die, he shall live. And whoever lives and believes in Me shall never die. Do you believe this?" John 11:25, 26
"I am the vine, you are the branches. He who abides in Me, and I in him, bears much fruit; for without Me you can do nothing." John 15:5 John 8:58 **Jesus answered**, "I tell you the truth, **before Abraham was** even born, **I AM!**" Exodus 3:14, "God said to Moses, **"I AM WHO I AM"**; and He said, "Thus you

shall say to the sons of Israel, **'I AM'** has sent me to you."

"**I AM the good shepherd. The good shepherd gives His life for the sheep.**" John 10:11

Jesus said to her, "I AM the resurrection and the life. He who believes in Me, though he may die, he shall live. And whoever lives and believes in Me shall never die. Do you believe this?" John 11:25, 26

Jesus said to him, "I AM the way, the truth, and the life. No one comes to the Father except through Me." John 14:6

So then, with all these Bible passages in mind **CONCERNING JESUS AND 'I AM,'** let's start with Matthew's statement' concerning **ABRAHAM.**

Go from your country and your kindred and your father's house to the land that I will show you. ***And I will make of you a great nation, and I will bless you and make your name great, so that you will be a blessing. I will bless those who bless you, and him who dishonors you I will curse, and in you all*** *the families of the earth. Look around from where you are, to the north and south, to the east and west. All the land that you see, I will give to you and your offspring forever. I will make your offspring like the dust of the earth, so that if anyone could count the dust, then your offspring could be counted. Go, walk through the length and breadth of the land, for I am giving it to you."* **(Genesis 13:14-17**).

The **original promise of land and blessings** started to come into focus as the Lord refers to Abraham's offspring, for the first time. Only one problem, Abraham was now 85 years old, with no children of his own, and married to a woman who was herself unable to have children.

(**Genesis 12:1-3**, ESV).
I will make you a great nation;
I will bless you
And make your name great;
And you shall be a blessing.
[3] **I will bless those who bless you,**
And I will curse him who curses you;

And in you all the families of the earth shall be blessed."
This man will not be your heir, **but a son who is your own flesh and blood will be your heir."** *He took him outside and said, "Look up at the sky and count the stars — if indeed you can count them." Then he said to him, "So shall your offspring be."* (**Genesis 15:4-5**). **Possibly unsure of how this would happen, or maybe even growing a bit impatient, it didn't take long for Abraham and his wife to take matters into their own hands. This resulted in Sarah's female servant becoming pregnant with Abraham's first child, Ishmael (Genesis 16:3-4**).
"...No longer shall your name be called Abram, but your name shall be Abraham, **for I have made you the father of a multitude of nations. I will make you exceedingly fruitful, and I will make you into nations, and kings shall come from you... And I will give to you and to your offspring after you the land of your sojournings, all the** *land of Canaan, for an everlasting possession,* **and I will be their God."** (v. 4-8). God makes that

clear <u>13 years later when the promise is seen once again in</u>

Genesis 17

THIRTEEN YEARS LATER, God told Abram that He would give him a son through Sarai. This son—**ISAAC**— not Ismael would BE THE SON OF HIS **COVENANT.** THE LORD CHANGED ABRAM'S NAME TO **ABRAHAM, MEANING "FATHER OF A MULTITUDE" AND** HE CHANGED SARAI'S NAME TO SARAH, MEANING "<u>MOTHER OF NATIONS</u>." GOD FULFILLED HIS PROMISE TO <u>ABRAHAM</u> AND SARAH GAVE BIRTH TO <u>ISAAC</u> (<u>GENESIS 21:1</u>). Sarah believed in the living God and in His unchanging Word. **Even though she was 90 and Abraham was 100,** she trusted that the Lord will fulfill His promise by giving them a son in their old age. She died at the age of 127 (<u>Genesis 23:1</u>). **During her life, Sarah respected Abraham and submitted to his headship in the home** (<u>Genesis 18:12</u>). The apostle Peter points to her as the matriarch of all godly wives (<u>1 Peter 3:5–6</u>).

(NOTE IN LUKE with the ORIGINAL CREATION, GOD CREATED ADAM AND EVE UNIQUELY <u>IN GOD'S OWN IMAGE,</u> AND HE called them "mankind.' He commanded them to " be fruitful, multiply, fill the earth and subdue it, and have dominion over... every living thing." (Genesis 1:27-28, 5:1-<u>Genesis 17</u> this with <u>Genesis 9:1-2</u>:

AND GOD <u>BLESSED NOAH AND HIS SONS, AND SAID UNTO THEM, BE FRUITFUL, AND MULTIPLY, AND REPLENISH THE EARTH.</u>
<u>And the fear of you and the dread of you shall be upon every beast of the earth, and upon every fowl of the air, upon all that moveth upon the earth, and upon all the fishes of the sea; into your hand are they delivered.</u>

ADAM

Adam and Eve were <u>created without sin</u> and because they were perfect, they were meant to live forever. In Adam's time, people lived to be 900 years old and Adam himself died at 930.(If Adam had lived a century more, he would have been alive in Noah's time.) Now we all know the story how Adam brought sin into the world because he and Eve went against God's instructions about eating of the one tree of forbidden fruit in the garden. Before the flood, there was no rain because the earth was covered with a water type canopy like a greenhouse effect and sheltered the earth and people from harmful rays of the sun.(Genesis 1:6-7) The garden 'would have been perfect for a lifetime, 'work free' atmosphere.
Because God told Adam to name the animals, it sort of made him the first **zoologist**. Then, because later of having to work the land because of his sin, he would have been the first landscaper and horticulturist. He was not only man but the 'first man and the father' of all humankind. He was the only man without a mother and a father.(However... keep this in mind for later in the book.)

(Adam)- You may freely eat of every tree of the garden but 'of the tree of knowledge of good and evil', you shall not eat of it, for in the day that you eat of it, you shall die. (Genesis 2:16)

Disobedience is a **rebellion against God.** It is going against what God has commanded and **disobeying** how He wants us to live. **Adam and Eve** then became another 'first' because they **were the first to disobey God when** in the Garden of Eden they ate forbidden fruit, as we see in **Genesis 3:1-24.** As a result of their 'disobedience', WE 'ALSO' inherited the same Adamic sinful and rebellious nature that we all have, that naturally makes us rebellious and disobedient to God. **(Psalms 51:5).**

(For **rebellion is as the sin** of witchcraft and **stubbornness is as iniquity and idolatry. 1 Samuel 15:23).**

They profess to 'know God', BUT BY THEIR DEEDS, THEY 'DENY HIM', being detestable, **disobedient,** and worthless for any good deed. **Titus 1:16**

Let no one deceive you with empty words, for because of these things the wrath of God comes upon the sons of **disobedience. Ephesians 5:6.**

'SINS' <u>ARE THE WORKS OF THE FLESH</u> because they **all** fall into the **DISOBEDIENCE** to God.

There are many different 'avenues' connecting with Adam and Eve's lives.
Adam's son, Cain, was the earth's 'first' <u>murderer</u>. God gave Adam another son, Seth, and with 'Seth', people began to worship God. (Genesis 4:26) It seems Adam and Eve repented of their sin which had brought corruption and death into the world.(Romans 5:12-21) We must remember God is slow to anger and abounds in steadfast love. (Psalms 103:8) The clue to their repentance was when they heard the voice of God and they felt ashamed because they were naked, and 'were aware' of their disobedience with fear.

So then, when you 'walk' **in the 'flesh' and 'not' in the spirit**, you will find the **'cesspool' of sinful activity which reaps negativity of** feelings, actions, and emotions which in turn lead to frustration, despair, disappointments, depression, anxiety, and futile thoughts. **Those 'sins' are, immorality, impurity, licentiousness, idolatry, sorcery, enmity, strife, jealousy, anger, selfishness, dissention, party spirit ,envy, drunkenness, carousing, and the like .** (Galatians 5:19-21).

Archangel Michael attended Adam's death and he was buried with his murdered son Abel.

Adam ... and Eve

(Adam)- **You may freely eat of every tree of the garden but of the <u>tree of knowledge of good and evil you shall not eat of it</u>, for in the day that you eat of it, you shall die. (Genesis 2:16)**
This is interesting here 'because' it is actually telling us right here that there <u>is already</u> ... an evil. Before creation of Man, good AND evil existed!
 Disobedience is a **rebellion against God.** It is going against what God has commanded and **disobeying** how He wants us to live.
Adam and Eve WERE the first to <u>disobey God</u> in the Garden of Eden by eating the forbidden fruit (as seen in **Genesis 3:1-24.)**
As a result of **their** disobedience, **WE** 'ALSO' inherited the same Adamic sinful and **rebellious nature that we all have which naturally makes us rebellious and disobedient to God.** (Psalms 51:5).
We weren't even given a chance to see what 'we' would do. We didn't have a choice to see

if we would follow Adam's example or do it differently. (Sort of sounds like a DNA attached situation.)
For **rebellion is as the sin** of witchcraft and **stubbornness is as iniquity and idolatry.** 1 Samuel 15:23a.
They profess to know God, BUT BY THEIR DEEDS, THEY DENY HIM, being detestable, **disobedient,** and worthless for any good deed. **Titus 1:16**
Let no one deceive you with empty words, for because of these things the wrath of God comes upon the sons of **disobedience. Ephesians 5:6.**
SINS ARE THE WORKS OF THE FLESH because they **all** fall into the **DISOBEDIENCE** to God. Galatians 5:22 - **GOD IS the 'fruit of the spirit:'** ... **LOVE, JOY, PEACE, PATIENCE, KINDNESS, GOODNESS, FAITHFULNESS, GENTLENESS, SELF-CONTROL. If we live in the spirit, we have to walk with the spirit with no self-conceit, no provoking of another, no envy of another.**

So then, when you 'walk' **in the 'flesh'** and **'not' in the spirit,** you will find the **'cesspool' of sinful activity which reaps negativity of** feelings, actions, and emotions which in turn lead to frustration, despair, disappointments, depression, anxiety, and futile thoughts. **Those 'sins' are immorality, impurity, licentiousness, idolatry, sorcery, enmity, strife, jealousy, anger, selfishness, dissention, party spirit, envy, drunkenness, carousing, and the like. (Galatians 5:19-21).**

If people would live their lives according to God's Ten Commandments, we would be living the way God wishes us to live and it would be a **better and safer place.** The Commandments are recorded virtually identically in Exodus 20:2–17 and Deuteronomy 5:6–21.
There are many different versions as to Adam and Eve's lives so depending on where you look and whose version you use, you can come up with a long range of accounts. I will give a sort of summation with trying to blend them together and will use a few Bible verses to help.
Adam and Eve were created without sin and because they were perfect, they were meant to live almost forever. In Adam's time, people lived to be 900 years old and Adam himself died at 930 . If Adam had lived a century more, he would have been alive in Noah's time. Now we

all know the story of how Adam brought sin into the world because he and Eve went against God's instructions about eating of the one tree of forbidden fruit in the garden. Before the flood, there was no rain because the earth was covered with a water type canopy like a greenhouse effect and sheltered the earth and people from harmful rays of the sun. (Genesis 1:6-7) After the first sin, things changed and the longevity in Genesis 1:28 eventually found man living 125 years compared to 900. You will find the reason for the difference with a variety of reasons depending on whether you are going according to God or mankind's 'theories'. (It boils down to... DO YOU BELIEVE IN GOD?) Adam's son, Cain, <u>was the earth's first murderer</u>. God gave Adam another son, Seth, and from Seth, people began to worship God. (Genesis 4:26) It seems Adam and Eve repented of their sin which had brought corruption and death into the world. (Romans 5:12-21) We must remember God is slow to anger and abounds in steadfast love. (Psalms 103:8) Remember! The clue to their repentance was when they heard the voice of God and they felt ashamed and were aware of their disobedience with fear. Archangel Michael attended Adam's death and he was buried with his murdered son Abel.

Remember! Because God told Adam to name the animals, it 'sort of' made him the first **zoologist**. Then because of having to work the land because of his sin, he would have been the 'first landscaper' and 'horticulturist'. He was not only the first man but the first man and the 'father' <u>of all humankind.</u> He was the only man without a mother and a father. (However... remember this for later in the book.)

ISAAC

In about a dozen places in the Bible, the Lord God is referred to as the **God of Abraham, Isaac, and Jacob.** (e.g., Genesis 50:24; Exodus 3:15; Acts 7:32). Right now, we cover **Isaac and although 'some' may have mentioned Jesus as having children, most others say they are nuts, They are usually referring to Jesus' life 'while being Jesus'.** The **Bible DOES actually reveal Jesus as being married and having many children, BUT it was a 'pre-Jesus' incarnation... one as... Isaac. TO BEGIN WITH, ISAAC HIMSELF WAS A 'SUPERNATURAL' BIRTH AS THE ONLY SON OF ABRAHAM AND SARAH. (GENESIS17:16)-SARAH SHALL BE HER NAME.** I will give you a son by her and moreover I will bless her and **she will be a mother of nations; kings of people shall come from her**. Then Abraham fell on his face and laughed and said unto him, "Shall a child be born to a man who is a hundred years old? **Shall Sarah, who is ninety years old, bear a child?"** There are more verses if you wish to read them on your own but in **Genesis 21:1-7, the Lord came at the foretold time and gave Abraham and Sarah a son Isaac.** (I'm going to add this here but will mention it again in other places. It IS in the Bible. God's days are like a thousand years!) The rest of the story of <u>Isaac</u> continues to chapter 23 but I will give you my own words for what it is revealing to shorten it. Abraham and Sarah were beyond years to have children, but God gave them a special gift of having a son anyway. They named him Isaac and eight days after his birth, they circumcised him as was done to all males of Abraham's household because of a covenant made with Yahweh who was the name revealed to Moses when Isaac was **circumcised**, the eighth day after his birth, which was needed to be done for all males of Abraham's household in order to be in compliance with '**Yahweh**'. (From Wikipedia, the free encyclopedia)

Yahweh was the <u>name of God</u> 'as revealed by' <u>Moses</u> and is linked to God's redeeming act in the history of God's chosen people. He saved his people from government's power of slaves in Egypt and is there to be near to save

us from our sins. Right now, we cover **Isaac** and although 'some' may have mentioned over time about Jesus as having children and most others say they are nuts. The **Bible actually does** reveal Jesus as being married and having many children, **but** it was a '**pre-Jesus incarnation**' like one of **Isaac.**
To begin with, Isaac himself was a 'supernatural' birth as the **only son of Abraham and Sarah. (Genesis17:16)-"Sarah** shall be her name. I will give you a son by her and moreover I will bless her and **she will be a mother of nations; kings of people shall come from her**. Then Abraham fell on his face and laughed and said unto him, "Shall a child be born to a man who is a hundred years old? **Shall Sarah, who is ninety years old, bear a child?"** There are more verses if you wish to read them on your own but in **Genesis 21:1-7,** the **Lord came at the foretold time and gave Abraham and Sarah a son, Isaac.** (The rest of the story of Isaac continues to chapter 23 but I will give you my own words for what it is revealing to shorten it.)

In the **Epistle to the Hebrews**, it tells how Abraham willingly followed God's command to 'sacrifice' his son Isaac to show his 'faith' he had in God. (**MY thoughts** on **that** situation are found in the section of Abraham.)
The early Christian church continued to develop with **the New Testament theme of Isaac AS a type of Christ and the Church** as both "the son of the promise" and the "father of the faithful".
Tertullian, known as the church history father of Latin theology, drew a parallel between **Isaac's bearing the wood for the sacrificial fire with Christ's carrying his cross. (I sort of picked up on that myself, even though there would have been no way 'I' could have done that!, no matter how prophetic the occasion might have been. I still stick with 'my thoughts'** mentioned in the 'Abraham section'.

(I 'could' go on further with that theory about the wood signifying the wood for carrying the cross, to the sheep or lamb **given in** Isaac's place. Who was the shepherd or lamb of God who gave **his life** 'in place of' us' for 'our sins'? I could lie and say I feel Abraham did the right thing, (and he did, '**because**' HE had faith! ('**I**' need ... **a whole lot more work.**)

Because of Genesis 24:63 where "Isaac went out to meditate in the field at the eventide",-the Jewish people claim him as the one who started the afternoon prayer.

In Genesis 24:19, that author views the **release of Isaac from** being **SACRIFICED** as being 'similar to himself being father to Jacob and Esau and **grandfather** of the <u>**TWELVE TRIBES OF ISRAEL**</u>. **Faith in them to do right and be there to for**give.

Isaac was the only patriarch who stayed in Canaan during his whole life and although once he tried to leave, God told him not to do so. Rabbinic tradition gave the explanation that Isaac was almost sacrificed and <u>anything dedicated as a sacrifice may not leave the Land of Israel.</u> Isaac was the oldest of the biblical patriarchs at the time of his death, and the only patriarch whose name was NEVER changed.

(Genesis 25:20) Before Isaac was THE AGE OF 40, <u>Abraham</u> sent his steward to find a <u>wife</u> for Isaac from his nephew's family, and the steward chose Rebekah. (I guess this would be the 'lazy man's way out, or for one who makes poor choices, or can't make decisions, but for someone else to make the decision as to who 'I will be living with day in and day out for the rest of <u>MY life', it</u> sounds like a brewing 'storm of life' for the future. (If you get nothing else from this book, you may see we sort of have things 'better' now days in many things even with all that is wrong! Course, if anyone gets married and then divorced in 'these' days, you can't blame it on someone else's choice made!).

Like his father, Isaac also pretended that his wife, Rebekah, was his sister, **due to 'fear that <u>someone</u> would kill him in order to have her**. (If they wanted her but she was married, they could only have her IF her husband was 'dead!) The one thing you may 'pick up on' is the women were really not treated as having 'feelings' or wishes in those days.

After many years of marriage to Isaac, Rebekah had still not given birth to a child and was believed to be barren. Isaac prayed for her and she conceived. (You've heard the saying '"watch out what you pray for"? This came with a double-edged sword. REBEKAH GAVE BIRTH to <u>**TWIN**</u> **boys,** Jacob and Esau. Isaac was 60 years old when his two sons were born. and **Isaac favored Esau, while Rebekah favored Jacob**. Nothing good ever comes from showing favoritism. We see the concept all the time in our lives. Favorite sports with our likes for one team versus the team a relative or friend likes can be fun and cause of healthy competition, but when one or both sides become obsessive and combative, violent, or deceitful, negative aspects to life occur. If it concerns people competing for 'same males or females' as boyfriends, girlfriends, or even 'just' friends, more is at stake. The worst would be one parent having a special favorite for a child in the household.

That could be a whole story in itself because some children could feel completely unloved and left out while another is getting everything they themselves would like to have. In **ISAAC'S case, they didn't both favor the 'same son' but each had their own of the** two. This not only put the two boys at odds against each other, but a strong parental hold between the parents.

This brings to mind another set of twins earlier in time.

Because of "those', these two **may be** a **reincarnation of** them.!

REBEKAH

Her sin consisted in aiming at a right object by sinful means.
The punishment of Rebekah came in a form she little anticipated — she lost the son for whom she had plotted and sinned. Her example speaks plainly and solemnly also to all who are parents amongst 'us'. **It tells us that children are easily led into sin.** Deceit and falsehood are bound up in the heart of every child that breathes, and it is as easy to call them **into** action as to get their tongues to speak or their feet to move. It is easy also to find motives that **seem** good, for prompting the lie, or sanctioning, or concealing the lie; but there is a God living in heaven, and the evil we encourage or tolerate in our children will come down on our own heads. The curse of it will be on us. The negative may be aimed for others, but it **ends up ricocheting back to us.** Sometimes it may come from one's own child but other times it may come to us in some way in 'either' this lifetime, or a 'next'. In either case,...it WILL COME. 'Cause and effect'! ...Karma!
In Jacob's case because he is close to God, it seems God gets even more **displeased with**

any 'wrongs' He sees in him, and the more severe He punishes it. Jacob seemed to be the most beloved by God yet appeared to suffer the hardest.

His sin was complicated because <u>he</u> wasn't the one who instigated it. The idea came from his mother whom he loved and at first didn't go along with it. All those things that caused his beloved mother to form her plot to deceive started working on Jacob's mind. (How many times have 'you' thought something wasn't a good idea, but after thinking about it, changed your mind? Sometimes the change is for 'good', but other times it is just the body making up their mind it is. Adding fuel to the fire would be for them to believe that they would actually be helping someone.) Jacob used someone's 'need' to get them to give up something they were expected to have. (Giving food in exchange for turning over his birthright.) Then even worse was using his own father's failing eyesight to trick him into giving Jacob the blessing intended for his brother rightly for his brother. Jacob's punishment for his sin lasted his entire lifetime. It followed him wherever he went. The 'blessing' was to make his life

better, but no matter what 'good' there seemed to be, there was always doubt in his mind as to whether the people he was with, or what people were saying or telling him was really the truth. He always felt they were trying to 'scam' him and he could never trust 'anyone'. He always thought they were lying to him, like he had done.
Recalling Genesis 25:29–34, Esau had previously sold his birthright to Jacob for 'bread and stew of lentils'. When the time for the blessing had come and Esau realized what his brother had done by fooling their near blind father into giving him the blessing instead. Esau vowed he would kill Jacob but with his father near death he would wait until after that took place. In the meantime, Jacob had to leave town in fear for his life. His father ended up living twenty more years and all that time Jacob was 'looking over his shoulder in fear.'

After 20 years working for his uncle, Jacob returned home. He reconciled with his twin brother Esau, but even though Esau was really trying to give him things or do something for him, Jacob was always thinking it was just a way to then kill him.

Their father died at 180 years old and he and Esau buried their father, Isaac.
According to local tradition, the graves of Isaac and Rebekah, along with the graves of Abraham and Sarah and Jacob and Leah, are in the Cave of the Patriarchs.
The Eastern Orthodox Church and the Roman Catholic Church consider Isaac as
a saint along with other biblical patriarchs.
The Quran mentions **Isaac** as a prophet and a righteous man of **God**. Isaac and Jacob are mentioned as being bestowed upon Abraham as 'gifts' of God, who then worshipped God only and were righteous leaders in the way of God.

I have to add this in case you forgot! You just read what Jacob did. How he fell short of being who God wished him to be. Remember the name of this book? Jacob 'was' one of JESUS' own incarnations! (Hang on…there will be proof of this to be told later!)

Jacob

Jacob was born a twin of Esau and when born was grasping his brother's foot. In Genesis 25:26, his name was translated as 'he deceives.' God told their mother Rebecca that **she was the mother of two nations and they would be divided with one being stronger than the other, with the older (Esau) serving the younger. (Jacob) (Genesis 25:23)**

Esau loved being out in the outdoors and was **favored by his father Isaac** because he loved the wild game Esau brought home from his hunting trips. **Jacob,** on the other hand, was **favored by his mother** and was a 'stay at home' type person, living within the tents. **(Genesis 25:27/28.)**

Choosing favorites within a family can be hurtful and harmful to the other children and is the cause of many destructive experiences as found when Jacob too carried on with choosing a favorite, later in life, with his own son Joseph, (which almost cost Joseph his life.) **When their father Isaac was old with failing eyesight** and close to dying, Isaac felt

it was time to pass on the 'expected blessings' that is due to go to the firstborn son, **Esau. (Genesis 27:1-4).**
With their mother Rebekah favoring Jacob, she came up a plan to **deceive Isaac** into giving the blessing to Jacob instead. **It worked, and so Jacob received the blessing instead of Esau**. Esau came in with food from his hunt, prepared the food, and offered it to his father expecting he would get the 'blessing' in return. He then learned of the deceptive episode.
Esau vowed he would kill Jacob for this but would wait until his father's days for mourning were past. (Genesis 27:41). However, it turned out, Isaac didn't die but lingered for another twenty years. **(Genesis 35:27–29**). Jacob quickly departed from the area.

(Keep something in mind here. God had already told Rebecca she had two nations within her and that the 'older would serve the younger!' God already knew that! (Sometimes it seems as if we on earth are nothing but a 'game' with pawns to be moved around for some kind of a strategy!)

During Jacob's journey, 'he' had a dream of a ladder to heaven with <u>God at the top and angels ascending and descending.</u> <u>This imagery is mirrored in Jesus' words to His disciple Nathanael. John 1:51</u>
"And he saith unto him, Verily, verily, I say unto you, Hereafter ye shall see heaven open, and the angels of God ascending and descending upon the Son of man." John 1:51 (KJV)

God gave Jacob the assurance of His presence and reiterated His promise to Abraham. Genesis 28:13-15.
"And he dreamed, and behold a ladder set up on the earth, and the top of it reached to heaven: and behold the angels of God ascending and descending on it." Genesis 28:12 (KJV)
"And behold, the LORD stood above it, and said, I am the LORD God of Abraham thy father, and the God of Isaac: the land

whereon thou liest, to thee will I give it, and to thy seed;" Genesis 28:13 (KJV)
"And thy seed shall be as the dust of the earth, and thou shalt spread abroad to the west, and to the east, and to the north, and to the south: and in thee and in thy seed shall all the families of the earth be blessed." Genesis 28:14 (KJV)
"And behold, I am with thee, and will keep thee in all places whither thou goest and will bring thee again into this land; for I will not leave thee, until I have done that which I have spoken to thee of." Genesis 28:15 (KJV)
"And Jacob awaked out of his sleep, and he said, 'Surely the LORD is in this place; and I knew it not.'" Genesis 28:16 (KJV)
As a result of this experience, Jacob renamed the place 'Bethel' meaning 'house of God' and he vowed to serve God.

After <u>Jacob</u> settled in Haran, Laban offered him payment for the work he had been doing AS <u>A SHEPHERD</u> looking after his flocks. Jacob offered to work for Laban for

seven years in return for Laban's daughter Rachel whom he loved very much. HOWEVER, JACOB WAS TO DISCOVER THAT HIS UNCLE LABAN **COULD BE JUST AS MUCH A DECEIVER AS HE HIMSELF HAD BEEN**. <u>On Jacob's wedding night, Laban **substituted** his older daughter, **Leah,** for **Rachel. Genesis 29:23-25**</u>
However, **Laban agreed to give Jacob Rachel as well, <u>provided Jacob finish the wedding week with Leah before taking Rachel as a wife, and THEN work 'another seven years' for him. Jacob agreed to this</u>** <u>so both women</u> remained Jacob's wives but **Jacob loved Rachel more. <u>Genesis 29:30</u> This caused strife within the marriage as you can imagine.** (Hmmm. He had caused strife by deceiving his brother, and now he is experiencing strife because of wanting one thing but getting another!)

Rachel, his 'love', seemed to be barren while Leah <u>gave birth to Jacob's firstborn son</u>, Reuben. **<u>Then followed the birth of eleven more sons from Leah</u>, Rachel, and**

their two handmaidens. These sons would be the progenitors OF THE TWELVE TRIBES OF ISRAEL. (There are more strange competitive stories that can be taking place through what is happening in his life.) After the birth of Joseph, **Rachel's first child... and Jacob's eleventh**, Jacob asked Laban to send him back to his homeland, but **Laban asked him to stay telling him to name his wages**. JACOB REQUESTED ONLY THE SPECKLED AND SPOTTED SHEEP AND GOATS FROM ALL LABAN'S FLOCKS THAT HE TENDED in order to MAKE FLOCKS OF HIS OWN. It was never mentioned why or **how it worked, but Jacob put striped branches in front of the flocks when they mated, and it resulted in speckled and spotted offspring that he could claim for himself.** (YOU TALK ABOUT STORIES IN THE Bible that are strange and' people' being the ones who chose what would be used...**this** shows **'anything' can be 'true', and how in the heck did people choose some of this stuff...ALSO how can you 'pooh, pooh'** this **BOOK. The Bible stories are far weirder than 'this.' I have to laugh**

though. I think of this story whenever I see all the different markings of the animals in the pastures by my house. There are some pretty strange markings and don't resemble anything else there.

Jacob did this only with the strong animals so that his flocks grew strong while Laban had weak flocks. **Genesis 30:31–43** Jacob recognized that Laban and Laban's son's attitude toward him had changed. It was then that God commanded Jacob to return to the land **of his fathers** along with His promise, "**And I will be with you.**" **Genesis 31:3**

Jacob left Haran, taking with him his wives and children and all the vast flocks he had accumulated. When Laban learned that Jacob left, he pursued him. But God told Laban **in a dream** to "be careful not to say anything to Jacob, either good or bad." Genesis 31:24 Laban did ask Jacob why he'd left secretly saying that if it weren't for God's warning, he could have greatly harmed him.

(By now you are seeing a lot of ways God has communicated with people. Voices, weather issues, dreams, through other people's ways without them even knowing about it, and the list goes on. THIS book is no different. I did one book which actually had the pen racing across the page without any guidance from me, but at the end came out with a profound message— "Spiritually Yours". In fact I get phone calls every week from someone wanting to 'redo' the book and give it publicity. They have no idea what that book is. The wrong sentences and misspelled words are from the 'spirit' and you don't make changes to please the 'general' public's correct language. This book is different in that I have to compose what is being said but the places that keep cropping or 'popping up' is almost more than I can keep up with. Am 'I' special? HECK NO! ...But from what the stuff is revealing, I am also learning NOT to NOT LISTEN!)

Laban also accused Jacob of '**stealing**' his household **idols.** Jacob's own life was filled of '**deceptions**', by himself, and then others to him. His wife had taken the idols and it wasn't known by Jacob. She hid them from her father during his search. **Laban and Jacob eventually parted company after swearing an oath not to invade one another's lands.** (You are remembering aren't you, that this incarnation WAS JESUS 'living during one of HIS' lifetimes, don't you?)

So now, **Jacob had to face his brother, Esau**. Even though it had been twenty years since they last saw each other, Esau's 'threat' to kill him had never left him. **Genesis 32:11** (Think of how long he had to live with the fact of what he had done to his brother. You can try to pretend to cover up deceptions you did, but when it has your very 'life' hanging over your head, it is sort of hard to sweep under the rug.

Jacob sent messengers ahead of him with gifts, telling them to tell Esau that he was coming soon. The messengers returned to Jacob telling him that Esau was coming to meet him along with four hundred men.

Afraid that Esau was coming to destroy him, Jacob divided his family into two groups, hoping at least one group could escape attack. **Jacob prayed for God to save him, <u>reminding God that</u> HE had sent Jacob back to the land of Abraham and had promised to make him prosper and his descendants numerous. <u>Genesis 32:9–12</u>**

Jacob sent ahead more gifts with his servants. He spaced them out.
That night he sent his wives and sons away. In the middle of the night, alone and scared for his life, Jacob wrestled with a man who touched Jacob's hip, putting it out of socket, yet even at daybreak Jacob still refused to let the man go but asked for a blessing and was told, **"YOUR NAME WILL NO LONGER BE JACOB, BUT ISRAEL**, <u>because</u> you **have struggled with God <u>and</u> with humans and have overcome." <u>Genesis 32:28</u> JACOB THEN REALIZED IT WAS GOD!** Jacob named the place Peniel, (**face of God**) for I have seen Elohim face to face." (Genesis 32:30) Recognizing that HE had seen God and yet God had spared

his life. This wrestling match and name change marked a new beginning for Jacob.

The reunion with Esau was not the attack he had feared: "Esau ran to **meet Jacob and embraced him; he threw his arms around his neck and kissed him. And they wept."
Genesis 33:4**

Esau offered to accompany Jacob the rest of the way but he refused saying he had a large family. He also declined Esau's offer to leave some of his men with them. Actually, Jacob didn't really 'trust' his brother and instead of meeting Esau where mentioned, Jacob took his family on another route where they purchased and settled on a plot of land in Elohe Israel or "Mighty is the God of Israel." **Even with the new name** given to him by God, Jacob, who was the deceiver himself, would **never trust anyone**. He had been deceived by others and was always wary of others so would never trust 'anyone' again. He lived his entire life with always thinking someone could be 'deceiving' him. Here we see that the 'mind' of those who plot to deceive is always suspicious of the motives of others and can never fully be at rest. Think of your own 'conscience'. Have you ever done something, ever so small, to someone and it seems to remain within your thoughts? You can make amends in order to 'right the wrong' or live as Jacob did being tormented for his entire life. There IS ONE MORE THING TO REMEMBER. People will 'pay' for their wrongs until they pay for what they did, even if it means reincarnation to another time! DO YOU WANT TO LIVE 'ANOTHER' life tormented for mistakes of 'today?' (Use Jesus as an example. The first ADAM brought sins into the world and even though he perfected himself as Melchizedek, he STILL had to pay for bringing sins into the world and had to come as Jesus to take away our sins!

Genesis 34 records the rape of Jacob's only daughter, Dinah, and the revenge her brothers carried out on the rapist's entire community. See how the deviousness of the parents is passed on to the children in the **deceitful**

way. Jacob was angry with his sons and, in obedience to God's guidance, moved his family back to **Bethel. <u>Genesis 35:1</u>** In Jacob's meeting with God, he received the promise **that kings and many nations would come from him and that the land God had promised his forefathers would be his . <u>Genesis 35:11-12</u>**

Jacob and his family later moved from Bethel to Eder. On the way, **Rachel gave birth to her second son, Jacob's twelfth. Rachel died in childbirth.** <u>Jacob was reunited with his father, Isaac, and when his father died</u>**, both** <u>Jacob and Esau buried him.</u>

Like his mother, Jacob also had favorites, with Rachel being his favorite wife, and her children, Joseph and Benjamin, were his favorite sons. In fact, **Joseph was <u>so</u> favored that his brothers became JEALOUS and sold him into slavery. But God was with Joseph, and he eventually was okay and in Egypt was able to rescue his family**. Besides a lot of deceiving going on, there seems to be a lot of 'jealousy' linked to people's lives in many ways. Jacob included. Jacob died in Egypt and was embalmed at Joseph's request. **Genesis 49:29—50:3** Joseph and his brothers took Jacob's body back to Canaan to be buried alongside Abraham, Sarah, Isaac, Rebekah, and Leah. Before his death, Jacob blessed his twelve sons and asked to be buried in the cave that Abraham had bought for burial. Jacob had also blessed Joseph's two sons but **gave the blessing of the firstborn to the younger son. Unlike his father who had been deceived into giving the blessing of the firstborn to Jacob, Jacob crossed his hands to purposefully give the uncustomary blessing**.

THE SIMILARITIES IN THE LIVES OF ABRAHAM, ISAAC, AND JACOB ARE STRIKING. IN THEIR STORIES. We see **the importance of family** and how **'influence can become something passed on** even if it's bad. NEVER trusting 'anyone' and such things as deceit, favoritism, family strife, unexpected blessing, reconciliation, and faith flow forth like water

from a faucet. However, through it all we see **GOD and his faithful** endeavors to keep his promises. He chooses to accomplish His kingdom's purpose and is seen through sinful people who are willing to believe Him.
He makes those sinful people new and with a new start with even giving a new name.
(Abram the name Abraham, Jacob the name Israel, and making those who believe in Jesus Christ, new creations.) **2 Corinthians 5:17 Though our sinful patterns might still plague us, in Christ we find forgiveness for our sins as well as power to overcome.** We are invited to participate in God's work in the world.
Jacob's name, "deceiver," does seem to characterize **much of Jacob's life**. But he was also Israel, one to whom God made promises to which He **remained faithful**. God appeared to Jacob, and Jacob believed God's promises. **Despite Jacob's faults, God chose him to be the <u>LEADER OF A GREAT NATION</u> that <u>still bears his name today</u>**— (Israel). If it wasn't for this, we probably would never know **MUCH ABOUT JACOB WHO APPEARS TO**

BE IN THE MIDDLE OF EVENTS WHILE THE KEY PLAYERS ARE THOSE AROUND HIM. THERE IS NO GREAT WISDOM OR BRAVERY IN JACOB to speak of, and we are tempted to see him as little more than God's passive instrument. (If 'we' tend to think that because we aren't in the spotlight performing great acts for God and we are unimportant to Him, then we should consider the life of Jacob. In spite of our failings, God can and WILL <u>still use us</u> in His plan. God proves Himself faithful time and time again.

REINCARNATION

Are Jacob and Esau the reincarnated Cain and Abel?

Jeremiah 29:11 FOR I KNOW THE <u>PLANS I HAVE FOR YOU, DECLARES THE LORD,</u> **<u>PLANS FOR WELFARE AND NOT FOR EVIL, TO GIVE YOU A FUTURE AND A HOPE.</u>** (Here it is saying God has plans for everyone to do 'good and not evil. In His plans, it is for a better future.)

Let's look at CAIN AND ABEL. They were SONS OF ADAM and not only did Adam sin by not doing as 'he' was told by God, but Adam ended up with **one of his sons <u>KILLING HIS OTHER SON</u>** because of another sin, **'<u>jealousy</u>'**. So he then, also, added **MURDER** to his list.(Remember **CAIN WAS <u>JEALOUS</u>**!)

Jacob and Esau   (Twins later in time)
When Rebekah had conceived children by one man, our forefather Isaac,   **<u>THOUGH THEY WERE NOT YET BORN AND HAD DONE NOTHING EITHER GOOD OR BAD</u>**—in order that <u>God's PURPOSE</u> MIGHT CONTINUE, she was told, **"The older will serve the younger."** (Keeping the 'thought' of 'reincarnation' in

mind, Gods 'purpose' is to make people <u>pay</u> for the wrongs they did. ARE <u>THESE</u> TWINS 'reincarnations' of the others, Cain and Abel? AS IT IS WRITTEN, "JACOB I LOVED, BUT ESAU I HATED ." Romans 9:10-13   A future baby to be born <u>with a purpose</u> is one thing, but here are '<u>common folks</u>' also <u>being known before being born</u> and one is **HATED BY GOD**. Think about it. Why would God put an innocent child to be destined to fail because he **hated him**! How could he **HATE** an **UNBORN BABY**? (Is it because Cain was a murderer (Esau) before and was now coming back to 'pay' for what he did?

 So **MY THOUGHTS**... are **Jacob and Esau** '<u>reincarnations of</u> **Cain and Abel?) ARE THEY BACK AGAIN TO be together to work out their lesson from previous LIFE'S MISTAKES ?**

God put a curse on Cain and may be showing up in the new set of twins.

JEREMIAH 1:5 "BEFORE I FORMED YOU IN THE WOMB I KNEW YOU, and before you were born, I consecrated you; I <u>appointed you</u> a <u>prophet to the nations."</u>

 ISAIAH 49:1 Listen to me, O coastlands, and give attention, you <u>peoples</u> from afar. **THE LORD CALLED ME FROM THE WOMB, FROM THE BODY OF MY MOTHER <u>HE NAMED MY NAME</u>**.

REINCARNATION

PSALM 139:13 For you formed my inward parts; you knitted me together in my mother's womb. Psalm 139:13-16 Wonderful are your works; my soul knows it very well. My frame was not hidden from you, when I was being made in secret, intricately woven in the depths of the earth. Your eyes saw my unformed substance; **IN YOUR BOOK WERE WRITTEN, 'EVERY ONE OF THEM', THE DAYS THAT WERE FORMED FOR ME, WHEN AS 'YET' THERE WAS NONE OF THEM. ISAIAH 49:5** And now the **LORD SAYS, HE WHO FORMED ME FROM THE WOMB TO BE HIS SERVANT, TO BRING JACOB BACK TO HIM; AND THAT ISRAEL MIGHT BE GATHERED TO HIM— FOR I AM HONORED IN THE EYES OF THE LORD, AND MY GOD HAS BECOME MY STRENGTH. ISAIAH 44:24** (Jacob was 'created' by God- I AM.) REINCARNATION? Much has been 'lost' through people living lives of being who they were and going against God. In asking that JACOB be <u>returned BACK</u> to him might be reincarnations of the people who 'strayed' that will come back to Jacob, 'original creation' of God.
(Psalms) **Thus says the Lord,** your Redeemer, who formed you from the womb: **"I am the Lord, <u>WHO MADE ALL THINGS, WHO ALONE</u>**

Pauline E. Petsel

STRETCHED OUT THE HEAVENS, WHO SPREAD OUT THE EARTH BY MYSELF. GALATIANS 1:15
BUT when he who **HAD SET ME APART BEFORE I WAS BORN,** and called me by H
is grace.

JOSHUA

Joshua was the son of Nun (Exodus 33:11, Numbers 11:28) from the tribe of Ephraim. Numbers 13:8 He was born in Egypt into slavery. His name was originally Hoshea. Numbers 13:16 Moses called him Joshua, which means "Savior" or "the person by whom God will save." This name in Greek would be equivalent in the Greek to "Jesus" which also means "Savior."

He lived his first 40 years of his life in the wilderness with the Israelites in Egypt in slavery. (www.bible gateway.com)
He lived during the late Bronze Age around 1200 B.C. and was responsible for dividing up the land amongst the tribes of Israel. Joshua 13:8-21:45 He led the Israelites into the Promised Land (Deuteronomy 31:1-8) where he lived, until he died at the age of 110. Joshua 24:29

Joshua was filled with faith. Numbers 14:6-8 He stood up for what was right even if it seemed ridiculous. Joshua 5:13-6:27 He was dedicated to doing the right thing (Joshua 7:1-26) and was humble before the Lord. (Joshua 7:6-9; 8:30-31 He knew that God was responsible for his success.

Joshua was a 'people pleaser'. Despite God's earlier instruction to completely destroy all the Canaanites, he caved into the lies and wishes of the Gibeonites and permitted them to live in the Promised Land alongside the Israelites. Joshua 9:1-27

Overall, Joshua had a positive impact on others. He was the leader who helped the Israelites realize the promises originally given to Abraham. He led in a fair way and in a direct way.

(Obviously, Joshua had a NEGATIVE IMPACT ON THE CANAANITES AS THEY WERE ALMOST COMPLETELY DESTROYED BY THE ISRAELITES UNDER JOSHUA'S LEADERSHIP.)

Joshua had a close relationship with God similar to his predecessor, Moses. Throughout the book of Joshua, it states "The Lord said to Joshua…" Joshua 1:1; 3:7; 4:15; 5:2,9; 6:2; 7:10; 8:1; 11:6; 13:1; 20:1

Even though Joshua's 'spiritual life' was pretty consistent, Joshua was still human and he made the treaty with the Gibeonites relying on feedback from his fellow Israelites rather than 'consulting' with the Lord.

He provided a beautiful sendoff speech before he died (Joshua 23) but he failed the Israelites by not bringing up a successor like Moses had done for 'his' death. Joshua left Israel without a leader. This would soon lead to Israel's decline and departure from God's ways. Judges 2:10-15 (A disappointment to God.)

He had courage, endurance, gifts of intelligence, speech, and was distinguished to the worship of God, yet by not consulting with God and failing to

appoint a replacement for his death, it eventually led to Israel's downfall and peoples going away from God.
 Keep God first in everything. Whether or not we succeed in man's eyes, we need to keep God first in everything.

Do you not know that in a race, all the runners run, but only one gets the prize? Run in such a way as to get the prize. **I Corinthians 9:24**

NOT THAT I HAVE ALREADY OBTAINED ALL THIS, OR HAVE ALREADY BEEN MADE PERFECT, BUT I PRESS ON TO TAKE HOLD OF THAT FOR WHICH CHRIST JESUS TOOK HOLD OF ME. Brothers, I do not consider myself yet to have taken hold of it. But one thing I do: FORGETTING WHAT IS BEHIND AND STRAINING TOWARD WHAT IS AHEAD, I PRESS ON TOWARD THE GOAL TO WIN the prize for which God has called me heavenward in Christ Jesus. Philippians

REINCARNATION

3:12-14 (Think of these words with 'reincarnation' behind them!)

SOLOMON

Solomon's life is found in 2 <u>Samuel</u>, 1 <u>Kings,</u> and 2 <u>Chronicles</u> of the Bible. His two names mean "<u>peaceful</u>" and "<u>friend of God</u>".

Childhood

Solomon was the second born child of <u>David</u> and his wife <u>Bathsheba</u>. The first child died at childbirth when **David had an adulterous affair with Bathsheba so sent her husband to war hoping he would be killed and then would cover up what they'd done. After Bathsheba's husband died, David married Bathsheba and was then forgiven. Solomon was then born like a peace offering**. .

Solomon went to the throne when he was only about fifteen when he magnified his military strength. Solomon was the Bible's most wealthy of Israelite kings and known for how wise he was.

When God appeared to him in a dream and asked him what he wanted, he asked for wisdom in order to better rule and guide his people. This made God very happy and He gave him <u>**GREAT wisdom**</u> because he didn't ask for things for himself.

Of all David's many sons, God chose SOLOMON to sit on the throne of the LORD's kingdom over Israel. God told him '**Solomon' would be the one who would build HIS house and courts because he had chosen him as <u>HIS SON</u>, AND HE would be HIS FATHER** and establish **his kingdom forever, IF** he carries out GOD'S commandments and ordinances, as was being done **tha**t day.' Remember all the Bible verses saying '**<u>ONLY</u>** ' BEGOTTEN SON! THIS THEN is a **NEW** 'reincarnation' **for Jesus**, after he 'screwed up' the last one.
<u>**1 Chronicles 28:6** And He said to me,
I will establish his kingdom forever, IF HE RESOLUTELY CARRIES OUT MY COMMANDMENTS AND ORDINANCES AS IS BEING DONE THIS DAY.'....(Notice again that God says he will be HIS SON IF... That 'same condition' was with EVERY 'incarnation' God said when he said he would make them HIS SON. It always came with 'IF' they followed his ways. (It started with ADAM!)</u>
And He said to me, '**SOLOMON YOUR SON IS THE ONE WHO WILL BUILD MY HOUSE AND MY COURTS FOR I HAVE CHOSEN HIM AS MY SON** and I will be his Father.
It is this reason why he was given his name, which means peace. Because

Solomon knew of David's adultery, a very serious offense, the prophet held great influence over David.
SOLOMON SURROUNDED HIMSELF WITH LUXURIES AND HIS GOVERNMENT became very prosperous. HE BUILD city after city in his name. The Bible claimed he had 700 wives and 300 concubines but the wives were AS FOREIGN PRINCESSES for which <u>GOD DISAPPROVED</u> <u>because</u> SOLOMON let <u>those WIVES</u> import THEIR own National gods and goddesses AND BUILD TEMPLES TO THEM. THEN <u>SOLOMON</u> himself 'also' FELL INTO 'WORSHIPING IDOLS' because of 'their influence!'
1 KINGS 11:9–13 (Here again we have 'others' being able to be 'influenced' by those around them even when they know it is wrong. Also… remember,…you' just read' something of what 'JESUS' (GODS <u>ONLY</u> BEGOTTEN SON) did during another INCARNATIOIN!)
IN DEUTERONOMY 17:16–17, A KING IS COMMANDED NOT TO MULTIPLY. <u>SOLOMON SINNED IN ALL THREE THINGS.</u> <u>ALL THE WIVES HE HAD, PLUS, HIS HUGE COLLECTION OF TALENTS OF GOLD EACH YEAR (1 KINGS 10:14), AND A</u>

MULTITUDE OF HORSES AND CHARIOTS FROM EVERYWHERE INCLUDING EGYPT WHERE HE TOOK THEM BACK IN SPIRIT. 1 KINGS 11:30–34 AND 1 KINGS 11:9–13

*** **THE LORD WAS ANGRY WITH SOLOMON BECAUSE HIS HEART HAD TURNED AWAY FROM THE LORD.** GOD APPEARED TO HIM TWICE COMMANDING ABOUT THIS AND SHOULD NOT GO AFTER OTHER GODS, <u>BUT HE DIDN'T LISTEN TO HIM</u>.

Therefore, the Lord said to Solomon, "**SINCE THIS HAS BEEN YOUR PRACTICE AND YOU HAVE NOT KEPT MY COVENANT AND MY STATUTES THAT I HAVE COMMANDED YOU, I WILL SURELY TEAR THE KINGDOM FROM YOU AND WILL *GIVE IT TO YOUR SERVANT*.** YET FOR THE SAKE OF DAVID YOUR FATHER, I WILL NOT DO IT IN YOUR DAYS, BUT I WILL TEAR IT OUT OF THE HAND OF YOUR SON. HOWEVER, I WILL NOT TEAR AWAY ALL THE KINGDOM, **BUT I WILL GIVE ONE TRIBE TO YOUR SON**, (FOR THE SAKE OF DAVID MY SERVANT) AND FOR THE SAKE OF JERUSALEM THAT I HAVE CHOSEN.

1 Chronicles 28:6 And he said to me

All of this information is one thing, and to have it been done by a person who was good and favored, yet worse when you realize, THIS WAS <u>ONE OF</u>... JESUS'... PREVIOUS INCARNATIONS. (Don't completely freak out and say I'm crazy!. I WILL show it is TRUE shortly...and with using the BIBLE as the means.)

He would be cursed by God of all who curses Abraham. Abraham and Sarah his wife with him. When he came to the land the Canaanites possessed, God told him this land would be possessed by Abraham's descendants so Abraham built an altar there but continued onward. Many more stories come from Abraham but the one to remember is that his wife Sarah was unable to have children so Abraham, with Sarah's direction, did have a child with their maidservant. However God told Abraham that he and Sarah would have a child of their own and that seemed impossible because they were old.

... Raising kids isn't easy... Solomon

1 Chronicles 22:9 He shall build a house for my name. HE SHALL BE MY SON, AND I WILL BE HIS FATHER, and I will establish his royal throne in Israel forever.

1 Chronicles 28:2 Then **King David rose to his feet and said**: "Hear me my brethren and my people. I had it in my heart to build the house of rest for the ark of the covenant of the Lord and for the footstool of our God; and I made preparations for the building. **But God said to me, 'You may not build a house in my name. For you are a warrior and have shed blood. YET** the Lord God of Israel chose me from all my father's house to be king over Israel forever; for he chose Judah, my father's house, and **among my father's sons, he took pleasure in me to make me king over all Israel.** (**Through offspring**)

1 Chronicles 28: 5-8

He said to me, **"IT IS SOLOMON YOUR SON WHO SHALL BUILD MY HOUSE AND MY COURTS FOR I HAVE CHOSEN HIM TO BE 'MY SON'.** I will establish his kingdom forever **IF** he continues resolute (* a firm fixed purpose, determined, unwavering*) in keeping my commandments and my ordinances.

AND YOU, <u>SOLOMON MY SON</u>, "Know the God of your father, and serve him with a whole heart and a willing mind; FOR THE LORD <u>SEARCHES</u> ALL HEARTS AND UNDERSTANDS EVERY PLAN AND THOUGHTS<u>. IF YOU SEEK HIM, HE WILL BE FOUND BY YOU</u>. BUT <u>IF YOU FORSAKE HIM</u>, HE <u>WILL CAST YOU OFF FOREVER</u>. TAKE HEED NOW, FOR THE LORD <u>HAS CHOSEN YOU</u> TO BUILD A HOUSE FOR THE SANCTUARY; BE STRONG AND DO IT".

Acts 2:34 For David did not ascend into the heaven but he himself says, "The Lord said to my lord, sit at my right hand 'til I make the enemies a stool for thy feet."

(JESUS/SOLOMON)

Solomon sits upon the royal throne. Moreover, the King's servant came to congratulate our lord King David saying, **"YOUR GOD MAKE THE NAME SOLOMON MORE FAMOUS THAN YOU AND MAKE HIS THRONE GREATER THAN YOUR THRONE. AND <u>THE KING BOWED HIMSELF UPON THE BED</u>, AND <u>THE KING</u> ALSO SAID, "BLESSED BE THE LORD, THE <u>GOD OF ISRAEL</u> WHO HAS '<u>GRANTED ONE OF</u>**

MY OFFSPRING' TO SIT ON MY THRONE THIS DAY, MY OWN EYES SEEING IT.
1 Kings 9:1 **When Solomon had finished building the house of the Lord** and the king's house and all that Solomon desired to build, the **LORD APPEARED TO SOLOMON**............... And as for you, **IF you will walk before me** as David your father walked, **with integrity of heart and uprightness,** doing according to all that I have commanded you **and keeping my statues and my ordinances. THEN I SHALL ESTABLISH** your **royal throne over Israel forever, as I promised David** your Father saying, "**There shall not fail you a man upon the throne of Israel. BUT IF YOU TURN ASIDE FROM FOLLOWING ME, YOU OR YOUR CHILDREN, AND DO NOT keep my commandments and my statues** which I have set before you **but go serve other gods and worship them, THEN I will cut off Israel from the land which I have given them**. (NOTICE SOMETHING BEING REVEALED HERE. It says IF **YOU OR YOUR CHILDREN**! The 'eventual Jesus' is being seen as many different persons who were given the **'promise' of being with God and reaping** everything he had. (However, they were **'each'** missing the chance because they sinned and **didn't follow what God**

commanded of them. However, they came back again and were given another chance, yet were connected in 'some way' with who they had been before. (Reincarnation!)

1 Kings 11: 9-13 AND THE LORD WAS ANGRY WITH SOLOMON BECAUSE HE HAD TURNED AWAY FROM THE LORD, THE GOD OF ISRAEL, <u>WHO HAD APPEARED TO HIM TWICE</u> AND <u>COMMANDED HIM CONCERNING THIS THING</u>, THAT HE SHOULD <u>NOT</u> GO AFTER <u>OTHER GODS</u>; BUT HE <u>DID NOT KEEP WHAT THE</u> LORD HAD COMMANDED. Therefore, **the Lord said to Solomon "Since this has been <u>your mind</u> and <u>you</u> have NOT kept <u>my covenant and my statues</u>** which I have commanded you, **I WILL SURELY TEAR THE KINGDOM FROM YOU AND GIVE IT TO YOUR SERVANT.**
(***<u>Remember</u>, the beginning of this section IS where <u>JESUS</u> had asked the Pharisees who <u>they say</u> <u>CHRIST</u> <u>is</u>? THEY said, the son of David. JESUS then says...why <u>then,</u> did 'David' call <u>HIM</u> Lord. (Jesus himself 'just said' THE WORD 'HIM' (Him... pertaining to Christ!)... 'SOLOMON' WAS '<u>CHRIST</u>! (In

another incarnation, back in time and who went against God by going after 'other gods'.) (THUS…SOLOMON <u>WAS ONE OF THE REINCARNATIONS OF JESUS.</u>)

"RAISING KIDS ISN'T AN EASY JOB"

ISAIAH 1:2-6 Hear, O heavens, and give ear, O earth; for the Lord has spoken; **"SON<u>S</u> HAVE I REARED AND BROUGHT UP BUT <u>THEY</u> HAVE REBELLED AGAINST ME.** The ox knows its owner, and the ass its master's crib; but Israel does not know, my people does not understand." **AH, SINFUL NATION, A PEOPLE LADEN WITH INIQUITY, OFFSPRING OF EVIL DOERS, SONS WHO DEAL CORRUPTLY! THEY HAVE FORSAKEN THE LORD, THEY HAVE DESPISED THE HOLY ONE OF ISRAEL, THEY ARE <u>UTTERLY ESTRANGED</u>.**
('<u>Pieces</u>' from <u>other</u> scriptures throughout Isaiah 1….
---To what purpose is your multitude of sacrifices to me…

<u>Incense</u> is an 'abomination to me'...
<u>New moons, appointed feasts</u>, 'my soul I hadith'...
When you make many prayers, I will not hear. Your hands are full of blood...
Wash yourself and make you clean. seek judgement...do no evil...be willing and obedient....If you refuse, you will be devoured!

***<u>THIS PAGE</u> 'SUMS UP' AND REVEALS, THE '<u>ENTIRE</u>' BOOK'S 'MESSAGE.' ***

This page is showing that <u>**all those**</u> 'scholars' and <u>**supposed**</u> '**BIBLE <u>INTERPRETERS</u>** 'who <u>don't believe in 'reincarnation'</u>, **ALSO DON'T KNOW WHAT THEY ARE TALKING ABOUT. HERE, in the 'very Bible,' THEY CLAIM** <u>it says nothing about 'reincarnation',</u> <u>Is **GOD** revealing there **IS**, and... **VERY MUCH SO.**</u>

(So then are they '<u>also wrong</u>' about the Bible passages mentioning, "Let <u>US</u> make man in

OUR image, MALE AND FEMALE, he made them... Especially since DNA brings thousands of that very thing forward in births even in 'this day and age, as there is 'NOTHING NEW' under the sun!)

13 And I haue also giuen thee that which thou hast not asked, both riches, and honour: so that there shall not be any among the Kings like vnto thee, all thy dayes.
14
15 And Solomon awoke, and behold, it was a dreame: and he came to Ierusalem, and stood before the Arke of the Couenant of the Lord, and offered vp burnt offerings, and offered peace offerings, and made a feast to all his seruants.

Nehemiah 13:26 | Read whole chapter
Did not Solomon king of Israel sinne by these things? yet among many nations

was there no king like him, who was beloued of his God, and God made him king ouer all Israel: neuerthelesse, euen him did outlandish women cause to sinne.

2 Chronicles 1:7 | Read whole chapter
¶ In that night did God appeare vnto Solomon, and saide vnto him;
Aske what I shall giue thee.

1 Kings 5:12 | Read whole chapter
And the Lord gaue Solomon wisedome, as hee promised him: and there was peace betweene Hiram and Solomon, and they two made a league together.

Behind the story of the divided kingdom is the fall of Solomon. He did so well at first, yet he sank to a shameful low —as two sweeping chapters describe. 1Kings 10 and 11   The factors behind Solomon's sin and fall from glory, his excess, his disobedience, and his neglect.

1 *Solomon's Excess*

- *Solomon's Disobedience* (17:14-20).

- "The king shall not multiply horses for himself, nor shall he cause the people to return to Egypt to multiply horses..."
- "Neither shall he multiply wives for himself lest his heart turn away..."
- "Nor shall he greatly multiply silver and gold for himself..."
- "When the king sits on the throne... he shall write for himself a copy of this law on a scroll... And it shall be with him, and he shall read it all the days of his life... carefully observing all the words of this law... that he may not turn aside from the commandment"
-

Solomon did the very opposite —a warning for us to "pay closer attention to what we have heard lest we drift away." Hebrews 2:1-3

2 *Solomon's Repentance*

The book of Ecclesiastes was almost certainly written by Solomon, "King over Israel in Jerusalem." Ecclesiastes 1:1,12 It was written after all his works and acquisitions were accomplished. On reflection, he pronounces them "vanity and chasing after the wind." Ecclesiastes 1:14

Solomon recognizes that God's works and word are eternal and all that really matters. Ecclesiastes 3:14, 12:13-14 This indicates a reformed and penitent Solomon who followed again after the heart of his father David. Like David, Solomon is forgiven. The temporal consequences of his sins had to stand, but from the eternal consequences he was saved.

3 *Solomon Divided*
Behind this story is the fact that, no matter how strong our faith might be, we can, like Solomon, let it slip by not paying sufficient attention to God's word daily.

4 *The Kingdom Divided*
We find God saying to Solomon, "I will tear the kingdom away from you." 1Kings 11:9-11 While Benjamin clung to Judah, the other ten tribes were rebellious. When Solomon died, they rejected Solomon's son, Rehoboam, as king, and made Solomon's servant, Jeroboam, their king instead.

5 *The World Divided*
The Bible says, "Behold the goodness and severity of God —on those who fell severity, but to you kindness, if you continue in his kindness, otherwise you also will be cut off."

God Dumps Solomon

The story of Solomon begins very well. He began to reign with humility and dedication. In Gibeon, God appeared to him in a dream, and invited Solomon to ask for anything he wanted. Solomon pleased God with his reply: "Give me wisdom to rule your people well."

God gave him great wisdom, as well as many blessings he had not asked: "riches and honor, so there will not be any among the kings like you all your days if you walk in my ways keeping my commandments and laws." 1Kings 3:3-15

God later appeared to Solomon a second time.

Pauline E. Petsel

Sons... IF YOU!

***THIS PAGE 'SUMS UP' AND REVEALS, THE 'ENTIRE' BOOK'S 'MESSAGE.'

Things that disappointed God.
(1) Adam- ate of the forbidden fruit
(2) Isaac- Played favoritism
(3) Jacob-Deception
(4) Joshua- Failed to consult with God and also didn't make arrangements for when he passed away, thus leaving an atmosphere away from God.

Zechariah 6:11 Take from them silver and gold and **make a crown and set it upon the head <u>of Joshua, the son of</u>** Jehozadak, the high priest, and say to him, "**Thus says the Lord of hosts, <u>BEHOLD THE MAN</u> WHOSE <u>NAME 'IS' THE BRANCH</u>: FOR HE SHALL GROW UP IN HIS PLACE, AND HE SHALL BUILD THE TEMPLE OF THE LORD. IT IS HE <u>WHO SHALL BUILD THE TEMPLE OF THE LORD</u> AND <u>SHALL SIT AND RULE</u> <u>UPON HIS THRONE</u>. AND THIS SHALL COME TO pass, IF** you will <u>diligently obey</u> the <u>voice of the Lord your God</u>." **(JOSHUA DID NOT SEEK THE LORD BEFORE MAKING A**

DECISION WHICH WITHOUT HIM REALIZING IT, THE LORD HAD BEEN AGAINST.

And when **Abram** was ninetie yeres old and nine, the LORD appeared to Abram, and said vnto him, I am the almightie God, **WALKE BEFORE ME, AND BE THOU PERFECT**. (Promised **a son in their old age and would be the parents of the nation.**)

In the <u>**Epistle to the Hebrews**, **Abraham's willingness to follow God's command to sacrifice Isaac 'is used as an example of faith as is Isaac's action in blessing Jacob and Esau with reference to the 'future promised' by God to Abraham.**</u>-

<u>SOLOMON</u>
AND 'IF' THOU WILT WALK IN MY WAYES, TO KEEPE MY STATUTES AND MY COMMANDEMENTS, <u>as thy father Dauid did walk</u> 'THEN' I WILL LENGTHEN THY DAYES.

SOLOMON ACCUMULATED ENORMOUS QUANTITIES OF SILVER AND GOLD, (1KINGS 10:14-21,27), HAD STOCKS, AND TRADES IN HORSES FROM

EGYPT, (1 KINGS 10:26,28-29), HAD 700 WIVES, WITH SOME BEING THE DAUGHTERS OF FOREIGN KINGS, AND HE HAD 300 CONCUBINES. 1 KINGS 11:1-3 IN HIS OLD AGE, HE WORSHIPPED OTHER GODS OF HIS PEOPLE.
So toward the end of Solomon's reign, his relationship with God had become reversed: because the Lord was angry with him. <u>So once again, another incarnation of someone who was to be **GOD'S Son** was squelched.</u>
Each one of these showed things the persons did to please God but God was unimpressed and why the different **incarnations** <u>'displeased'</u> God. (<u>other</u> scriptures throughout Isaiah 1....)
(From God) All these people did things to show their love <u>for</u> God at the beginning.
'THIS' is GOD'S response:
-To' <u>what **purpose'** IS YOUR MULTITUDE OF SACRIFICES to me</u>...
-**'Incense'** IS AN **'ABOMINATION TO ME'**...
-**'<u>New moons, appointed feasts</u>'**, ...'MY SOUL I <u>HATETH'</u>...
'<u>When you make many prayers</u>', I WILL <u>NOT HEAR</u> ...YOUR '<u>HANDS' ARE FULL OF BLOOD</u>...

-**Wash yourself and make you clean, seek judgement...do no evil...be willing and obedient....** If you refuse you will be devoured!
"It is sown in dishonour; it is raised in glory: it is sown in weakness; it is raised in power:"
1 Corinthians 15:43 (KJV)

"RAISING KIDS ISN'T AN EASY JOB"

ISAIAH 1:2-6 Hear, O heavens, and give ear, O earth; for the Lord has spoken; "**SONS HAVE I REARED AND BROUGHT UP BUT THEY HAVE REBELLED AGAINST ME.** The ox knows its owner, and the ass its master's crib; but Israel does not know, **my people do not understand**." **AH, SINFUL NATION, A PEOPLE LADEN WITH INIQUITY, OFFSPRING OF EVIL DOERS**, 'SONS' WHO DEAL CORRUPTLY! **THEY HAVE FORSAKEN** You. It can't be any more 'revealing' than 'that'!!)
"Hear, O heavens, and give ear, O earth: for the LORD hath spoken, I have nourished and brought up children, and they have rebelled against me." Isaiah 1:2 (KJV)

Pauline E. Petsel

THE LORD, THEY HAVE DESPISED THE HOLY ONE OF ISRAEL, THEY ARE UTTERLY ESTRANGED.

"For as we have 'many members in one body' and all members have not the same office:" Romans 12:4 (KJV)

THIS IS TELLING RIGHT HERE that there were other incarnations for whom God was saying His son would be. I doubt that God chose one person to be His son and then when he didn't work out, he went around to 'look for' someone else. The passages throughout the Bible tells of GOD'S 'ONLY BEGOTTEN' Son.

Melchizedek

The name **Melchizedek** would probably merely be a name discussed at some time during a Bible study and would be no different than any other person studied. However, this is just like other times when **important things might be being missed because of us not paying attention to what the Bible is reveling to us**. 'This name' is not only showing something important to us as to who Melchizedek was...but **the Bible is also showing so much more. It reveals the subject of 'reincarnation'. In fact, 'this is one of two Bible verses that is the 'reason' for my doing this book to begin with.
"Your father Abraham rejoiced to see my day: and he saw it and was glad."
Then said the Jews unto him, Thou art not yet fifty years old, and hast thou seen Abraham? Jesus said unto them, Surely, verily I say unto you, Before Abraham was, I am.**

Then took they up stones to cast at him: but Jesus hid himself, and went out of the Temple, going through the midst of them, and so passed by.

Melchizedek's name means "king of righteousness" and was a king of Salem (Jerusalem) plus a priest of the Most High God. Genesis 14:18–20; Psalm 110:4; Hebrews 5:6–11; 6:20—7:28 ***His appearance and disappearance in Genesis is mysterious***. Melchizedek and Abraham first met after Abraham's defeat of Chedorlaomer and his three allies. Melchizedek presented bread and wine to Abraham and his men, showing friendship. He gave Abraham a blessing in the name of *El Elyon* ("God Most High") and praised God for giving Abraham a victory in battle. Genesis 14:18–20

Abraham presented Melchizedek with a tenth of all the items he had gathered. By

doing this, Abraham showed that he recognized Melchizedek as a priest who ranked higher 'spiritually' than himself. In Psalm 110, a messianic psalm written by David (Matthew 22:43), **Melchizedek is presented as a type of Christ**. This is repeated in the book of Hebrews, where **both Melchizedek and Christ are considered kings of righteousness and peace**. Melchizedek and his 'different kind of priesthood showed it as something that Christ's new priesthood is superior to the old Levitical order and the priesthood of Aaron. Hebrews 7:1–10

Hebrews 6:20 says, "[Jesus] **has become a high priest forever, in the order of Melchizedek**." Order usually meant a successor but because no priests were between Melchizedek's time and when Jesus appeared, it indicates the two were the same person.

Hebrew 7:3 says that Melchizedek was "**without father or mother, without genealogy, without beginning of days or**

end of life, resembling the Son of God, <u>he remains a priest</u> FOREVER."
(Again remember 'those words'......"**ONLY** Begotten Son." Then add to this the... "I AM that I AM" indicating he always 'was' (no beginning or end). Being a 'priest forever,' Melchizedek sits at the right hand of God (where LATER JESUS joins him there ...as one 'after the **order** of Melchizedek.') 'Earthly' kings don't "remain a priest forever," and no ordinary human is "without father or mother."
ALSO, **Melchizedek was addressed BY GOD** who welcomed 'him' AS, "Finally <u>**I have gotten** my **ONLY BEGOTTEN SON.**"</u>
If therefore perfection were by the Levitical priesthood where people received the law, there would have been no reason for another priest to rise after the order of Melchizedek, and not be called after the order of Aaron.
For unto which of the angels said he at any time, "<u>**Thou art my Son, this day have I begotten thee.**</u>" Which of the angels said he," **Thou art my Son. THIS day have I begotten thee."**

"So also, Christ glorified not himself to be made a high priest; but he that said unto him, **Thou art my Son. TODAY have I begotten thee.**" **Hebrews 5:5 (KJV)**

For unto which of the angels said he at any time, "Thou art my Son. This day have I begotten thee." **And again, "I will be to him a Father, and he shall be to me a Son." Hebrews 1:5 (KJV)**
So also Christ glorified not himself to be made a high priest; but he that said unto him, "**Thou art my Son. Today have I begotten thee.**"
Hebrews 5:5 (KJV)
"I will declare the decree: the LORD hath said unto me, **Thou art my Son; 'THIS DAY' HAVE I BEGOTTEN THEE.**" Psalms 2:7 (KJV)
God hath fulfilled the same unto us their children, in that he hath raised up Jesus again; as it is also written in the second psalm, "**Thou art my Son. This day have I begotten thee.**"
Acts 13:33 (KJV)
I can hear all the dissention loud and clear!!
"WHAT ARE YOU SAYING MELCHIZEDEK WAS— THE 'Only BEGOTTEN SON'! Are you crazy?!!!

That is declared by God at Jesus' death **after he was crucified!!**...Again you have to read what is being said. **There are two 'similar' statements by God**. ONE, **NOW, when he got Melchizedek as his longed for 'ONLY BEGOTTEN SON** who had been perfected....and THEN ...**when Jesus died on the cross.**
And lo, **a voice from heaven saying**, "THIS IS MY BELOVED SON, **IN WHOM I AM WELL PLEASED**." MATTHEW 3:17 (KJV)

When **Melchizedek is welcomed as God's "ONLY BEGOTTEN" Son, those are the words said. WHEN 'JESUS DIED ON THE CROSS' IT 'CHANGED' TO GOD SAYING, "THIS IS MY SON, WHOM I AM WELL PLEASED.** (I will give you the places it is found in the Bible, so if you think it is repetition, it is just showing the 'different' BIBLE verses where it is being said.
And there came a voice from heaven, saying, "THOU ART MY BELOVED SON, IN

WHOM I AM WELL PLEASED." Mark 1:11 (KJV)

While he yet spake, behold, a bright cloud overshadowed them: and **behold a voice out of the cloud, which said,** "THIS IS MY BELOVED SON, IN WHOM I AM WELL PLEASED; HEAR YE HIM."
Matthew 17:5 (KJV)

"Behold my servant, whom I have chosen; my beloved, in whom my soul is well pleased: I will put my spirit upon him, and he shall shew judgment to the Gentiles."
Matthew 12:18 (KJV)

And the Holy Ghost descended in a bodily shape like a dove upon him, and a voice came from heaven, which said, "THOU ART MY BELOVED SON; IN THEE I AM WELL PLEASED." Luke 3:22 (KJV)

(Jesus as)Melchizedek had become perfected and became God's always wanted son. If therefore perfection were by the Levitical priesthood, (for under it the people received the law,) **what further**

need was there that another priest should rise after the order of Melchizedek, and not be called after the order of Aaron?
The only thing was,...<u>Melchizedek had not died for our sins so therefore, even though he had been perfected, Jesus, the 'first Adam' who had brought sin</u> **into the world still had to take away our sins by dying for us and removing it.**
"And said, by myself have I sworn, saith the LORD, for because thou hast done this thing, and hast not withheld thy son, thine only son." Genesis 22:16 (KJV)

So also, Christ glorified not himself to be made a high priest; but he that said unto him, "Thou art my Son, today have I begotten thee." Hebrews 5:5 (KJV)
I will declare the decree: the LORD hath said unto me, "Thou art my Son; this day have I begotten thee." Psalms 2:7 (KJV)
God hath fulfilled the same unto us their children, in that he hath raised up Jesus again; as it is also written in the second psalm, "<u>Thou</u> art my Son. This day have I begotten thee." Acts 13:33 (KJV)

REINCARNATION

THE WORDS ARE DIFFERENT WHEN JESUS DIED FOR US ON THE CROSS.

And lo, a voice from heaven saying, "This is my beloved Son, in whom I am well pleased." Matthew 3:17 (KJV)

"For God so loved the world, that he gave His only begotten Son, that whosoever believeth in him should not perish, but have everlasting life." John 3:16 (KJV)

And said, "By myself have I sworn, saith the LORD, for because thou hast done this thing, and hast not withheld thy son, thine only son." Genesis 22:16 (KJV)

"For God so loved the world, that he gave his only begotten Son, that whosoever believeth in him should not perish, but have everlasting life." John 3:16 (KJV)

Pauline E. Petsel

TIE THESE TOGETHER

What started me on this book was JESUS telling the Jews HE KNEW Abraham and they rebuked him because he was only 50 years old and that was impossible. I then went back in the Bible and found the incident 'Jesus' SPOKE about but found HE had been MELCHIZEDEK! **JESUS IS THE ONE WHO JUST REVEALED THIS HIMSELF!**

NOW-

The **BIBLE** tells about (JESUS) having 'reached' PERFECTION (...BUT it was through his name of 'MELCHIZEDEK' who 'sits at the' RIGHT HAND of GOD in heaven.) There would have been 'NO REASON' for ANOTHER to 'EVER' have to COME! However, God made the 'rules' for people paying for sins and because Jesus had been Adam who 'brought sin' INTO the world and Melchizedek had not paid for that, the 'PREDICTION' of JESUS 'HAVING TO COME AGAIN' AS THE SECOND ADAM TO TAKE AWAY SINS still had to be done!

This then is revealing 'another incarnation' of Jesus: ADAM! He brought SIN 'into the world' and now had to take it 'out'. (So, in JESUS' OWN WORDS, he is revealing THREE of his incarnations: Adam, Melchizedek, and Jesus!)

There is some interesting information 'hidden behind' all this. Adam had no parents but was placed by God on the earth. He sinned. All of Jesus' other incarnations he had parents but even 'they' were indirectly for there 'was' a father and mother but the father 'had not' made the incarnation through sex in some cases or was given fertility by God after some long period of time, in others. Each of these offspring did well for long periods of time, then fell into going against God by succumbing to 'earthly' wants and wishes. Incarnation after another of Jesus' characters fell into this mode.

It seemed as if GOD decided to change the way to bring the SON he wanted into the world. At least when you look at Bible verses ...it appears so. There is a story behind Melchizedek where in several scriptures, it claims Melchizedek had no parents and if you read a lot of the various 'BIBLE BOOKS' found on the internet who 'claim' they are using The King James Bible for their interpretations, this is ONE they REALLY 'fall short' with their interpretation and give people 'false' information! (Remember I have warned

before to watch what you use to interpret the Bible with. There are a lot who 'say' they are using the King James Bible...but aren't, and it is only THEIR 'interpretation' of it.
(Then said they unto him, "Where is thy Father?" Jesus answered, "Ye neither know me, nor my Father: if ye had known me, ye should have known my Father also."
John 8:19 (KJV))

"Without father, without mother, without descent, having neither beginning of days, nor end of life; but made like unto the Son of God; abideth a priest continually."
Hebrews 7:3 (KJV)
The Bible says there is no beginning of days or end and is without mother or father. This, and the following scriptures are revealing an awesome TRUTH for you to realize, but people don't know what they are reading. I am going to place some scripture for you to compare.
LOOK AT THE   SCRIPTURES and FOLLOW THIS!

REINCARNATION

1-Priest of the <u>MOST HIGH</u> GOD! (Who is the MOST HIGH GOD!?) 3-Without mother or Father having NO BEGINNING OR ENDING of days. (*** "And God said unto Moses, "<u>I AM THAT I AM</u>." And he said, "Thus shalt thou say unto the children of Israel, I AM hath sent me unto you." Exodus 3:14 (KJV)) **10-FOR HE WAS YET IN THE 'LOINS OF HIS FATHER' WHEN MELCHIZEDEK MET HIM.** (Jesus had revealed '<u>HE</u>' **HAD BEEN THE ONE <u>TO BE WITH</u>** ABRAHAM, but also revealed 'it was **<u>AS</u>**' **MELCHIZEDEK. Therefore, 'JESUS' himself was merely in the 'loins' of his father, GOD, at the time of Melchizedek. (There were** about **2,000 years** before Jesus came to this earth. So He doesn't only 'represent Christ' but IS Christ, in another one of his many incarnations.

The difference here is that **HE WAS' PERFECTED' AS MELCHIZEDEK** and **WAS THE SON GOD ALWAYS WANTED** so there would not have been any reason for Jesus to have to come.

So also Christ glorified not himself to be made a high priest; but he that said unto him, "Thou art my Son. Today have I begotten thee." Hebrews 5:5 (KJV)

I will declare the decree: the LORD hath said unto me, "Thou art my Son; this day have I begotten thee." Psalms 2:7 (KJV)

For unto which of the angels said he at any time, "Thou art my Son, this day have I begotten thee? And again, I will be to him a Father, and he shall be to me a Son?" Hebrews 1:5 (KJV)

God hath fulfilled the same unto us their children, in that he hath raised up Jesus again; as it is also written in the second psalm, "Thou art my Son. This day have I begotten thee." Acts 13:33 (KJV)

And lo a voice from heaven, saying, "This is my beloved Son, in whom I

REINCARNATION

am well pleased." Matthew 3:17 (KJV)

"But with many of them, God was not well pleased: for they were overthrown in the wilderness." 1 Corinthians 10:5 (KJV)

"In this was manifested the love of God toward us, because that God sent his only begotten Son into the world, that we might live through him." 1 John 4:9 (KJV)
 Again, this can't be stressed enough. When you sin, those sins have to be dealt with and overturned. It could be something that can be dealt with during the lifetime you are in, or might have to have another lifetime to come back in. Jesus' soul had perfected itself but had not paid for the sin he brought into the world. He had to 'die' for our sins as designated. It seems so sad that after he did everything right, he still had 'old sins' that had to still be taken care of and had to reincarnate once more to do it. You would think and wish that if you perfected yourself, that everything done wrong would be wiped clean. I don't know if it was because Jesus' sin as Adam affected mankind so everyone

was affected, that he wasn't able to have his sin forgiven, or it is with 'everyone' and has to pay for what they did until it is rectified, but it gives you something to think about. Do today everything the best you can so you don't have something 'hanging over your shoulder!

Everything has a cause and effect. Reincarnation is paying for what wrongs you did purposely to others causing them problems and negative issues for their life. Wonder if the 'scammers', internet hackers, false advertisers, and price gougers are prepared? This brings something else to mind.

(I'm not even over covering the 'Melchizedek' having no mother or father subject, and I 'm off in a different direction first and will come back to THAT. Now 'most writers' would be putting their 'notes' together and compiling them in order, to cover everything together at the same time, but that isn't my style. I go where I'm being led, and I guess 'you the reader' has to conform and 'go with me'...or 'not read' the book! (Might 'be a lot of THAT'!) The FINAL JUDGEMENT is mentioned and that indicates there 'have been' other times but also indicates there 'will not' be anymore. That means it is the end and for your chances to get it right. Then there was the passage of knowing you before you were born, and 'reincarnation' to have another life to change yourself and get things right. What if 'this' is it? What if your cheating, stealing, scams, false information, and deeds to others is about to close and what you are doing is **YOUR FIINAL JUDGEMENT?**

There have been 'ages' of creation that have already passed by. I'm only going to give you a 'run down' with slight interesting information to know or 'learn about' but will just simply give you the 'source' where the topic can be found and researched on your own, should you like.

There are many people who believe we are at THE END OF TIME. Showing this information will show you just what the different ages of creation were lined up with.

The term **Golden Age** comes from **GREEK MYTHOLOGY**, particularly the **WORKS AND DAYS** of **HESIOD**, and is part of the <u>description of temporal decline of the state of peoples through five</u> Ages.

Pauline E. Petsel

In classical Greek mythology, **THE <u>GOLDEN AGE</u> was presided over by the leading** Titan **Cronus.** In some versions of the myth <u>Astraea</u> also ruled. **She lived with men until the end of the Silver Age. But in the Bronze Age, when men became violent and greedy, she fled to the stars, where she appears**

"Golden Age" denotes a period of **primordial <u>peace</u>, <u>harmony</u>, <u>stability</u>, and <u>prosperity</u>. During this age, peace and harmony prevailed in that people did not have to work to feed themselves for the earth provided food in abundance. They lived to a very old age with a youthful appearance, eventually dying peacefully, with spirits living on as "guardians".**

REINCARNATION

Book of Enoch

There is so much information 'out there' that 'I' had no idea existed, and <u>it wasn't</u> 'my' idea to cover the things I seem to keep being 'led to' for my 'proof of' the subject for my book... "REINCARNATIONS OF JESUS".
Remember that <u>all this began</u> with <u>just a Bible verse where Jesus</u> <u>indicated he had been 'Melchizedek'.</u> Had I known where all this was going to take me, believe me, I wouldn't have started it, but now I'm in too deep and have been writing it for almost two years, that to stop now so close to the end would be a crime. (Of course, it has been so 'close to the end' for nine months now that I feel like I'm going into labor with hopefully something good at the end of it all.) It's been about nine months since I thought I had about two weeks more to do and it would be done. I still have 'two more weeks!
www.learn religions.com is where I have found the material that I will be sharing here right now, but I am <u>far from</u> covering all of what 'they' have to say! You may wish to 'plug into their site' and, in fact, I highly recommend that you do (or some place else that also has information on this.)

Classical and modern <u>scholars rejected the Apocryphal books</u> of the Bible because the <u>Jewish scribes of the common era</u> rejected them. They felt the **Apocrypha was not inspired or authorized by Jesus or the early church. They believed they had falsehoods and contradictions.** (Who hasn't read the Bible that haven't said those same things? Some of the things we read seem just as 'farfetched' at times as any books in the Apocrypha.) However, it is said that **<u>WITHOUT</u> THE BOOKS OF THE APOCRYPHA, THERE CAN'T BE THE CONNECTION TO THE MESSIAH IN THE NEW TESTAMENT.**

They say, **'Those books are the 'thread' that sews them together.' The books appeared in the 1611 King James Bible and were placed between the Old and New Testament for 274 Years until removed in 1885 A.D. Now think of that. They had once been there 'with' what we have now, but then got 'moved' to a special place where they were still recognized as filled with**

information but didn't quite fill the bill' of the people with 'final' say to be 'part of the Bible!'

Enoch is actually mentioned in Genesis 5:18-24, 1 Chronicles 1:3, Luke 3:37, Hebrews 11:5-6, and Jude 1:14-15[1] of the Bible.

> **The BOOK OF Enoch** is found in the 'later writings' not included in the Hebrew Bible or even in a lot of places.

Enoch, mentioned in Genesis 5:18, **was the descendant of Adam.** The **book of Hebrews states that, "By faith, Enoch was taken from this life, so that he did not experience death."**
'**He could not be found, because God had taken him away.'** He was said to be one who pleased God and was one of only two people in the Bible who were chosen to escape death by God, the other being **Elijah.** (***keep 'this' in mind, for later)

Jude 1:14

> 14 Enoch, **THE SEVENTH FROM ADAM, PROPHESIED ABOUT THEM**:

"And Enoch walked with God after he begat Methuselah three hundred years, and begat sons and daughters." Genesis 5:22 (KJV)

Genesis 4:17

Cain made love to his wife, and she became pregnant and gave birth **to Enoch.**

John 11:26

"And whoever lives by believing in me, will never die. Do you believe this?"

Jude 1:14-16

Enoch, the seventh from Adam, prophesied about them: "See, the Lord is coming with thousands upon thousands of his holy ones **TO JUDGE EVERYONE, AND TO CONVICT ALL OF THEM OF ALL THE UNGODLY ACTS THEY HAVE COMMITTED IN THEIR UNGODLINESS, AND OF ALL THE DEFIANT WORDS UNGODLY SINNERS HAVE SPOKEN AGAINST HIM."

15 These people are grumblers and faultfinders; <u>they follow their own evil desires; they boast about themselves and flatter others for their own advantage.</u>

<u>Hebrews 8:1-5</u>

Now the main point of what we are saying is this: We do have such a **high priest who sat down at the right hand of the throne of the Majesty in heaven**.

<u>Genesis 5:18-24</u>

18 When Jared had lived 162 years, he became the father of Enoch.
19 After he became the father of Enoch, Jared lived 800 years and had other sons and daughters.
20 Altogether, Jared lived a total of 962 years, and then he died.
21 When Enoch had lived 65 years, he became the father of Methuselah.
22 <u>After he became the father of Methuselah</u>, Enoch walked faithfully with God 300 years and had other sons and daughters.

**23Altogether, Enoch lived a total of 365 years.
24Enoch walked faithfully with God; then he was no more, because
25God took him away.**

The removal of the 7 books from the Bible by Martin Luther is an important part of the Reformation legacy. Luther believed that these books did not fit WITH <u>HIS INTERPRETATION</u> OF CHRISTIANITY, so CHOSE TO take them out of THE BIBLE. This decision had a major impact on Christianity, and it is something that continues to be debated today. The Protestant Bible consists of only 66 books — 39 books in the Old Testament and 27 books in the New Testament. The Catholic (i.e., the original canon) settled upon in the 4th century contains 73 books including Tobias, Judith, Wisdom, Sirach (i.e., Ecclesiasticus), Baruch, and 1 and 2 Maccabees — what Protestants call the *Apocrypha*.)

Luther's first German translation was missing 25 books, including **Genesis,**

Exodus, Leviticus, Numbers, Deuteronomy, Esther, Job, Ecclesiastes, Jonah, Tobias, Judith, Wisdom, Sirach (i.e., Ecclesiasticus), Baruch, 1 and 2 Maccabees, Matthew, Luke, John, Acts, Romans, Hebrews, James, Jude and Revelation. He referred to the Epistle of James as "straw not worthy to be burned in my oven as tinder." The rest he called "Judaizing nonsense." How anyone can think about the Bible the same way they have is more like being at a bowling alley and rolling the ball to knock down the pins. The only decision then would be as to if the ones knocked down would be Bible verses to leave in, or should it be the ones left standing? (Even a decision there would make a difference.)

WHAT HAPPENED TO THE BIBLE SAYING NO ONE IS TO PUT IN OR TAKE OUT THE BOOKS OF THE BIBLE?!

God works in mysterious ways and HE has a plan that shows us what to believe and he leaves 'breadcrumbs' for the birds, for us to find 'our' way. Remember God's days are 1000 years!

Pauline E. Petsel

In early 1946, in the region now known as the West Bank, a group of Bedouin teenagers were tending to their sheep and goats near the ancient settlement of Qumran. To pass the time, they threw around the rocks they found littered across the rugged desert terrain. When one rock was thrown into the dark cave, they heard a loud shattering noise echoing from inside. They found a collection of large <u>clay jars, one of which had been broken.</u>

Without realizing it, 'they' had made a <u>historic discovery</u>, for **INSIDE THE JARS WERE A SERIES OF ANCIENT SCROLLS. IN THE** following years, that **DISCOVERY** caused **ARCHAEOLOGISTS, HISTORIANS, AND TREASURE HUNTERS** to search and find additional scroll fragments in ten other caves in the area, their composition forming some 800 to 900 manuscripts collectively known as the <u>DEAD SEA SCROLLS</u>.
Among these manuscripts were large portions of a mysterious non-canonical religious text which had long been forgotten. IT WAS CALLED **THE BOOK OF ENOCH.**

(***It is here where I will tend to use the actual words for this information. They are too detailed and important to leave to any 'translating' I might do.*** In fact many of you may wish to look for more information. I feel this is VERY important and probably the 'most important' book of the Bible (Apocrypha).

IN ITS ENTIRETY, THE BOOK OF ENOCH IS MADE UP OF FIVE BOOKS – THE BOOK OF WATCHERS, BOOK OF PARABLES, THE ASTRONOMICAL BOOK, THE DREAM VISIONS, AND THE EPISTLES OF ENOCH – CONTAINING SOME 100 CHAPTERS. THESE CHAPTERS TELL THE STORY OF THE 7TH PATRIARCH IN THE BOOK OF GENESIS – ENOCH, THE FATHER OF METHUSELAH AND GRANDFATHER OF NOAH. (THE SAME NOAH IN THE BIBLICAL STORY OF NOAH'S ARK.)

YET, THIS WAS NOT THE 'BIBLICAL STORY' OF NOAH'S ARK. IN FACT, THE BOOK OF ENOCH PROVIDES AN

Pauline E. Petsel

<u>ENTIRELY DIFFERENT RECOUNTING OF THE EVENTS LEADING UP TO THE GREAT FLOOD OF NOAH'S TIME THAT IS A COMPLETELY DIFFERENT DOCTRINAL HISTORY</u>. THE STORY OF THE **BOOK OF ENOCH** TELLS A STORY OF THE <u>WATCHERS</u>, EXPLAINED IN BIBLICAL TERMS TO BE <u>FALLEN ANGELS</u> **SENT TO EARTH TO WATCH OVER HUMANS AT SOME UNDEFINED AND ANCIENT POINT IN TIME.** UNFORTUNATELY, **FAR FROM MERELY** *WATCHING* **HUMANS, THESE WATCHERS BECAME INFATUATED BY HUMAN WOMEN, AND IN SHORT ORDER, BEGAN TO ENGAGE IN DEPRAVED SEXUAL ACTS WITH THEM.** THE BOOK OF ENOCH TELLS OF THE CHILDREN BORN THROUGH THIS INTERBREEDING BETWEEN WATCHERS AND HUMANS CALLED THE NEPHILIM. THESE NEPHILIM <u>WERE</u> AS DESCRIBED: *"GIANTS AND SAVAGES THAT ENDANGERED AND PILLAGED HUMANITY"* OR SAID ANOTHER WAY, <u>*"SUPERNATURAL, 'MAN-EATING' GIANTS."*</u>

ANGERED WITH WHAT THE WATCHERS HAD DONE, THOSE DESCRIBED AS GODS CHAINED THEM IN A SUBTERRANEAN PRISON DEEP WITHIN THE EARTH. ENOCH BECAME THE GO-BETWEEN TO GODS AND IMPRISONED WATCHERS. THE BOOK <u>DESCRIBES</u> ENOCH'S JOURNEYS BETWEEN HEAVEN AND EARTH IN HIS ROLE AS AN INTERMEDIARY, HOW HE *"FLEW WITH THE ANGELS AND SAW THE RIVERS AND MOUNTAINS AND THE VERY ENDS OF THE EARTH FROM ABOVE."*
Despite Enoch's intervention, the gods said the earth had become so bad it had to be punished. <u>Which was to be a great flood</u>.. **THIS FLOOD WOULD DESTROY THE NEPHILIM AND CEMENT THE WATCHERS IN THEIR PRISON. HOWEVER, BEFOREHAND, ENOCH was 'TAKEN UP' TO HEAVEN IN A FIERY CHARIOT.**

In Genesis, it tells of the Flood, and references the **Nephilim** in Chapter 6, **<u>as</u>** *"heroes of old, warriors of renown."*
 In Numbers 13:32-33, Nephilim appear visiting the Israelites inhabited by

Nephilim, who are so large they make the Israelites look like *"GRASSHOPPERS."*

Things in the Bible times tend to be seen in today's time too but often referred to as allegorical, or more a myth than historical record. There is **ARCHAEOLOGICAL EVIDENCE** OF A GREAT FLOOD IN THE EARTH'S PAST and SPOKEN ABOUT IN many Religions AND CULTURAL TRADITIONS around THE WORLD.

YOU TUBE VIDEOs about dozens of enormous **GIANTS'** skeletons being unearthed across North America, many late 19th and early 20th century (USA) articles in newspapers claiming evidence that ancient giants were real and coexisted with early humans.

This belief seems to be all over the world. Enormous skeletons have been found in Africa's **Amazon Rainforest. (**www.ancientorigins.net**)**

The famed explorer Marco Polo once wrote of a race of giants in Zanzibar who were *"so strong they can carry as many as four ordinary men. (www* .desert sun story/life/)

The people of modern-day Tangier, Morocco claimed their city's founder was a giant. Many cultures have stories to tell, so maybe giants did exist. **THE BOOK OF ENOCH** may be less 'myth' and more 'grounded history.' (NOTE THAT FOR CENTURIES, THE **BOOK OF ENOCH** WAS AN IMPORTANT PART OF BOTH CHRISTIAN AND JEWISH RELIGIOUS TRADITIONS. **MANY, IF NOT MOST, SECTS ACCEPTED THE BOOK AS A SCRIPTURE. SOME think the BOOK OF ENOCH WAS THE <u>INSPIRATION</u> <u>FOR</u> THE BOOK OF GENESIS, because of their similar stories.)**

SO then, why is the Book of Enoch censored from the Bible? We have to go back to the early centuries AFTER THE DEATH OF JESUS CHRIST. Originally, there were numerous gospels and religious texts which made up the broad area of Christian tradition, so the Christian church decided to get some kind of control for what people need to believe. That has been discussed already at least for 'general' knowledge. Much of it was done with people's own personal beliefs even if at times 'over' knowledge.

Think of it in your own case. Those who believe in reincarnation would find a lot of examples to 'prove it', while the ones who want no part of it would look for places that speak of it, to get it deleted.

If it has vital information, how could the Book of Enoch be left out?

There were other books left out because of their unusual and unbelievable tales of things being seen and people either couldn't believe anything like it could be true or were afraid to think so. This became the list for being ignored. When you think about it and recall some of the things the Bible mentions that seem pretty 'farfetched' (Sarah having a baby in her old age, raising someone from the dead, making the blind see, etc. you wonder if they were just once again in the own minds of the people doing the 'cutting' and that perhaps we would learn some awesome things God had done.) Again, the Bible said nothing should be added nor 'taken away!

Like the Book of Enoch, these gospels tell extraordinary and history-challenging stories. The Book of Enoch may have been totally forgotten if not for its survival in small orthodox sects of <u>ETHIOPIAN JEWS</u>. The only pre-modern version of the text was written in an ancient African language. It was this version RICHARD LAURENCE, THE

ARCHBISHOP OF CASHEL, used in 1821 to produce the FIRST EVER **English translation of the book, the version used to inform STUDY OF THE DEAD SEA SCROLLS. (www.grunge.com)**

The Book of Enoch was omitted from the established Christian canon and then forgotten in all but the most obscure corners of religious tradition and theological study, the Bible does contain numerous references to it. (**www.reversespins.com**)
There are references to the Nephilim in **GENESIS** and NUMBERS. **Genesis also contains an extensive recounting of Enoch's lineage.** The Book of HEBREWS describes how *"God had taken [Enoch] away,"* seemingly a reference to his being taken to heaven via fiery chariot before the Great Flood. **JUDE,** meanwhile, **contains an entire paragraph transcribed almost word-for-word from Enoch, suggesting that the Book may, in fact, have served as an early inspiration for canonical biblical texts**.
(A lot of time when I find material, I will give the actual words the' source wrote' because it is so important and just giving you 'glimpses' isn't fair to you and the 'source' needs credit for their work .Again, that's why I'm putting the sources 'with' where I got it, so you can go to

their place right then and there if it is something you want to know more about.

From New Dawn Special Issue 8 (Winter 2009) Further, Corinthians 11:5-6 contains **instructions** from St. Paul that women should cover their heads while in church. (.www.newdawnmagazine)This is seemingly a direct reference to the fact that the <u>Watchers **in the Book of Enoch were attracted to women with long flowing hair. This is a practice which remains in Roman Catholicism and Islam to this day.**</u>

THOUGH IT WAS CENSORED, EVEN FORGOTTEN, THE BOOK OF ENOCH NEVER TRULY DISAPPEARED.

Enoch's description of his journey to meet the gods while keeping in mind the UFO sightings which often accompany and compliment these crop circles: *"I was taken to a kind of floating palace,"* Enoch said. *"It was huge, like carved glass. The floor had glass plates. Through the floor, you could see the stars we were crossing."*
Was the 'fiery chariot' which took Enoch away before the Great Flood an alien spacecraft?

REINCARNATION

Reincarnation of JESUS- John the Baptist

John the Baptist was LIKE Elijah in that he wore rough clothing and ate what he could from the land . **He was a strong-minded person who did not back away from confrontations of his mind.**
(You may think there is no reason to know so much about John the Baptist but trust me...THERE IS!)

This whole story can be found in THE KING JAMES BIBLE LUKE 1: 6-80 <u>for those who wish to see the 'Bible story' itself.</u>

For you others, I will give a quick rundown with 'my own' quick interpretation of what it says. John's parents had no children because his <u>mother was barren</u>. BEFORE JOHN THE BAPTIST WAS BORN, AN ANGEL OF THE LORD VISITED Zechariah his father explaining, "Your wife, Elizabeth, will <u>give you a son</u>, and <u>you are to name him John</u>." By this time, his parents were <u>old and</u>

beyond childbearing years. (Doesn't this sound a bit familiar as 'another person' in the Bible? Abraham and Sarah, who got Isaac under the same 'conditions'!)They were both 'godly people' but Zechariah was unable to 'believe' what he was told and because of his unbelief was stricken with the inability to speak until John was born. While still in his mother's womb, her cousin Mary, who was a 'virgin,' was also visited by an angel and was told the Holy Ghost would come to her and she would give birth to the son Of God. When the two women got together, JOHN, who was still in his mother's womb, jumped for joy as if recognizing 'Jesus' in Mary's womb. (To put a side note here for you to take into consideration. As adults, Jesus will be telling that 'Elijah' did come, but people didn't know him, so then people understood he spoke of 'John the Baptist...' (Reincarnation, my friends~!)

***What I found very interesting was this. In the **OLD TESTAMENT,** it tells of Moses being given instructions and said, 'Behold **I SEND YOU** ELIJAH **BEFORE** THE COMING OF THE GREAT AND **DREADFUL DAY OF THE LORD**. Malachi 4:4-6 That would have been Jesus's death on the cross!

Elijah should have been there to foretell it, but because Elijah was seen elsewhere shortly afterward, he couldn't have done it, but Bible predictions never change or are lied about. So the controversy among scholars, researchers, scholars, and such, disagree as to where Elijah was and that he 'couldn't have' been there.

However, ELI**SHA** was there instead. THIS is why in the Bible there is a Bible passage that says In the **NEW TESTAMENT** in **Luke 1: 17** "And he shall go before him in the **'spirit and power' OF ELIAS** to turn the hearts of the fathers to the children."

The Bible says 'Elijah will come before that fateful day to announce the end."

However, what you and I think was the fateful end of Jesus on the cross was NOT 'the end' the prediction is for. THAT day will be the end of life with the FINAL

JUDGEMENT. THAT is when Elijah <u>will</u> come.

.

***THIS IS VERY IMPORTANT AND SOMETHING TO KEEP IN YOUR MIND ***

<u>ELIJAH AND ELISHA</u> WERE <u>BOTH</u> PROPHETS IN THE <u>OLD TESTAMENT</u>, WHILE <u>JOHN THE BAPTIST</u> WAS A PROPHET IN THE NEW TESTAMENT [1].

<u>They were told he would be great in the sight of the Lord and that even from the womb he would be filled with the Holy Spirit.</u> Luke1:7, Luke 1;13,15,17, and Malachi 4:5...it said he will <u>come in the 'SPIRIT' OF</u> Elias (Elijah) to make ready a preparation for the Lord. *** This chapter is one to 'remember too!*** It also said John would not drink wine or strong drink.

"And thou, child, shalt be called the prophet of the Highest: for thou shalt go before the face of the Lord to prepare his ways." Luke 1:76 (KJV)

LATER, JOHN THE BAPTIST made the connection **BETWEEN HIS MISSION AND ISAIAH'S PROPHECY**, and declared," I am

the voice of one crying in the wilderness. Make straight the way of the Lord, as said the prophet Esaias." John 1:23 (KJV)
Matthew confirms that John the Baptist is "the voice" ushering in the <u>beginning of</u> God's glorious future kingdom with the arrival of the King. **JOHN'S ROLE WAS TO PREPARE THE WAY FOR THE KING'S ADVENT.**

HE '<u>WILL BE</u>' A MAN WITH THE 'SPIRIT AND POWER' <u>OF</u> <u>ELIJAH</u>.(Notice it says 'in the 'spirit' <u>OF</u> Elijah. <u>HE</u> WILL PREPARE THE PEOPLE FOR THE COMING OF THE LORD.)
And thou shalt have joy and gladness; and many shall rejoice at his birth.

For he shall be great in the sight of the Lord and shall drink neither wine nor strong drink; and he shall be filled with the Holy Ghost, even from his mother's womb.

16And many of the children of Israel shall he turn to the Lord their God. **17**AND HE SHALL GO BEFORE HIM **IN THE SPIRIT AND POWER OF ELIAS**, TO TURN THE HEARTS OF THE FATHERS TO THE CHILDREN, AND THE DISOBEDIENT **TO MAKE READY A PEOPLE PREPARED FOR THE LORD** THE WISDOM OF THE JUST.

THROUGH THE TESTIMONY OF MATTHEW, MARK, LUKE, JOHN, ZECHARIAH, AND JOHN THE BAPTIST HIMSELF, GOD emphasizes that the RUGGED WILDERNESS PREACHER IS THE fulfillment OF ISAIAH'S PROPHECY because John the Baptist called upon people TO REPENT OF THEIR SINS AND BE BAPTIZED—an 'act' that 'outwardly' <u>demonstrated</u> their' inward' <u>giving</u> of their lives to GOD. It started their "Faith" and <u>baptism</u> represented a 'new way' of doing things.
AS A RELIGIOUS PRACTICE, BAPTISM WAS GENERALLY ONLY OBSERVED BY OUTSIDERS (GENTILES) CONVERTING TO JUDAISM. TO PREPARE THE WAY OF THE

LORD AND MAKE HIS PATHS STRAIGHT, JOHN NEEDED THE JEWS TO UNDERSTAND THAT THEIR ANCESTRAL HERITAGE WOULD NOT SAVE THEM. FAITH IN JESUS CHRIST AS LORD AND SAVIOR WOULD REQUIRE A PERSONAL COMMITMENT—A TURNING AWAY FROM SIN AND A NEW LIFE OF DEVOTION TO GOD.

As John encountered Jesus face to face, he understood that <u>**HIS LIFE MISSION**</u> **WAS TO REVEAL TO ISRAEL THAT CHRIST WAS THE SON OF GOD AND THEIR LONG-AWAITED MESSIAH.**

John (JESUS) prepared the way of the lord by introducing Jesus as "the chosen lamb of God who takes away the sin of the world". (Because of John's ministry, multitudes of sinners put their faith in Jesus Christ.)

JOHN WAS GOD'S MESSENGER CHOSEN TO PROCLAIM THE COMING OF JESUS CHRIST, ISRAEL'S MESSIAH, WHO IS KING OF KINGS AND LORD OF LORDS. JOHN PREACHED A GAME-CHANGING BAPTISM

OF REPENTANCE THAT LEADS TO A LIFE OF HOLINESS FOUND ONLY IN SURRENDERING TO JESUS CHRIST.
(AS CHRISTIANS, WE PREPARE THE WAY FOR THE LORD TO ENTER OUR HEARTS BY REPENTING OF OUR SINS SO THAT CHRIST CAN COME IN.)

Jesus saith unto him, "I am the way, the truth, and the life: no man cometh unto the Father, but by me." John 14:6 (KJV)

It is said very clearly in the Bible that the **Prophet Elijah, who never died, will return a little before the Second Coming of Christ**. In the same way that the disciples in Jesus' time were confounded because they didn't see Elijah coming before the Messiah (Christ), so many modern Christians are confused believing that Elijah was John the Baptist.

John the Baptist, a Nazarite

"For John the Baptist came neither eating bread nor drinking wine; and ye say, he hath a devil." Luke 7:33 (KJV)

"But camest back, and hast eaten bread and drunk water in the place, of the which the LORD did say to thee, Eat no bread, and drink no water; thy carcase shall not come unto the sepulcher of thy fathers." 1 Kings 13:22 (KJV)

"And he said unto them, Behold, when ye are entered into the city, there shall a man meet you, bearing a pitcher of water; follow him into the house where he entereth in." Luke 22:10 (KJV)

"But camest back, and hast eaten bread and drunk water in the place, of the which the LORD did say to thee, Eat no bread, and drink no water; thy carcase shall not come unto the sepulcher of thy fathers." 1 Kings 13:22 (KJV)

"But he said unto me, Behold, thou shalt conceive, and bear a son; and now drink no wine nor strong drink, neither eat any unclean thing: for the child shall be a Nazarite to God from the womb to the day of his death." Judges 13:7 (KJV)

"The words of Jonadab the son of Rechab, that he commanded his sons not to drink wine, are performed; for unto this day they drink none but obey their father's commandment: notwithstanding I have spoken unto you, rising early and speaking; but ye hearkened not unto me."
Jeremiah 35:14 (KJV)
"Now therefore beware, I pray thee, and drink not wine nor strong drink, and eat not any unclean thing:" Judges 13:4 (KJV)

Bible verses related to **Judges 13:4** (similar cross-references)

Numbers 6:2-3- Speak unto the children of Israel, and say unto them, When either man or woman shall separate *themselves* to vow a vow of a Nazarite, to separate *themselves* unto the LORD: He shall separate *himself* from wine and strong drink, and shall drink no vinegar of wine, or vinegar of strong drink, neither shall he drink any liquor of grapes, nor eat moist grapes, or dried.

Judges 13:14- She may not eat of any*thing* that cometh of the vine, neither let her drink wine or strong drink, nor eat any unclean *thing*: all that I commanded her, let her observe.

REINCARNATION

Luke 1:15- For he shall be great in the sight of the Lord and shall drink neither wine nor strong drink; and he shall be filled with the Holy Ghost, even from his mother's womb.

Leviticus 11:27- And whatsoever goeth upon his paws, among all manner of beasts that go on *all* four,
those *are* unclean unto you: whoso toucheth their carcase shall be unclean until the even.

Leviticus 11:47- To make a difference between the unclean and the clean, and between the beast that may be eaten and the beast that may not be eaten.

Judges 13:7- But he said unto me, Behold, thou shalt conceive, and bear a son; and now drink no wine nor strong drink, neither eat any unclean *thing*: for the child shall be a Nazarite to God from the womb to the day of his death.

Acts 10:14- But Peter said, "Not so, Lord; for I have never eaten anything that is common or unclean"

This was not just John the Baptist but rather because he was a Nazarite. They felt they could not do this until they did it with the Lord in heaven.
It had nothing to do with drinking 'water', but strong drink. There are places in the BIBLE that are mistakes and says 'water' instead of strong drink and wine. Therefore, when any of these verses are being quoted of the Bible and spelling is even wrong, don't hold it against my 'proofreader' but is as the Bible was.

Nazarite (noun)

    an Israelite who was consecrated to the service of God, under vows to abstain from alcohol, let the hair grow, and avoid defilement by contact with dead bodies (Numbers 6).

1<u>And the LORD spake unto Moses, saying,</u>
<u>2Speak unto the children of Israel, and say unto them, When either man or woman shall</u>
<u>separate</u> *themselves* <u>to vow a vow of a Nazarite, to</u>

separate *themselves* **unto the LORD:**
3He shall separate *himself* **from wine and strong drink, and shall drink no vinegar of wine, or vinegar of strong drink, neither shall he drink any liquor of grapes, nor eat moist grapes, or dried.**
4All the days of his separation shall he eat nothing that is made of the vine tree, from the kernels even to the husk.
5All the days of the vow of his separation there shall no razor come upon his head: until the days be fulfilled, in the which he separateth *himself* **unto the LORD, he shall be holy,** *and* **shall let the locks of the hair of his head grow.**
6All the days that he separateth *himself* **unto the LORD he shall come at no dead body.**
7He shall not make himself unclean for his father, or for his mother, for his brother, or for his sister, when they die: because the consecration of his God *is* **upon his head.**

8All the days of his separation he *is* holy unto the LORD.
9And if any man die very suddenly by him, and he hath defiled the head of his consecration; then he shall shave his head in the day of his cleansing, on the seventh day shall he shave it.
10And on the eighth day he shall bring two turtles, or two young pigeons, to the priest, to the door of the tabernacle of the congregation:
11And the priest shall offer the one for a sin offering, and the other for a burnt offering, and make an atonement for him, for that he sinned by the dead, and shall hallow his head that same day.
12And he shall consecrate unto the LORD the days of his separation and shall bring a lamb of the first year for a trespass offering: but the days that were before shall be lost, because his separation was defiled.
13And this *is* the law of the Nazarite, when the days of his separation are fulfilled: he shall be

**brought unto the door of the tabernacle of the congregation:
14 And he shall offer his offering unto the LORD, one he lamb of the first year without blemish for a burnt offering, and one ewe lamb of the first year without blemish for a sin offering, and one ram without blemish for peace offerings,
15 And a basket of unleavened bread, cakes of fine flour mingled with oil, and wafers of unleavened bread anointed with oil, and their meat offering, and their drink offerings.
16 And the priest shall bring** *them* **before the LORD, and shall offer his sin offering, and his burnt offering:
17 And he shall offer the ram** *for* **a sacrifice of peace offerings unto the LORD, with the basket of unleavened bread: the priest shall offer also his meat offering, and his drink offering.
18 And the Nazarite shall shave the head of his separation** *at* **the door of the tabernacle of the congregation**

and shall take the hair of the head of his separation and put *it* in the fire which *is* under the sacrifice of the peace offerings.
19And the priest shall take the sodden shoulder of the ram, and one unleavened cake out of the basket, and one unleavened wafer, and shall put *them* upon the hands of the Nazarite, after *the hair of* his separation is shaven:
20And the priest shall wave them *for* a wave offering before the LORD: this *is* holy for the priest, with the wave breast and heave shoulder: and after that the Nazarite may drink wine.
21This *is* the law of the Nazarite who hath vowed, *and of* his offering unto the LORD for his separation, beside *that* that his hand shall get: according to the vow which he vowed, so he must do after the law of his separation.
22And the LORD spake unto Moses, saying,
23Speak unto Aaron and unto his sons, saying, On this wise ye shall

bless the children of Israel, saying unto them,
24The LORD bless thee, and keep thee:
25The LORD make his face shine upon thee, and be gracious unto thee:
**26The LORD lift up his countenance upon thee and give thee peace.
27And they shall put my name upon the children of Israel; and I will bless them.**

Pauline E. Petsel

Seven Facets of Jesus

THIS HAS BEEN THE MOST FRUSTRATING, TIME CONSUMING, MIXED-UP BOOK I HAVE EVER WRITTEN. Even though my 'usual' books, which are written about weird and strange things which have happened in my life, those things' seem NORMAL' in comparison to the 'REAL THINGS' that the BIBLE REVEALS. **Things we've never realized, yet even though it is 'right in the open' for us 'all' to see, we haven't seen it. There isn't 'anything' that the Bible doesn't have the answer for. The words "THERE IS NOTHING NEW UNDER THE SUN" AND "MAY THOSE WITH EYES SEE AND EARS HEAR" ARE BOTH THE SUMMATION OF THE BIBLE!**

I had the 'computer 'add duplicates at times and then there were times when what I 'thought' were 'repeats' because I was sure I'd read this before, happened to be that different 'characters/persons' had similar and 'almost' <u>exact description to their background.</u> (Apparently from a previous incarnation, but sure messes up trying to write a book!)

(This will have also had to be a 'nightmare' for the person having to 'proofread' through all this. Because I have 'tried' to make it easier for YOU the 'reader' to BE ABLE TO UNDERSTAND what is being revealed, in 'some ways' it may have made it 'worse' for proofreading! So 'we all are in this together because for 'your part' you need to be forgiving and understanding. With some of the 'strange things I found, the book should have been 'DISCOVERY' rather than REINCARNATION'! I came close to saying 'just forget this whole thing'…it isn't worth it. Then some new, 'strange' information seemed to 'be sent' my way, which 'boggled' my mind! Was I being 'given' this stuff for a reason? Well, my 'solving' a mystery of Elijah and Elisha was worth it. (I think!)
YOU DECIDE!

Pauline E. Petsel

How Jesus Found the Church

https://las.depaul.edu/Pages/default.aspx
The pope today claims universal ecclesial authority, and because the Vatican is a nation-state, he is a head of state and has diplomats. There are many differences between the original Jesus movement and the Catholic Church now. So how is the Catholic church the same one that Jesus founded? (Keep in mind that the APOSTLES' CREED being said every time we recite it says, **"I believe in the HOLY CATHOLIC CHURCH"**!
Roman Catholicism has understood the church to be instituted by Christ. (based on Matthew's gospel. (16:18) Jesus said, "You are **Peter,** and on **this rock I will build my church**." He chose Peter over all the Apostles and said **here i**s where **HE would build HIS c**hurch.
Apostle and **disciple** to many people are the same thing, but they are not. The main difference is that AN **APOSTLE is one who has been given authority BY JESUS CHRIST to teach** others about Him. A DISCIPLE is someone who **follows a mentor.**
Roman Catholics have tended to understand the church as institution under the **primacy of**

Peter's successor as being the same as with the "kingdom of God" proclaimed by Jesus. Jesus directly founded the institution, the offices, and <u>procedures</u> within the church.

On its own, this view is no longer the dominant understanding because the church is more than an institution. According to the Second Vatican Council, **A SACRAMENTAL COMMUNITY ANNOUNCED BY JESUS WHO "INAUGURATED HIS CHURCH BY PREACHING THE . . . COMING OF THE KINGDOM OF GOD."** The church is not identical with the kingdom of God, but **its purpose is** to announce the kingdom even if making short connections.

Jesus found something more with a life-giving community with presence of the Holy Spirit. As Luke's gospel shows, Jesus begins proclaiming the Good News of God's kingdom by reading Isaiah's words, "The **SPIRIT OF THE LORD IS UPON ME."** Luke 4:18 **IN JOHN'S GOSPEL, THE HOLY SPIRIT TAKES A LEADING ROLE IN FOUNDING AND SUSTAINING THE CHURCH.** So while the church may live on in a much different form than its early beginnings, <u>**THE SPIRIT REMAINS THE GLUE BETWEEN JESUS AND HIS CHURCH. HE DID INDEED FOUND IT ON THE ROCK OF PETER, BUT PETER AND THE**</u>

APOSTLES ARE TO BE ALWAYS GUIDED BY, STRENGTHENED BY, AND ACCOUNTABLE TO THE HOLY SPIRIT OF JESUS THE CHRIST. JESUS SENT THE SPIRIT AND THE CHRISTIAN COMMUNITY CALLED THE CHURCH WAS BORN.
(a little repetition here)
I AM
Exodus 3:14
GOD GIVES HIS NAME REVEALED DIRECTLY TO MOSES, TRANSLATED AS, "I AM THAT I AM" OR "I SHALL BE WHAT I AM". IT IS THE PERSONAL NAME OF GOD.
In the New Testament it is recorded to have been used mainly by Jesus, especially in **the Gospel of John**.

I AM the
- Bread of Life (John 6)
- the Light of the World (John 8:12)
- the Door (John 10:9)
- the Good Shepherd (John 10:11,14)
- the Resurrection and the Life (John 11:25)
- I am the Way and the Truth and the Life (John 14:6)
- I am the Vine (John 15:1,5) (interpreted as a self-declaration by Jesus, identifying Himself as God.

Jesus says: "For unless you believe that I am, you will die in your sins." John 8:58

21 (For those priests were made without an oath; but this with an oath by him that said unto him, The Lord sware and will not repent, Thou *art* **a priest for ever after the order of Melchisedec:)**
22 By so much was Jesus made a surety of a better testament.
23 And they truly were many priests, because they were not suffered to continue by reason of death:
24 But this *man*, **because he continueth ever, hath an unchangeable priesthood.**
25 Wherefore he is able also to save them to the uttermost that come unto God by him, seeing he ever liveth to make intercession for them.
26 For such an high priest became us, *who is* **holy, harmless, undefiled, separate from sinners, and made higher than the heavens;**

Actually, all that Jesus did, has been summed up within some of the other people's lives already mentioned. He preached about repenting of sins and having 'faith' in God, keeping the ten commandment, love one another, be baptized and born again, and warning the day of judgement is at hand to decide if you live forever in heaven with God, or sent to a fiery end with Satan. Most people don't even think about this because the Bible is representing him and his life, but Jesus ministry was only three and a half years!

[17]"And the disciples came, and said unto him, Why speakest thou unto them in parables?" Matthew 13:10 (KJV)
"He answered and said unto them, Because it is given unto you to know the mysteries of the kingdom of heaven, but to them it is not given." Matthew 13:11 (KJV)
"For whosoever hath, to him shall be given, and he shall have more abundance: but whosoever hath not, from him shall be taken away even that he hath." Matthew 13:12 (KJV)

"And in them is fulfilled the prophecy of Esaias, which saith, By hearing ye shall hear, and shall not understand; and seeing ye shall see, and shall not perceive:" Matthew 13:14 (KJV)

"For this people's heart is waxed gross, and their ears are dull of hearing, and their eyes they have closed; lest at any time they should see with their eyes, and hear with their ears, and should understand with their heart, and should be converted, and I should heal them." Matthew 13:15 (KJV)

"But blessed are your eyes, for they see: and your ears, for they hear." Matthew 13:16 (KJV)

"For verily I say unto you, That many prophets and righteous men have desired to see those things which ye see and have not seen them; and to hear those things which ye hear and have not heard them." Matthew 13:17 (KJV)

Jesus and Melchizedek (Same person)
John 8:48-58 "Truly, truly, I say to you **IF** anyone keeps my words, he will never see death. The Jews said to him, "Now we know you have a demon. <u>Abraham died, as did the prophets</u> and you say "If anyone keeps 'my' word, he will never taste death. <u>Are you greater than our father Abraham</u>, who died,

<u>and the prophets died</u>! Who do you claim to be? Jesus answered. "If I glorify myself, my glory is nothing; it is my Father who glorifies me, or whom you say that he is your God. But you have not known him; I know him. If I said, I do not know him, I should be a liar; but I do know him and I keep his word. Your father Abraham 'rejoiced' to <u>see 'MY' day</u>, <u>he saw it</u> and <u>was glad</u>. The Jews then said TO HIM, "<u>You are not yet fifty years old, and have you seen Abraham?</u>" <u>I SAY TO YOU, 'BEFORE Abraham' was, 'I am'</u>. So they took up stones to throw at him. Genesis 14:18-20
And Melchizedek king of Salem brought out bread and wine; he was priest of God Most High, and he blessed him and said, "Blessed to Abram by God Most High, maker of heaven and earth; and blessed be God Most High, who has delivered your enemies into your hand!" And Abram gave him a tenth of everything.

Hebrews 7:1- For this Melchizedek, king of Salem, priest of the Most High God, met Abraham returning from the slaughter of the kings and bless him; and to him Abraham apportioned a tenth part of everything. He is first by translation of his name, king of righteousness, and then he is also king of Salem, that is, <u>king of peace</u>. He is without father or mother or genealogy and has neither beginning of days nor end of life, but resembling the Son of God he continues a priest forever. <u>See how great he is</u>. <u>Abraham the patriarch</u> gave him a tithe of the spoils. And those <u>descendants</u> of Levi (third son of Jacob) <u>who receive the priestly office</u> have a commandment in the law to take tithes from people, that is, from their brethren, though these also are descended from Abraham. But <u>this man</u> who has <u>not their genealogy received tithes from</u> Abraham and blessed who had the promises. It is beyond dispute that the inferior is blessed by the superior. Here tithes are received by mortal men; there, but one of whom it is testified that he lives. One might even say that Levi himself, who 'receives' tithes, paid tithes through Abraham, for he was still in the loins of his ancestor when Melchizedek met him. (Resembling=to be 'like' in appearance or similar in character)

(7: 11) Now if perfection had been attainable through the Levitical priesthood, (for under IT the people received the law) what further need would there have been for another priest to arise after the order of Melchizedek, rather than one named after the order of Aaron. For when there is change in the <u>priesthood</u> there is necessarily a change in the law as well. For our Lord 2-(Jesus/Melchizedek) was descended from Judah and in connection with THAT tribe, Moses said nothing about priests. (7:15) This becomes even more evident when '<u>another</u>' <u>priest arises</u> in the <u>likeness of</u> Melchizedek, who has become a priest <u>not according to a legal requirement</u> concerning bodily descent but by the power of an indestructible life. For it is witnessed of him, "Thou art a priest forever, <u>after the order of Melchizedek</u>." (On the one hand, a former commandment is <u>set aside</u> because of the weakness and uselessness (for the law made nothing perfect.) On the other hand a better hope is introduced through which we draw near to God.

(****Remember the <u>start</u> of <u>this</u> section... <u>Jesus was telling the Jews</u> that '<u>Abraham was glad to</u> <u>see HIS day</u>... "and before Abraham 'I am'...when you read the above scriptures, it means he <u>stood before</u> Abraham...If Jesus is revealing 'those days' and is using the statement that <u>Abraham rejoiced to see</u> MY day, he is revealing that HE <u>was</u> MELCHIZEDEK!)

Regeneration and Born Again

What is regeneration? Being born again? Are these synonymous with each other? I always believed that at Pentecost is when man first became born again. Old Testament saints were saved through faith and obedience to the law, and when they died, they went to Abraham's bosom until Jesus took them to paradise because their sins hadn't been atoned for yet and they weren't born again.

Being born again is when you confess that you're a sinner and ask the Lord to forgive you and come into your heart. The authority to ask this was made possible by the Lord's death and resurrection. **John 1:12** Although the Greek word translated regeneration (KJV) or rebirth (NIV) in **Titus 3:5** is different from the one translated born again in **John 3:3,** they both come from the same root which means to become or come into existence. Therefore, regeneration is another way of saying born again.

You're correct in saying that Old Testament saints waited in Abraham's Bosom until the Lord's death because it took the shedding of Jesus' blood to give humanity access to Heaven. But Abraham's Bosom and Paradise

REINCARNATION

are two names for the same place. The first is a Hebrew idea and the 2nd is Greek. Jesus took the Old Testament saints to Heaven.

 Most people have heard the words "BORN AGAIN "but for non-religious people, it is a bunch of 'crap' and is simply some of that 'gibberish' people who 'claim to be' religious, use. For religious people 'sometimes' those words seem to be confused as to what is meant too, and so 'even religions themselves' seem to differ with its use.
 Some say that '<u>you agree you believe in God and heaven and are changing your ways of living to be worthy of God's blessing.</u>' To acknowledge that proclamation, they go to church to be blessed with the 'water ceremony' for being <u>born again with the 'spirit</u>'. Here is where the problem lies. The people leave, <u>knowing</u> they have verbally been 'born again' and professed their life to Christ, but on the way home someone cuts you off with their car and you chase after them with yelling and honking the horn. An argument enters with a few gestures and when it is over, more of the rage is shared with your family members about what just happened! <u>God is love! Love is patient, kind, doesn't act unbecomingly, is not</u>

<u>provoked, or takes an account of having a wrong suffered. Oops! Was the 'water' ceremony worth anything?</u> (Well yes, because of the fact you '<u>admitted</u>' **there IS a GOD and 'BELIEVE' Jesus died for our sins. Once that has been admitted, it is 'sealed', never to be erased. (Too bad some people's** <u>actions,</u> **though, are 'testing the 'forgiveness of sins' part.) BORN AGAIN IS MORE THAN A HUMAN PERSON DOING A 'RITUAL' ON ANOTHER HUMAN BEING. The water is a symbolic gesture to believing and admitting there is a God but is NOT a true meaning and commitment to being BORN AGAIN!**
BEING BORN AGAIN FALLS UNDER SEVERAL WORDS: CONVERSION-JOHN 3:1-8; **REGENERATION** JEREMIAH 24:7,EZEKIEL 11:19-20;36:26-29; **SALVATION** ACTS 4:12. THESE BIBLE VERSES MIGHT HELP...
John 3:5 There was a man of the Pharisees named Nicodemus, a ruler of the Jews. [2] This man came to Jesus by night and said to Him, "Rabbi, we know that You are a teacher <u>come from God</u>; FOR NO ONE CAN DO THESE SIGNS THAT YOU DO <u>UNLESS GOD</u> IS WITH HIM.

REINCARNATION

³ JESUS ANSWERED AND SAID TO HIM, "MOST ASSUREDLY, I SAY TO YOU, <u>UNLESS ONE IS BORN AGAIN, HE CANNOT SEE THE KINGDOM OF GOD."</u> (<u>Look at this closely.</u> JESUS is SAYING **A 'PERSON'** 'CAN NOT ' DO THE TYPE OF THINGS HE DOES '**UNLESS**' GOD ' IS' WITH HIM.)

Nicodemus said to Him, "**How can a man be born when he is old? Can he enter a second time into his mother's womb and be born?**" ⁵Jesus answered, "Most assuredly, I say to you, **'<u>Unless</u>' one is BORN OF <u>WATER</u> '<u>AND</u>' <u>THE SPIRIT</u>, he cannot enter the kingdom of God.** ⁶ That which is born of the <u>flesh is flesh</u>, and that which is <u>born</u> of the <u>spirit is spirit.</u> ⁷ Do not marvel that I said to you, "You must be born again." ⁸ The wind blows where it wishes, and you hear the sound of it, but cannot tell where it comes from and where it goes. <u>So is everyone who is born</u> OF THE SPIRIT."

(You can't <u>see</u> the wind or where it is, yet you <u>can see what it does.</u> You can 'feel it with your body. Is 'born again' when the body takes on a 'ghostlike or invisible' type nature? Are the verses where it says 'the waters above the heavens, separated from waters below' could then be implying the water ABOVE would be like 'steam' where it is still water, but in a 'form' you can see through.)

Jesus answered, "Very truly I tell you, **no one can enter the kingdom of** God <u>**unless they are born of 'water' AND The Spirit.**</u> (The Bible says man dies but the spirit/soul does not, and lives forever. If the soul is then 'reincarnated' into another body where it can learn to better itself, it still comes back in flesh. IF and when the body has perfected itself and no longer needs to come back, it is born again in spirit, but <u>also with</u> the water consistency of seeing through. Think about this. When the body has 'sinned' and not yet perfect, it reincarnates to 'try again.' However, they are returning again with a **'flesh'** body. The 'baptizing with water' is showing they 'believe there is a GOD, but with my example of the man reacting with a 'less than Godly way' when someone does something to them causing an <u>earthy reaction,</u> it doesn't keep them from having to 'do life again' in flesh until they get it right.

Jesus answered and said unto him, "Verily, verily, I say unto thee, except a man be born again, he cannot see the kingdom of God." John 3:3 (KJV)

"Not by works of righteousness which we have done, but according to his mercy he saved us, by the washing of regeneration, and renewing of the Holy Ghost;" Titus 3:5 (KJV)

"For with the heart, 'man believeth' <u>unto righteousness</u>; and with the <u>mouth</u>, 'confession' is made <u>unto salvation</u>." Romans 10:10 (KJV)

Then Peter said unto them, "Repent, and be baptized every one of you in the name of Jesus Christ for the remission of sins, and ye shall receive the gift of the Holy Ghost." Acts 2:38 (KJV)

<u>Whoever 'believes in the Son' has eternal life</u>; WHOEVER DOES 'NOT OBEY' THE SON SHALL' <u>NOT SEE LIFE</u>', BUT THE WRATH OF GOD REMAINS ON HIM. <u>(You can believe there is a GOD and get 'eternal life'...BUT... if you don't obey his ways, there are 'two places' where eternal life can go.)</u>

Then Jesus came from Galilee to the Jordan to John, to be baptized by him. John would have prevented him, saying, "I need to be baptized by you, and do you come to me?" But Jesus answered him, "Let it be so now, for thus it is fitting for us to fulfill all righteousness." Then John consented. And when **Jesus was baptized, immediately he went up from the water, and behold,** the heavens were opened to him, and he saw the Spirit of God descending like a dove and coming to rest on him; and **behold, a voice from heaven said, "This is my beloved Son, with whom I am well pleased."** (***Notice here he is saying, "This is my son with whom I AM WELL PLEASED!")

(Here Jesus himself was baptized by the 'water' as some of our churches do today, (Complete submersion) but the Holy Spirit in heaven recognized it, sending a dove as recognition thus opening the heavens 'born again in spirit' process. THIS IS THE BEGINNING FOR ALL THAT WILL TRANSPIRE BEFORE LONG FOR JESUS DYING FOR OUR SINS.

"And it shall come to pass afterward, that I will pour out my spirit upon all flesh; and your sons and your daughters shall prophesy, your old men shall dream dreams, your young men shall see visions:" Joel 2:28 (KJV)

"And also upon the servants and upon the handmaids <u>in those days will I pour out my spirit</u>." Joel 2:29 (KJV)

"And I will shew wonders in the heavens and in the earth, blood, and fire, and pillars of smoke." Joel 2:30 (KJV)

There cometh a woman of <u>Samaria</u> to draw water: Jesus saith unto her, "Give me to drink." John 4:7 (KJV) Then saith the woman of Samaria unto him, "How is it that thou, being a Jew, askest drink of me, which am a woman of Samaria? For the Jews have no dealings with the Samaritans." John 4:9 (KJV) Jesus answered and said unto her, "If thou knewest the gift of God, and who it is that saith to thee, 'Give me to drink', thou wouldest have asked of him, and he would have given thee living water." John 4:10 (KJV) The woman saith unto him, "Sir, thou hast nothing to draw with, and the well is

deep: from whence then hast thou that living water?" John 4:11 (KJV)   Jesus answered and said unto her, "Whosoever drinketh of this water shall thirst again." John 4:13 (KJV) "But whosoever drinketh of the water that I shall give him shall never thirst; but the water that I shall give him shall be in him a well of water springing up into everlasting life." John 4:14 (KJV)

The woman saith unto him, "Sir, give me this water, that I thirst not, neither come hither to draw." John 4:15 (KJV) (It continued with the woman not accepting the concept of God.) Jesus answered and said unto her, "If thou knewest the gift of God, and who it is that saith to thee, 'Give me to drink', thou wouldest have asked of him, and he would have given thee living water." John 4:10 (KJV) (Notice it is saying <u>when</u> people are met with God they too <u>will have</u> the abilities Jesus spoke of when he said **ONLY THOSE of GOD** <u>could do the things he does. So all must be born again of spirit and water.)</u>

REINCARNATION

Nicodemus answered and said unto him, "How can these things be?"
"Blessed be the God and Father of our Lord Jesus Christ, which according to his abundant mercy hath begotten us again unto a lively hope by the resurrection of Jesus Christ from the dead," 1 Peter 1:3 (KJV) and John 3:9 (KJV)

"For we have not a high priest which cannot be touched with the feeling of our infirmities; but was in all points tempted like as we are, yet without sin."

"Seeing ye have purified your souls in obeying the truth through the Spirit unto unfeigned love of the brethren, see that ye love one another with a pure heart fervently:" 1 Peter 1:22 (KJV) and Hebrews 4:15 (KJV)

"That if thou shalt confess with thy mouth the Lord Jesus, and shalt believe in thine heart that God hath raised him from the dead, thou shalt be saved." Romans 10:9 (KJV)

"Beloved, let us love one another: for love is of God; and everyone that loveth is born of God, and knoweth God." 1 John 4:7 (KJV)

"If ye know that he is righteous, ye know that everyone that doeth righteousness is born of him." 1 John 2:29 (KJV)

"Seeing ye have purified your souls in obeying the truth through the Spirit unto unfeigned love of the brethren, see that ye love one another with a pure heart fervently:" 1 Peter 1:22 (KJV)

"Being born again, not of corruptible seed, but of incorruptible, by the word of God, which **liveth** and **abideth forever."** 1 Peter 1:23 (KJV)

"And now why tardiest thou? Arise, and be baptized, and wash away thy sins, calling on the name of the Lord." Acts 22:16 (KJV)

"Which were born, not of blood, nor of the will of the flesh, nor of the will of man, but of God." John 1:13 (KJV)

"For whatsoever is BORN OF GOD 'overcometh' the world: and this is the **VICTORY** THAT OVERCOMETH THE WORLD, even our faith." 1 John 5:4 (KJV)

"NOW THIS I SAY, BRETHREN, THAT 'FLESH AND BLOOD' CANNOT INHERIT THE KINGDOM OF GOD; 'NEITHER DOTH' CORRUPTION INHERIT INCORRUPTION." 1 CORINTHIANS 15:50 (KJV)

REINCARNATION

(***As long as you have to keep coming back 'because of' sinful ways,...You will NOT be 'reborn' IN THE SPIRIT!)
"But the natural man receives not the things of the Spirit of God: for they are foolishness unto him: neither can he know them, because they are spiritually discerned." 1 Corinthians 2:14 (KJV)
"And as Jesus passed by, he saw a man which was blind from his birth." John 9:1 (KJV) And his disciples asked him, saying, "Master, who did sin, this man, or his parents, that he was born blind?" John 9:2 (KJV) **Jesus answered, "Neither hath this man sinned, nor his parents: but that the <u>works of God should be made manifest in him</u>." John 9:3 (KJV)**
"I must work the works of him that sent me, while it is day: the night cometh, when no man can work." John 9:4 (KJV)
<u>"As long as I am in the world, I am the light of the world." John 9:5 (KJV) "When he had thus spoken, he spat on the ground, and made clay of the spittle, and he anointed the eyes of the blind man with the clay," John 9:6 (KJV)</u> And said unto him, <u>"Go, wash in the pool of Siloam, (which is</u>

by interpretation, Sent.) He went his way therefore, and washed, and came seeing." John 9:7 (KJV)
AND JESUS SAID, <u>FOR "JUDGMENT"</u> I AM COME INTO THIS WORLD, THAT <u>THEY WHICH SEE NOT MIGHT SEE</u>; AND THAT THEY WHICH SEE MIGHT BE MADE BLIND." JOHN 9:39 (KJV)
This is a 'major issue' to be BORN AGAIN!...
"I've come to judge those who see and MAKE THEM 'BLIND' SO THEY CAN NOT SEE!
And some of the Pharisees which were with him heard these words, and said unto him, "Are we blind also?" John 9:40 (KJV)
Jesus said unto them, "IF YE WERE BLIND, YE SHOULD HAVE NO SIN." But now ye say, "We see; therefore your sin remaineth." John 9:41 (KJV)

It is saying right here that until you are blind AS ADAM WAS BLIND 'before' he sinned, you cannot enter the Kingdom of Heaven. ADAM came into this world not knowing SIN... good and evil ... until they went <u>against God</u>.
(ONCE WE FOLLOW GOD'S

COMMANDMENTS, WE TOO will be 'free from sins'...and **WILL BE** BORN BLIND!
(Refer to, Genesis) .... **(Adam)**- You may freely eat of every tree of the garden but of the tree of knowledge of good and evil you shall not eat of it, for in the day that you eat of it, you shall die. (Genesis 2:16)
"And they were both naked, the man and his wife, and were not ashamed." Genesis 2:25 (KJV)
"For God doth know that in the day ye eat thereof, THEN YOUR EYES SHALL BE OPENED, and ye shall be as gods, knowing good and evil." Genesis 3:5 (KJV)
(Remember all the sins occurring are for wanting to be the 'top guy'.)
"AND THE 'EYES OF THEM BOTH' WERE OPENED, and they knew that they were naked; and they sewed fig leaves together and made themselves aprons." Genesis 3:7 (KJV)

"Verily, verily, I say unto you, He that entereth not by the door into the sheepfold, but climbeth up some other way, the same is a thief and robber. [2] But he that entereth in by the door is the shepherd of the sheep. ³To him the porter openeth; and the sheep hear his voice: and he calleth his own sheep by name, and leadeth them out. ⁴And when he putteth forth his own sheep, he goeth before them, and the sheep follow him: for they know his voice. ⁵And a stranger will they not follow but will flee from him: for they know not the voice of strangers." ⁶This parable spake Jesus unto them: but they understood not what things they were which he spake unto them. ⁷Then said Jesus unto them again, "Verily, verily, I say unto you, I am the door of the sheep. ⁸All that ever came before me are thieves and robbers: but the sheep did not hear them. ⁹I am the door: by me if any man enter in, he shall be saved, and shall go in and out, and find pasture. ¹⁰The thief cometh not, but for to steal, and to kill, and to destroy: I am come that they might have life, and that they might have *it* more abundantly."

[11] "I am the good shepherd: the good shepherd giveth his life for his sheep. [12] But he that is an hireling, and not the shepherd, whose own the sheep are not, seeth the wolf coming, and leaveth the sheep, and fleeth: and the wolf catcheth them, and scattereth the sheep. [13] The hireling fleeth, because he is a hireling, and careth not for the sheep. [14] I am the good shepherd, and know my *sheep*, and am known of mine. [15] As the Father knoweth me, even so know I the Father: and I lay down my life for the sheep. [16] And other sheep I have, which are not of this fold: them also I must bring, and they shall hear my voice; and there shall be one fold, *and* one shepherd. [17] Therefore, doth my Father love me because I lay down my life, that I might take it again. [18] No man taketh it from me, but I lay it down of myself. I have power to lay it down, and I have power to take it again. This commandment have I received of my Father."

'Water' <u>represents</u> the 'Holy Spirit's <u>ability</u>' to <u>refresh us</u>, <u>quench</u> our <u>spiritual</u> thirst, <u>cleanse us</u>, and bring forth life.

Now on the last day, the great day of the feast, Jesus stood and cried out, saying, "IF ANYONE IS THIRSTY, LET HIM COME TO ME AND DRINK. **He who believes in Me**, as the Scripture said, **from his innermost being** will flow **rivers of living water.**' BUT THIS HE SPOKE **OF THE SPIRIT WHOM THOSE WHO BELIEVED** IN HIM **WERE TO RECEIVE**; FOR **THE 'SPIRIT' WAS NOT YET GIVEN BECAUSE JESUS WAS NOT YET GLORIFIED.** JOHN 7:37-39 (If any would have been perfected and didn't need to be reincarnated in a body, they would have gone to one of those 'many mansions' the Bible tells about, until Jesus was glorified, and **then** would be with him.)

1 Corinthians 12:13 (Verse Concept)
For <u>by one Spirit</u> we were all baptized into one body, whether Jews or Greeks, whether slaves or free, **and we were all made to <u>drink of one Spirit.</u>**

Genesis 1:7-9 (KJV)
⁷ And God made the firmament, and **divided the WATERS WHICH <u>WERE UNDER</u> THE FIRMAMENT FROM THE WATERS WHICH WERE <u>ABOVE</u>** THE FIRMAMENT: AND IT WAS SO.
⁸ **AND GOD CALLED THE FIRMAMENT <u>HEAVEN</u>.**
⁹ And God said, **<u>Let the waters under</u> the heaven** be gathered together unto one place, and let **the dry land appear.**

JOHN 4:13-14 (KJV) JESUS ANSWERED AND SAID UNTO HER, "WHOSOEVER DRINKETH OF THIS WATER SHALL **THIRST** AGAIN, **BUT WHOSOEVER DRINKETH OF THE WATER <u>THAT I SHALL GIVE HIM</u> SHALL NEVER** THIRST."

JESUS ANSWERED HIM, "TRULY, TRULY, I SAY TO YOU, **UNLESS ONE IS BORN AGAIN HE CANNOT SEE THE KINGDOM OF GOD."**
(One can be baptized with water to show their belief and love for GOD, however it **will be the MOUTH** <u>that tells</u> if you 'really' **are** with

God, **by the things you say and how you treat others in all situations of life.)**
 "The Lord is not slack concerning his promise, as some men count slackness; but is longsuffering to us-ward, not willing that any should perish, but that all should come to repentance." 2 Peter 3:9 (KJV)
(If you read this with 'reincarnation' in mind, it is saying GOD IS PATIENT and allows us to better ourselves until we get it right!)
So, BORN AGAIN isn't just something you 'say' and it is done. It is something you have to earn.

Born Again

 Most people have heard the words "BORN AGAIN "but for non-religious people, it is a bunch of 'crap' and is simply some of that 'gibberish' people who 'claim to be' religious, use. For religious people, 'sometimes' those words seem to be confused as to what is meant too, and so 'even religions themselves' seem to differ with its use.
Some say that '<u>you agree you believe in God and heaven and are changing your ways of living to be worthy of God's blessing</u>.' To acknowledge that proclamation, they go to church to be

REINCARNATION

blessed with the 'water ceremony' for being <u>born again with the 'spirit'</u>. Here is where the problem lies. The people leave, <u>knowing they have verbally been 'born again' and professed their life to Christ</u>, but on the way home someone cuts you off with their car and you chase after them with yelling and honking the horn. An argument enters with a few gestures and when it is over, more the rage is shared with your family members about what just happened! <u>God is love! Love is patient, kind, doesn't act unbecomingly, is not provoked, or takes an account of having a wrong suffered. Oops! Was the 'water ceremony worth anything?</u> (Well yes, because of the fact you '<u>admitted</u>' **there IS a GOD and 'BELIEVE' Jesus died for our sins. Once that has been admitted, it is 'sealed', never to be erased. (Too bad some people's <u>actions</u> though are 'testing' the 'forgiveness of sins' part. BORN AGAIN IS MORE THAN A HUMAN PERSON DOING A 'RITUAL' ON ANOTHER HUMAN BEING. The water is a symbolic gesture to believing and admitting there is a God but is NOT a true meaning and commitment to being BORN AGAIN! BEING BORN AGAIN FALLS UNDER SEVERAL WORDS. CONVERSION** JOHN 3:1-8;

REGENERATION JEREMIAH 24:7, EZEKIEL 11:19-20; 36:26-29; and **SALVATION** ACTS 4:12. THESE BIBLE VERSES MIGHT HELP...
John 3:5 There was a man of the Pharisees named Nicodemus, a ruler of the Jews. ² This man came to Jesus by night and said to Him, "Rabbi, we know that You are a teacher come from God; FOR NO ONE CAN DO THESE SIGNS THAT YOU DO UNLESS GOD IS WITH HIM."
³ **JESUS ANSWERED AND SAID TO HIM, "MOST ASSUREDLY, I SAY TO YOU, UNLESS ONE IS BORN AGAIN, HE CANNOT SEE THE KINGDOM OF GOD."** (Look at this closely. JESUS is SAYING **A 'PERSON'** 'CAN NOT ' DO THE TYPE OF THINGS HE DOES '**UNLESS**' GOD ' IS' WITH HIM.)
Nicodemus said to Him, "**How can a man be born when he is old? Can he enter a second time into his mother's womb and be born?**" ⁵Jesus answered, "Most assuredly, I say to you, **'Unless' one is BORN OF WATER 'AND' THE SPIRIT, he cannot enter the kingdom of God.** ⁶ That which is born of the flesh is flesh, and that which is born of the spirit is

REINCARNATION

spirit. <u>⁷</u> Do not marvel that I said to you, 'You must be born again.' **⁸** The wind blows where it wishes, and you hear the sound of it, but cannot tell where it comes from and where it goes. <u>So is everyone who is born</u> OF THE SPIRIT."

(You can't <u>see</u> the wind or where it is, yet you <u>can see what it does.</u> You can 'feel it with your body. Is 'born again' when the body takes on a 'ghostlike or invisible' type nature? Are the verses where it says 'the waters above the heavens, separated from waters below' could then be implying the water ABOVE would be like 'steam' where it is still water, but in a 'form' you can see through)

Jesus answered, "Very truly I tell you, **no one can enter the kingdom of** God **unless they are born of '<u>water</u>' AND The <u>Spirit.</u>**
(The Bible says man dies but the spirit/soul does not, and lives forever. If the soul is then 'reincarnated' into another body where it can learn to better itself, it still comes back in flesh. IF and when, the body has perfected itself and no longer needs to come back, it is born again in spirit, but <u>also with</u> the water consistency of seeing through. Think about this. When the body has 'sinned' and not yet

perfect, it reincarnates to 'try again.' However, they are returning again with a **'flesh'** body. The 'baptizing with water' is showing they 'believe there is a GOD, but with my example of the man reacting with a 'less than Godly way' when someone does something to them causing an <u>earthy reaction,</u> it doesn't keep them from having to 'do' life again in flesh until they get it right.

Jesus answered and said unto him, "Verily, verily, I say unto thee, except a man be born again, he cannot see the kingdom of God." John 3:3 (KJV)

"Not by works of righteousness which we have done, but according to his mercy he saved us, by the washing of regeneration, and renewing of the Holy Ghost;" Titus 3:5 (KJV)

"For with the heart, 'man believeth' <u>unto righteousness;</u> and with the <u>mouth,</u> 'confession' is made <u>unto salvation</u>." Romans 10:10 (KJV)

Then Peter said unto them, "Repent, and be baptized every one of you in the name of Jesus Christ for the remission of sins, and ye shall receive the gift of the Holy Ghost." Acts 2:38 (KJV)

<u>"Whoever 'believes in the Son' has eternal life;</u> WHOEVER DOES 'NOT OBEY' THE SON

SHALL' <u>NOT SEE LIFE', BUT THE WRATH OF GOD REMAINS ON HIM</u>."
<u>(You can believe there is a GOD and get 'eternal life'... BUT... if you don't obey his ways, there are 'two places where eternal life can go.)</u>

Then Jesus came from Galilee to the Jordan to John to be baptized by him. John would have prevented him, saying, "I need to be baptized by you, and do you come to me?" But Jesus answered him, "Let it be so now, for thus it is fitting for us to fulfill all righteousness." Then he consented. And when **Jesus was baptized, immediately he went up from the water, and behold,** the heavens were opened to him, and he saw the Spirit of God descending like a dove and coming to rest on him; and **behold, a voice from heaven said, "This is my beloved Son, with whom I am<u> well pleased."</u>** <u>(***Notice here he is saying 'This is my son with whom I AM WELL PLEASED!')</u>
(Here Jesus himself was baptized by the 'water' as some of our churches do today,

(Complete submersion) but the Holy Spirit in heaven recognized it sending a dove as recognition, thus opening the heavens 'born again in spirit' process. THIS IS THE BEGINNING FOR ALL THAT WILL TRANSPIRE BEFORE LONG FOR JESUS DYING FOR OUR SINS.

"And it shall come to pass afterward, that I will pour out my spirit upon all flesh; and your sons and your daughters shall prophesy, your old men shall dream dreams, your young men shall see visions:" Joel 2:28 (KJV)

"And also upon the servants and upon the handmaids in those days will I pour out my spirit." Joel 2:29 (KJV)

"And I will shew wonders in the heavens and in the earth, blood, and fire, and pillars of smoke." Joel 2:30 (KJV)

There cometh a woman of Samaria to draw water: Jesus saith unto her, "Give me to drink." John 4:7 (KJV) Then saith the woman of Samaria unto him, "How is it that thou, being a Jew, askest drink of me, which am a woman of Samaria? For the Jews have no dealings with the Samaritans." John 4:9 (KJV) Jesus

answered and said unto her, "If thou knewest the gift of God, and who it is that saith to thee, 'Give me to drink', thou wouldest have asked of him, and he would have given thee living water." John 4:10 (KJV) The woman saith unto him, "Sir, thou hast nothing to draw with, and the well is deep: from whence then hast thou that living water?" John 4:11 (KJV)
Jesus answered and said unto her, "Whosoever drinketh of this water shall thirst again." John 4:13 (KJV)
"But whosoever drinketh of the water that I shall give him shall never thirst; but the water that I shall give him shall be in him a well of water springing up into everlasting life." John 4:14 (KJV)

The woman saith unto him, "Sir, give me this water, that I thirst not, neither come hither to draw." John 4:15 (KJV) (It continued with the woman not accepting the concept of God.) Jesus answered and said unto her, "If thou knewest the gift of God, and who it is that saith to thee, 'Give me to drink', thou wouldest have asked of him, and he would have given thee living water." John 4:10 (KJV) (Notice it is saying <u>when</u> people are met with God, they too <u>will have</u> the abilities Jesus spoke of when he said **ONLY THOSE of GOD** <u>could do the things he does. So all must be born again of spirit and water.</u>)

Nicodemus answered and said unto him, "How can these things be?"

"Blessed be the God and Father of our Lord Jesus Christ, which according to his abundant mercy hath begotten us again unto a lively hope by the resurrection of Jesus Christ from the dead." 1 Peter 1:3 (KJV) and John 3:9 (KJV)

"For we have not a high priest which cannot be touched with the feeling of our infirmities; but was in all points tempted like as we are, yet without sin."

"Seeing ye have purified your souls in obeying the truth through the Spirit unto unfeigned love of the brethren, see that ye love one another with a pure heart fervently:" 1 Peter 1:22 (KJV) and Hebrews 4:15 (KJV)

"That if thou shalt confess with thy mouth the Lord Jesus, and shalt believe in thine heart that

God hath raised him from the dead, thou shalt be saved." Romans 10:9 (KJV)

"Beloved, let us love one another: for love is of God; and everyone that loveth is born of God, and knoweth God." 1 John 4:7 (KJV)

"If ye know that he is righteous, ye know that everyone that doeth righteousness is born of him." 1 John 2:29 (KJV)

"Seeing ye have purified your souls in obeying the truth through the Spirit unto unfeigned love of the brethren, see that ye love one another with a pure heart fervently." 1 Peter 1:22 (KJV)

"Being born again, not of corruptible seed, but of incorruptible, by the word of God, which <u>liveth</u> and <u>abideth forever."</u> 1 Peter 1:23 (KJV)

"And now why tardiest thou? Arise, and be baptized, and wash away thy sins, calling on the name of the Lord." Acts 22:16 (KJV)

"Which were born, not of blood, nor of the will of the flesh, nor of the will of man, but of God." John 1:13 (KJV)

"**For** whatsoever is **BORN OF GOD** <u>'overcometh' the world</u>: and <u>this is the</u> **VICTORY** THAT OVERCOMETH THE WORLD, even our faith." 1 John 5:4 (KJV)

"NOW THIS I SAY, BRETHREN, THAT '<u>FLESH AND BLOOD</u>' CANNOT <u>INHERIT THE</u>

KINGDOM OF GOD; 'NEITHER DOTH' CORRUPTION INHERIT INCORRUPTION."
1 CORINTHIANS 15:50 (KJV)
(***As long as you have to keep coming back 'because of' sinful ways,...You will NOT be 'reborn' IN THE SPIRIT!)

"But the natural man receives, not the things of the Spirit of God: for they are foolishness unto him: neither can he know them because they are spiritually discerned." 1 Corinthians 2:14 (KJV)

"And as Jesus passed by, he saw a man which was blind from his birth." John 9:1 (KJV)
And his disciples asked him, saying, "Master, who did sin, this man, or his parents, that he was born blind?" John 9:2 (KJV)
Jesus answered, "Neither hath this man sinned, nor his parents: but that the <u>works of God should be made manifest in him</u>." John 9:3 (KJV)
"I must work the works of him that sent me, while it is day: the night cometh, when no man can work." John 9:4 (KJV)
<u>"As long as I am in the world, I am the light of the world." John 9:5 (KJV)</u>

"When he had thus spoken, he spat on the ground, and made clay of the spittle, and he anointed the eyes of the blind man with the clay." John 9:6 (KJV)

And said unto him, "Go, wash in the pool of Siloam," (which is by interpretation, Sent.) He went his way therefore, and washed, and came seeing. John 9:7 (KJV)

AND JESUS SAID, FOR 'JUDGMENT' I AM COME INTO THIS WORLD, THAT THEY WHICH SEE NOT MIGHT SEE; AND THAT THEY WHICH SEE MIGHT BE MADE BLIND." JOHN 9:39 (KJV)

This is a 'major issue' to be BORN AGAIN!... "I've come to judge those who see and MAKE THEM 'BLIND' SO THEY CAN NOT SEE!

And some of the Pharisees which were with him heard these words, and said unto him, "Are we blind also?" John 9:40 (KJV)

Jesus said unto them, "IF YE WERE BLIND, YE SHOULD HAVE NO SIN: but now ye say, We see; therefore your sin remaineth." John 9:41 (KJV)

It is saying right here that until you are blind AS ADAM WAS BLIND 'before' he sinned, you cannot enter the Kingdom of Heaven. ADAM came into this world not knowing SIN ... good and evil ... until they went against God.
(ONCE WE FOLLOW GOD'S COMMANDMENTS, WE TOO will be 'free from sins'...and **WILL BE BORN BLIND!**
(Refer to Genesis) .... **(Adam)**- You may freely eat of every tree of the garden but of the tree of knowledge of good and evil you shall not eat of it, for in the day that you eat of it you shall die. Genesis 2:16
"And they were both naked, the man and his wife, and were not ashamed." Genesis 2:25 (KJV)
"For God doth know that in the day ye eat thereof, THEN YOUR EYES SHALL BE OPENED, and ye shall be as gods, knowing good and evil." Genesis 3:5 (KJV)
(Remember all the sins occurring are for wanting to be the 'top guy'.)
"AND THE 'EYES OF THEM BOTH' WERE OPENED, and they knew that they were naked; and they sewed fig leaves together and made themselves aprons." Genesis 3:7 (KJV)

"Verily, verily, I say unto you, he that entereth not by the door into the sheepfold, but climbeth up some other way, the same is a thief and robber. 2 But he that entereth in by the door is the shepherd of the sheep. 3 To him the porter openeth; and the sheep hear his voice: and he calleth his own sheep by name, and leadeth them out. 4 And when he putteth forth his own sheep, he goeth before them, and the sheep follow him: for they know his voice. 5 And a stranger will they not follow but will flee from him: for they know not the voice of strangers. 6 This parable spake Jesus unto them: but they understood not what things they were which he spake unto them.
7 Then said Jesus unto them again, Verily, verily, I say unto you, I am the door of the sheep. 8 All that ever came before me are thieves and robbers: but the sheep did not hear them. 9 I am the door: by me if any man enter in, he shall be saved, and shall go in and out, and find pasture. 10 The thief cometh not, but for to steal, and to kill, and to destroy. I am come that they might have life, and that they might have *it* more abundantly.
11 I am the good shepherd: the good shepherd giveth his life for the sheep. 12 But he that is a hireling, and not the shepherd, whose own the sheep are not, seeth the wolf coming, and leaveth the sheep, and fleeth: and the wolf catcheth them, and scattereth the sheep. 13 The hireling fleeth,

because he is a hireling, and careth not for the sheep. ¹⁴ **I am the good shepherd, and know my** *sheep*, **and am known of mine.** ¹⁵ **As the Father knoweth me, even so know I the Father: and I lay down my life for the sheep.** ¹⁶ **And other sheep I have, which are not of this fold: them also I must bring, and they shall hear my voice; and there shall be one fold,** *and* **one shepherd.** ¹⁷ **Therefore doth my Father love me, because I lay down my life, that I might take it again.** ¹⁸ **No man taketh it from me, but I lay it down of myself. I have power to lay it down, and I have power to take it again. This commandment have I received of my Father.**
'Water' <u>represents</u> the 'Holy Spirit's <u>ability</u>' to <u>refresh us</u>, <u>quench</u> our <u>spiritual</u> thirst, <u>cleanse us</u>, and bring forth life.

Now on the last day, the great day of the feast, Jesus stood and cried out, saying, "IF ANYONE IS THIRSTY, LET HIM COME TO ME AND DRINK. **<u>He who believes in Me</u>**, as the Scripture said, **f<u>rom his innermost being</u>**, will flow **<u>rivers of living water.</u>**' BUT THIS HE SPOKE **<u>OF THE SPIRIT</u> WHOM THOSE WHO BELIEVED** IN HIM **<u>WERE TO RECEIVE</u>**; FOR **THE 'SPIRIT' WAS NOT YET GIVEN, BECAUSE JESUS WAS NOT YET GLORIFIED."** JOHN 7:37-39

(If any would have been perfected and didn't need to be reincarnated in a body, they would have gone to one of those 'many mansions' the Bible tells about, until Jesus was glorified, and **then** would be with him.)
1 Corinthians 12:13 (Verse Concept)
For <u>by one Spirit</u> we were all baptized into one body, whether Jews or Greeks, whether slaves or free, **and we were all made to <u>drink of one Spirit.</u>**
Genesis 1:7-9 (KJV)
[7] And God made the firmament, and **divided the WATERS WHICH <u>WERE UNDER</u> THE FIRMAMENT FROM THE WATERS WHICH WERE <u>ABOVE</u>** THE FIRMAMENT: AND IT WAS SO.
[8] **AND GOD CALLED THE FIRMAMENT HEAVEN<u>.</u>**
[9] And God said, **<u>Let the waters under</u> the heaven** be gathered together unto one place, and let **the dry land appear**:

JOHN 4:13-14 (KJV) JESUS ANSWERED AND SAID UNTO HER, "WHOSOEVER DRINKETH OF THIS WATER SHALL **THIRST** AGAIN: **BUT WHOSOEVER DRINKETH OF THE WATER <u>THAT I SHALL GIVE HIM</u> SHALL NEVER** THIRST."

JESUS ANSWERED HIM, "TRULY, TRULY, I SAY TO YOU, **UNLESS ONE IS BORN AGAIN HE CANNOT SEE THE KINGDOM OF GOD."**
(One can be baptized with water to show their belief and love for GOD, however it **will be the MOUTH** <u>that tells</u> if you 'really' **are** with God, **by the things you say and how you treat others in all situations of life.)**
"The Lord is not slack concerning his promise, as some men count slackness; but is longsuffering to us-ward, not willing that any should perish, but that all should come to repentance." 2 Peter 3:9 (KJV)
(If you read this with 'reincarnation in mind, it is saying GOD IS PATIENT and allows us to better ourselves until we get it right!)
So BORN AGAIN isn't just something you 'say' and it is done. It is something you have to earn.

REINCARNATION

TIMELINE FOR DEATH OF JOHN THE BAPTIST AND JESUS' DEATH

When 'we' read the Bible, we 'don't have to' **read** for 'thirty years' before we read when Jesus **started his ministry,** but simply 'can read the whole life of Jesus' as fast as 'we' wish. We can sit and read it in a day **or** stretch our readings over days or weeks, or even months, or years. It's up to us. So, too, can we get caught off guard because the timeline between 'events' of the verses seem to have happened fairly close together. That is 'not' necessarily so in some cases.

An example of this is that 'should you' look up 'Bible studies' on the internet or, in our churches Bible study, and they are from people who **do not** believe in 'reincarnation', you will get either the Bible interpretations from a person's **personal views** or, verses not quite interpreted the **way it is written** but changing the small words like 'the', 'is', 'was', 'am', etc. to fit their ideas of 'what is **meant**', thus changing 'what the Bible' **actually says**! An example of this **is with** 'John the Baptist'. Although the 'Bible itself' **says** and **reveals** that John the Baptist **was Elijah**, 'non reincarnation believers'

will change those 'just mentioned' small words, when giving their interpretations to say, "what is meant here... "thus **changing** the **'truth' being revealed** to **us**.
'They' like to use the fact that before Jesus' death when he is in the wilderness praying and his disciples saw him speaking with Moses and **Elijah that John the Baptist couldn't have been** Elijah and this proves it. (Matthew 17:3) **LET'S LOOK AT THIS.**
The 'belief' of the time 'was' that Jesus **'could be'** John the Baptist who **had been beheaded**. This indicates they believed **both** in reincarnation, and the fact he **could already be back** since they did that deed of cutting his head off. Mark 6:14-16 ; Matthew 14:1-2; Luke 9:7-9, 9:19; Matthew 21:11
ONE VERSE IN LUKE says the appearance of Elijah with Moses and Jesus a little differently and a **'few words' change the ones** people try to quote from other books of the Bible of **this experience**.... Luke 9:30-31 And behold two men talked with him, Moses and Elijah, **who appeared in glory** ,spoke of his departure, which he was to accomplish at Jerusalem.
BUT let's see **the timeline** from **John's death** 'to' Jesus' Life and death **taken from Mark 6:14-29.**

REINCARNATION

John the Baptist is beheaded.
THEN, these things are what Jesus did **after that incident-**
- **Jesus told of John's death, goes to the area of his lost and lonely followers so Jesus started to teach them- five loaves and two fish fed five thousand**
- Jesus in the boat-walking on the water
- Jesus goes into villages, cities, or country to preach and heal
- **Jesus meets with Pharisees and scribes**
- **Jesus heals woman's daughter**
- **Jesus returns from Tyree through Siden, Sea of Galilee through Decapolis**
- **Jesus did many healings**

2- (Timeline)
- **Jesus greets a crowd- seven loaves of bread and a few fish- fed four thousand**
- **Jesus got in in boat and went to Dalmanutha-met Pharisee then went back to the other side**
- **Jesus went to Bethsaida- healed blind**
- **Jesus went to Caesarea Philippi – "Who do men say I am?"**
- **Jesus began to teach**
- **Jesus called the multitude**

- **Jesus after six days went to the mountains**
- **Elijah, Moses, <u>and</u> Jesus meet- Mark 9:9-13; Matthew 17:14-18; Luke 9:37-43; Malachi 4:5**

From 'My' COLLECTED THOUGHTS

For someone who has no education for Bible study, or the way creation began, and the way life has moved on from the beginning, I now give you what I have 'gained through the piles of information that seems to have been blown my way like debris blowing violently through a tornado. As I went through the book, I tried finding the Bible verses for 'each' subject I was covering in order to use the Bible as the proof for what I revealed. Just when I thought I had made headway and leaning toward an understanding to a possible close and end for the book, something else entered my brain cells with 'thoughts' to be covered. I am attempting here at this time to give you a quick (maybe not) overview of what I've gathered and from 'my' view. It may or may not even match the information I've revealed and with Bible verses to match.

This has taxed my brain, and I didn't have much to begin with when I started all this. Believe me... NOW I have 'less'. I'm not going to quote places where this or that was said as it is 'somewhere' in the book. I'm not going to stay with certain subjects or in an order of when mentioned. This is 'simply' what I've learned myself. **LEARNED** is an understatement! God created the world and everything in it. Because of scientists having proof of dinosaur relics and their timeline of their existence which makes the creation being more than in 'our thinking of seven days times', I've decided the creation's term 'day' was of a 'spiritual' definition of time. Later when Noah built the ark, the discrepancy as to how long that took went from 90 days to others thought of years! People lived for 500,700, 800, and 900 years, so how long were they 'actually' here 'spiritually' timed ? (More... or less?) I can't imagine having to live that long! We can't get along and do what we are supposed to with our now 'earthly' time, how bad would it have been then! Perhaps God gave them plenty of time to get things right and do what he wanted them to do but he found out humans aren't that good, and no amount of time seemed to do that. Another reason for my thinking of 'time' difference is that when the flood was about to happen, God changed the 'amount of years' a person can live to be one hundred twenty-five! THAT matches our timeline now in our way of thinking of 'time'! (Even with that, most people don't want to be around 'that' long!)

REINCARNATION

The next of my thoughts has to do with the color of people. There are people even today who are totally against blacks and whites being married. The black and brown races have been held back from obtaining the life where they can use their talents, skills, abilities, and stature just because of 'one thing'...Color! The thing is, COLOR of skin has nothing to do with anything but the fact where their body is living. We white people can hardly wait to go to the beach to lay in the sun and get a sunburn that turns our bodies tan. Yet just because we have a tan doesn't mean we aren't to go with someone who doesn't have one. This is a simple example for color. The color of a body depends on where they live in relation to the sun above. God provided inner protection to help the body be able to accept the atmosphere they live in. In time, that protection became an inbred DNA but that doesn't mean that if a group of relatives moved to an area where the skin is lighter that after 'thousands of years' their DNA might become different. God remarks that the color of skin makes no difference because it is what is 'inside a person' that counts, not the skin color. With my belief in reincarnation and the idea that whatever a person does or negatively adheres to, can be what they must face in a next lifetime so to learn from a person who was white but hated blacks and treated them badly, just might find their 'next' life being lived with that color skin. (I think of that when I see the commercial where a woman of color is stating her person of color was always told they were nothing because of their skin color and she is out to change that. I wonder if 'she' had at one time been against it.) Whatever the issue, people need to become aware of their own character and how they treat others. It can be an answer as to why their life isn't going the way they want. The Bible points to 'sin' being 'any action, feeling, or thought that goes against God's standards. (We are all screwed! It points to just how much we need to be thankful for Jesus dying for our sins.) How do we know if we are doing or saying something that is of God or if it is Satan and the 'false profits' God only 'acting' as God? That is why I have used Bible verses to back what I'm saying. Reincarnation is something many people don't believe in but don't realize it used to be in the Bible. As I've already covered that during the book, I will only add this here for now. Perhaps that is why people lived so long before. Because it was trying to give a chance for them to learn to do things better. That didn't work and it was so bad that God

decided to do it a different way. Those people would still live to be the same age type but in order to help them change, they could only live for at the most 125 years. At this point, they would die and go into heaven to one of the 'many mansions' it states as having to learn where and when they need to go back in what kind of person to learn the lessons, they need to learn with the hoped future outcome of being one with God. Thus, reincarnation with a way to learn the lessons a different way rather than living for hundreds of years.(At this point, some of you will 'see' the idea could be true…and others think I'm nuts! So, 'just my thought!")
Another thing I kept running into were times where God spoke of 'earthly material' things people were doing to please him but he was not really feeling its need but it was mainly for 'their own' thoughts. (ex.)

It's a thought that people are the reason things are done but is simply thought of and done by man's own thoughts and decisions. That is what I'm finding with 'sins' and things done in life; that are never covered or mentioned in the Bible but man is attached to an actual 'sin' of the Bible. Man has made things a sin in their own thoughts of attaching 'their own' thoughts and feelings. (abortion, life, suicide, when life begins, death, reincarnation, etc.)

So, I have given you my thoughts from what I have gleaned myself from the book. You may have gotten none of this. In fact, you may have gotten nothing and found this boring and a waste of time. (Just the fact of finding out about the Nephilim giants were why the flood came upon the earth should at least be worth the read.)

If these reincarnations of Jesus are true, then we have 'two things' to take from it. That even with Jesus being GOD'S ONLY BEGOTTEN SON, he had to earn his place and even he wasn't perfect. If 'he' had to learn his wrong ways and 'pay' for things he did wrong, WE may see that we 'can' change too, and because of seeing what took place with Jesus, we might learn and keep ourselves from doing wrong.

With 'that' thought mulling around in your mind', I am going to share something else, even though it has nothing to do with this book, or in fact 'religion' in any way.

Because I have something that I have shared with a lot of people and many of them reporting back with thanks for their experience which were helped by it, I am taking the time to share it in this book so 'readers' (if there is even 'only ONE OF YOU' (Ha!) might benefit. So I guess this should just be listed as, "**Free Fer Nothin'**."

I 'think' the idea to share this at the end was 'my' idea, but because after 'wondering' <u>if</u> I should do it, I had 'four things' happen to either confirm it that I should… or that <u>it wasn't 'my idea' to begin with.</u>
The first thing that 'coincidently' happened, was that I got a phone call from the fire department '<u>burn unit</u>' wanting a donation for tickets to an event for benefit of those who <u>suffer from burns</u>. It wasn't just a <u>fire department</u> asking for a donation or to buy tickets but was from the <u>BURN</u> unit! I shared my information with the person and they were most interested in what I said and said they would be 'passing' the information on. Then several 'television sit coms' had 'seemingly token episodes' involving 'burns of some kind' involved. One was a horrible sunburn, another was a burn while using a decorating torch, and another at an oven. ('TO ME', with them all showing up within days of each other after wondering if I should put it in the book, it made me think they were

showing up for verification. (May sound silly to you, but That seems to be the way my life works!)

This isn't to be a book in itself but certain things need to be told when I 'go off' on one of these 'side steps.'

When I was about four, we had a Halloween costume party at church. I was walking hand and hand with my little girlfriend who had a grass skirt on. As we passed the open flame, her grass skirt flung outwards and slipped between the wired protection grate into the heater and caught on fire. The flames swept upward onto her body and hair, and she was clinging to me, as I was trying to get away. My mother threw a heavy winter coat around her and put out the fire while someone called the fire dept and ambulance. She was in treatment for a long time, and it damaged her to the point that she never grew in size of height from that day.

Now move forward in time when I was married and living in a different state. I was a first- aid instructor, did 'healing' work, and hypnosis. I read a lot of books with 'spiritual' topics and read this one book, which the 'title' I don't remember, but the <u>information</u> stuck with me like glue.

It was about a 'touch healer' in the United States who had a friend who was studying to become a doctor. She was so shaken up when she had to go through the burn unit that she wasn't sure she could do it. The healer said, "The problem is, people NEVER HAVE TO GET THAT WAY WHEN THEY ARE BURNED IF THEY WOULD JUST POUR APPLE CIDER VINEGAR ON THEM. THE BURN WOULD BE GONE."

It wasn't long after that when the woman had a party at her house, and someone went to the kitchen and bumped a handle on the stove that had boiling liquid in it. It spilled all over the person's body, and the Dr. 'to be' remembered what her 'healer friend' had said, so she covered the person with vinegar. The next day there was <u>no burn</u> except for one the size of a fifty-cent piece that she had missed with the vinegar. The 'healer' healed 'that'.

After reading 'that' information, I kept apple cider vinegar handy and spread the word to everyone I knew. One day a neighbor came over to thank me for sharing that information with her. She had shorts on and was riding her motorcycle and touched her leg on the hot exhaust pipe. She used the vinegar, and the burn disappeared immediately. I was even amazed with that one because I hadn't thought for using it on 'every KIND' of burn. I do NOW. I have heard back from all kinds of different types of burns people have used it for. I even keep a couple bottles of vinegar in my car. Think of it. <u>ONE</u> person who shared the information has saved who knows how many people from suffering terrible scars from a burn just by sharing the knowledge. I pass it on so 'they', through 'me', might save even more!

So, there you have it. An 'added story' to a book <u>it has nothing to do with.</u>

Another bit of information that will be very helpful comes from country doctors coming to our house while growing up. (Ya... DOCTORS actually used to make 'house calls!') If someone had a cold, flu, or something that was 'catchy', the first thing the doctor did was ask for an onion. He peeled the onion and cut it in two placing it in two parts of the house. The theory behind this is that the 'onion' will absorb all the bacteria in the house and keep anything from being passed on to others. That onion could 'never' be eaten in 'any way' because it was filled with germs. However, anyone who had a respiratory condition should eat 'onion' sandwiches as thick as they can stand to kill the cause for the issue within them for it to go away. I have eaten 'many' onion sandwiches at the first sign of a cold, and needless to say, it 'always' warded it off.

So, while I am at it, I will pass on 'something else', which in a long roundabout way but could 'sort of' tie us back in with the book's subject matter. Even though it is from 'my' own thoughts in the making, I sort of made it into my 'own' Motto!

I thought about all the people out there who have completely messed up their bodies while following the 'FADS' of mankind. Tattoos covering their entire body, nose, eye, tongue, and nose piercing, weird colors and wearing of hairdos, and whatever some 'whim' caused someone to follow.

IT MAKES ME THINK BACK IN TIME TO 'MY' YOUTH when MY BROTHER WHO WENT INTO THE Navy got a large tattoo on the top of one arm. I wanted one too, but my 'wise' mother said I couldn't get one then, but if I still wanted one when I was a teenager, I could. Well, back then there wasn't the FAD like today, so luckily, I didn't want one. Instead,

Pauline E. Petsel

'our generation' was stuck with 'paper tattoos' that washed off. That was great because you could change the designs. When I see women with their entire body in permanent tattoos and years later are going to get married, those tattoos look horrible with a beautiful wedding gown. I overheard a conversation between two people who hadn't seen each other for some time and the woman didn't recognize the man. He explained he had shaved off his long beard and cut his hair.(However he still had a nose ring.) I wondered if he might someday remove that too, but the tattoo would still be there.) It got me wondering how many people out there might wish they could change the things they did to 'their bodies' just because they followed a "FAD"! a 'FAD... <u>made by</u> 'MAN.' With the book being on 'reincarnation' we are seeing that what we do in our lives 'now' can make a difference as to how, or IF, we will need to come back into another lifetime to 'pay', or 'make amends' for something we are 'doing wrong' now.'

Something happened while I was writing this, that brought home how, '<u>what we do in our life right now, can be a positive influence for others' lives and be in their memories for</u>

REINCARNATION

<u>years.</u> I got a phone call from a person who I knew about fifty years ago. I had taught her children to swim and back then, and I wrote a book about 'Teach your tot to swim". I recall It had my daughter of three months on the cover, swimming toward the underwater camera. Many swim instructors throughout the United Sates and Canada ,and beyond used the book to set up their own classes. (So, think of all the lives that have been saved) I <u>republished the same exact boo</u>k,' fifty years later' but with an 'update' on the kids who were then, grown. This woman stated how much they have talked about me over all these years, and she got the new book copy, because now, her 'grandchildren' are learning to swim. While the uplifting words of 'praise' were nice, it wasn't 'that' which got my attention. Why had this phone call shown up 'exactly at the same time I WAS WRITING ABOUT WHAT WE DO IN LIFE INFLUENCES OTHERS.(GOD WORKS IN MYSTERIOUS WAYS!)

The Influence can be in a 'positive ways...but... there 'could be 'negative' ways too. Do kids smoke or drink 'because they are doing what their parents do and are following their examples? Do they <u>not</u> go to church or not believe in God <u>because</u> of their parent's influence or someone else's who they look up too?)

Think about everything and everyone you meet during your everyday life. The services they provide that better your life in some way. EVERY 'ONE' OF THEM HAS IT! YOU do it!

So, all this made me put together everything I've just covered. What does the way you live your life and what you 'do' with your body <u>during FADS</u> have in common? Think about it. <u>DO WRONG WITH YOUR LIFE AND YOU WILL PAY FOR IT IN SOME WAY EITHER NOW OR IN ANOTHER LIFETIME</u>. So, THE ANSWER IS TO DO THINGS YOU 'DON'T HAVE TO CHANGE'. When they follow fads, they' must keep in mind' that people change their minds all the time, so don't get stuck with something you can't change. Thus...my MOTTO for life. ...

"DO ONLY THINGS IN YOUR LIFE THAT CAN BE CHANGED!"

This 'add in' has given you a 'break' to <u>rest your mind</u> and get ready for the rest of the book which is going to be intense and will need your mind fresh to focus on what is being revealed.

So, there you have it. An 'added story' to a book it has nothing to do with it.

"I SHOW YOU A MYSTERY"- ANSWER REVEALED

On the cover of 'this' book I said that I would reveal the answer to the "I SHOW YOU A MYSTERY" comment made by Jesus, concerning John the Baptist. Here it is, but it will take a while to reveal it.

Jesus began to say unto the multitudes concerning John, "What went ye out into the wilderness to see? A reed shaken with the wind? [8]But what went ye out for to see? A man clothed in soft raiment? Behold, they that wear soft *clothing* are in kings' houses. **But what went ye out for to see? A prophet? YEA, I SAY UNTO YOU, AND MORE THAN A PROPHET."**

Matthew 11:9 (KJV) **For THIS IS *HE*, of whom it is written, Behold, I send my messenger before thy face which SHALL 'PREPARE THY WAY' BEFORE THEE.** [11]Verily

I say unto **you,** among them that are **BORN OF WOMEN** there **HATH NOT RISEN** a greater than **John the Baptist**: notwithstanding he that is least in the kingdom of heaven."

(Let's 'back up'. Look at what happened about John's **BIRTH)**
Luke 1:5-25 (KJV)
There was in the days of Herod, the king of Judaea, a certain priest named Zacharias, and his wife Elisabeth.
[6] **And they were 'both' righteous before God, walking in all the commandments and ordinances of the Lord blameless.**
[7] And they **had no child** because that **Elisabeth was barren,** and they **both were** *now* **well stricken in years.**

[9] According to the custom of the priest's office, his lot was to burn incense when he went into the temple of the Lord.(*)
[10] And the whole multitude of the people were praying at the time of incense.(*)

¹¹**And there appeared unto him an angel of the Lord standing on the right side of the altar of incense.**(*)
¹²And when Zacharias saw *him*, he was troubled, and fear fell upon him.(*)
¹³But the angel said unto him, **Fear not, Zacharias: for thy prayer is heard; and THY WIFE ELISABETH SHALL BEAR THEE A SON, AND THOU SHALT CALL HIS NAME JOHN.**(*)
¹⁵For he shall be great in the sight of the lord, and shall drink neither wine nor strong drink; and **HE SHALL BE FILLED WITH THE HOLY GHOST, EVEN FROM HIS MOTHER'S WOMB.**(*)
¹⁶And many of the children of Israel shall he turn to the Lord their God.(*)
¹⁷And **he shall go before him IN THE 'SPIRIT AND POWER OF' ELIAS,** to turn the hearts of the fathers to the children, and the disobedient to the wisdom of the just;

TO MAKE READY A PEOPLE PREPARED FOR THE LORD.

¹⁸And **Zacharias** said unto the angel, **"Whereby shall I know this? for I am a<u>n old man, and my wife well stricken in years."</u>**

¹⁹And the <u>angel answering said unto him,</u> "I am **Gabriel,** that stand in the presence of God; and am sent to speak unto thee, and to shew thee these glad tidings.(*)

²⁰<u>**And, behold, thou shalt be dumb, and not able to speak, until the day that these things shall be performed**</u> because thou <u>believest</u> **not** my words **which shall be fulfilled in their season."**

²²<u>And</u> **when he came out, he could not speak unto them:** <u>and they perceived that he had seen a vision in the temple: for he beckoned unto them, and remained speechless.</u>

²⁴And after those days his wife Elisabeth **CONCEIVED.**

John's birth. **GOD HAD PERFORMED A MIRACLE AND BROUGHT JOHN INTO THE WORLD FOR A <u>SPECIAL PURPOSE</u>!**

<u>**He was to preach about repentance and to baptize people in water. He was also to preach about the Kingdom of God and prepare a people for the Messiah's coming**</u>.

(Doesn't this sound like someone earlier in the Bible?......

(READ THIS!)

............**Genesis Chapter 18**................

<u>³AND SAID, MY LORD, if now I have found favor in thy sight, pass not away, I pray thee, from thy servant</u>
¹⁰And he said, **"I will certainly return unto thee according to the time of life;** and, lo, **SARAH thy wife <u>SHALL HAVE A SON</u>."**
¹¹<u>**Now Abraham and Sarah were old *and* well stricken in age; *and* it ceased to be with Sarah after the manner of women.**</u> Genesis Chapter 21 <u>**And the LORD visited SARAH as he had said, and the LORD did unto Sarah as he had spoken.**</u>
FOR SARAH <u>CONCEIVED</u>, AND BARE <u>ABRAHAM</u> A SON IN HIS OLD AGE, AT THE SET TIME OF WHICH GOD HAD SPOKEN TO HIM.

And Abraham called the <u>name of his son</u> that was born unto him, whom Sarah bare to him, ISAAC.

(**BOTH '<u>ISAAC</u>' AND '<u>JOHN</u>' were '<u>BORN OF A WOMAN</u>', AND 'ALTHOUGH ONE <u>DID</u> COME FROM THEIR MOTHER'S OLD AND LIFETIME STERILE <u>BODY</u>, AND SHE <u>mysteriously</u> CONCEIVED <u>IN HER WOMB</u>, John the Baptist <u>mysteriously seemed to 'recognize Jesus while they were each within their mother's womb.</u> Jesus had just said, [11]**"Verily I say unto **you, AMONG THEM THAT ARE '<u>BORN OF</u> Women,' there HATH NOT RISEN a greater THAN John the Baptist:** notwithstanding he that is least."

('<u>Other</u>' <u>Biblical figures</u> who had 'miracle type' births, including Jesus, were of ' <u>Virgin</u>' mothers!)

Malachi 4:5–6 says, "Behold, **I will send you <u>Elijah</u>** the <u>prophet before the coming</u> of **the great and <u>DREADFUL</u> DAY OF <u>THE LORD</u>.** And he shall turn the heart of the fathers to the children, and the heart of the children to their fathers, lest I come and smite the earth with a curse."

(*** THIS is how I picked up that there is a difference with changed words. THIS is saying... **ELIAS**...<u>MY BIBLE</u> says **ELIJAH!!**)

You see, apparently <u>'I'</u> <u>saw the word AS</u> Elis<u>ha</u> (rather than Elias) and immediately looked that word up to prove 'the Bible' was wrong. When I did, I found there '<u>were</u>' actually <u>TWO</u> <u>PEOPLE,</u> and not only were they close in spelling, but ELIJAH was a <u>mentor for</u> ELISHA, so they were even 'CLOSE TO EACH OTHER.' <u>What the heck?!</u>

WELL, I then re-looked at the word the Bible had mentioned, and saw the spelling was <u>ELIAS</u>...NOT <u>ELISHA</u> which 'I' had looked up!! I found <u>MY</u> word <u>ELIJAH in my Bible wasn't a different person but merely a different, *language* **used of saying the same word.** I didn't know the Bible would be using two different pronunciations. So then, the **Bible** ended up being 'right' 'after' all!

HOWEVER, even though **'I' was wrong** and had looked up a spelling for a word I 'thought' was what the Bible had said…(ELISHA), something **MAJOR** happened.

With one of the two people mentioned that I looked up was **ELIJAH**. *In Mathew 11:7 **JESUS SAID JOHN THE BAPTIST WAS ELIAS (ELIJAH) which was to come. (ELIJAH was to break the news of Jesus' 'coming'.)** Little did I know where all of this was going to take me. I ended up with a 'side trip', looking for information that seemed to overtake me. One question's answer led to another question to be asked. I looked up things on the internet's Bing, on Websters dictionary, in my (KJV) Bible, Unger's Bible dictionary, and so much more. I wasn't looking for 'other people' to answer my question but rather to find out if other's thoughts were leaning my same way. **(These thoughts even plagued me** while trying to sleep at night. It was as if 'some' of the questions weren't even mine to look up!)

Jesus With Elijah. We read about the astounding ministry of **Elijah** in **1 Kings 17-21** and **2 Kings 1-2**. We don't know the family background of Elijah, **FOR SARAH CONCEIVED, AND BARE ABRAHAM A SON IN HIS OLD AGE, AT THE SET TIME OF WHICH GOD HAD SPOKEN TO HIM.**
And Abraham called the name of his son that was born unto him, whom Sarah bare to him, ISAAC.

(This may be indicating that nevertheless, He, (John), is the least of the two births of a woman, BECAUSE the 'FIRST' TIME (In both the Old and the New Testament) **GOD IS CALLED THE GOD OF ABRAHAM, ISAAC, AND JACOB BECAUSE WITH THEM GOD'S RELATIONSHIP OF 'PROMISE AND PURPOSE' WAS FIXED for**

ALL THOSE WHO 'DESCENDED FROM' THEM.
So that 'would' be the most important, but 'that promise' would also be <u>including John</u> and what his purpose '<u>would' be</u>.

SO... IS JOHN A 'REINCARNATION' (OR ONE OF them) **FROM Isaac?**

We know John was from the <u>other side of the tracks</u> **in Gilead.** He had a unique personality found within the Scriptures. He could go from being 'fearful' to 'all of a sudden 'being 'fearless.' He ran away from trouble one minute yet ran toward it and into another time. At times he was weak, but other times strong. He went from being 'discouraged' to 'other times' filled with 'confidence'. John was a loner, with feelings of abandonment at times, yet whatever life sent his way, he held deep faith and 'personal' relationship with God. He was always in prayer which held both deep and exceptional meanings.

Then, there is...Eli<u>sh</u>a with a similar story to that of the 'disciples'. HIS <u>MASTER,</u>

REINCARNATION

prophet ELIJAH, found him working in the fields. When ELIJAH called 'ELISHA' to 'follow' him, it was a 'symbolic gesture' of telling him that he would TRANSFER HIS POWER TO ELISHA in the future.
Elisha drops what he's doing and starts as an assistant to the prophet.
1 Kings 19:19-21

Reaching Mount Horeb, **Elijah** heard the **voice of God** tell him to anoint two kings **as well as Elisha as a prophet**. He did this, and **Elisha promptly joined him. 1 Kings 19:19-21**
I typed ON THE INTERNET "What's the difference between Elisha and Elijah?" (I had my own reason for this) At first when I 'did it', I had a 'series of two sentences'…one with **Elijah,** and then with the same question, but pertaining to **Elisha**. I darkened each one's name and put in parenthesis, plus I underlined each. I thought that would be easier for **you to compare**. However, with the names so close I was even confusing myself because I did it so many times. (You are going to sense it yourself just as you read it.) I decided that would also be confusing to the reader after a while. Instead, I decided to just do a 'paragraph' containing information for each person and that

way, **you** can compare them in 'sort of' a less confusing manner.
ELIJAH's name in Hebrew **means 'MY GOD IS YAHWEH' OR 'YAHWEH IS MY GOD.'** **Elijah** lived in despair in the desert and **wasn't a very 'subtle' man but instead sort of revealed 'who he was' by the 'way he was' in front of people.**

Elijah **was hairy**.... ELIJAH ran away from Jezebel wanting to die. **Elijah performed about 16** miracle accounts in his life... **Elijah was a prophet of judgment and gave testimonies against sin and evils of men and directed to the public. He dealt mostly with sinners and those that led them.** On a social level, **Elijah** came from a poor background. Elijah's story appears mostly in **1 Kings**. He was a **prophet during one of the most wicked times in Israel's history, when worship of Baal was at an all-time high**. **Elijah** personally **went head-to-head with one of the most evil royal couples in their history**: Ahab and Jezebel. **Elijah** was held back because he **didn't socialize** with people. (Compare all this to what had just been previously described for JOHN.)

REINCARNATION

According to <u>MALACHI 4:6</u>, **the reason for Elijah's return <u>WILL BE</u> to "turn the hearts" of fathers and their children TO EACH OTHER** with **<u>love and peace</u>**.
<u>Elijah</u> **technically does not die, and many have speculated that he is 'reincarnated' as John the Baptist .**

(So again, let's look at those comparisons.

(SWITCH Now to ELISHA!)

ELI<u>SH</u>A's name in Hebrew means '<u>GOD IS SALVATION</u>.'
Elisha was **more at <u>home in cities</u> and was often in the company of kings.**
Elisha was **more <u>even-tempered</u>**, without drama.
Elisha was **<u>bald,</u>**
Elisha seemed to HAVE **a more <u>influential personality</u>.**
Elisha HAD a more **'<u>able</u>' situation.**
Elisha was **more <u>graceful in tone</u> and his testimonies were more with salvation of people and preaching of God's mercy, and through God's compassion. He did many healings and miracles.**

ELISHA did ALMOST TWICE what **ELIJAH** performed.

Elisha was not only **active** but was often found **visiting** their **places of schooling or worship**.

Elisha performed about 21 recorded miracles.

ELISHA'S MINISTRY LASTED TWICE THAT OF ELIJAH'S.

(BOTH)

Elijah and Elisha LIVED during the time of the kings of Israel. In fact, **BOTH PROPHETS** completed **miracles** and **called down God's judgment on various evildoers. 1 Kings 18, 2 Kings 2**

BOTH were **GOD-ANOINTED prophets** who **served and helped people to be saved.**

BOTH served God with trust and faith and **considered to be** among the **most respected prophets in the Old Testament.**

BOTH came from Samaria and **had their close spellings** of their names.

(DIFFERENCES)

AT FIRST, THEIR MIRACLES WERE BASICALLY THE SAME… BUT THEN CHANGED.

ELIJAH healed a woman… but **ELISHA** restored a woman **BACK TO LIFE.**

MOST OF ELIJAH'S MIRACLES were directed from the 'destructions' people had while living their lives… while **ELISHA'S** consisted of **both restoration** and **ALSO BRINGING ONE'S FROM DEATH BACK TO LIFE**.

ELIJAH'S FIRST MIRACLE was prophesying that neither rain nor dew could be seen for a period of three and half years. ELISHA'S FIRST MIRACLE was PRAYING FOR AN UNCLEAN SPRING TO HAVE CLEAN WATER.

THERE WERE OTHER DIFFERENCES AS TO THE WAY THEY LIVED THEIR LIFE AS PEOPLE, And **THEIR DIFFERENCES EVEN IN DEATH.**

As diligent leaders and servants of people, **both feared God** and the Bible never speaks of either with any offenses. They committed their lives to God. **ELIJAH died through the fire on chariot and 'TAKEN UP' so he never saw death.**

ELISHA died in his old age.(**Elisha had fallen sick with the illness of which he was to die**, he gave a 'last prediction' to the king of Israel with an 'angry tone' because the king had not followed his direction precisely.

He **also left with a conclusion of 'doing a healing'! When he died and was buried, a man was being buried by a marauding band and the man was thrown into the grave of Elisha.** *AS SOON AS THE MAN TOUCHED THE BONES OF ELISHA, HE REVIVED AND STOOD ON HIS FEET.*
*** **EVEN THE <u>NEW TESTAMENT</u> TALKS OF THE <u>ANTICIPATED RETURN OF ELIJAH,</u> <u>(in a role TO BE MET BY JOHN THE BAPTIST</u>... <u>the one to announce the arrival of the messiah.)</u> (ELIJAH IS NOW REINCARNATED AS JOHN.)**

A Recap-
In <u>2 Kings 2</u>, <u>Elijah and Elisha</u> traversed the Jordan River on dry land, and <u>Elisha, was understanding that Elijah would soon pass away</u>,
5 The company of the **prophets** at Jericho **<u>went up to Elisha</u> and asked him, "Do you know that the LORD is going to take your master from you today?" "Yes, I know," he replied, "So be quiet."**

REINCARNATION

8 ELIJAH took his cloak, rolled it up and struck the water with it. The water divided to the right and to the left, and the two of them crossed over on dry ground.
9 When they had crossed, **ELIJAH said to ELISHA**, "TELL ME, WHAT CAN I DO FOR YOU BEFORE I AM TAKEN FROM YOU?" "LET ME INHERIT A DOUBLE PORTION OF YOUR SPIRIT," ELISHA REPLIED.
10 "YOU HAVE ASKED A DIFFICULT THING," ELIJAH SAID, "yet IF you SEE ME when I am taken from you, it will be yours—otherwise, it will not." (Pay attention to this.)
11 As they were walking along and talking together, **suddenly a chariot of fire and horses of fire appeared and separated the two of them and ELIJAH WENT UP TO HEAVEN IN A WHIRLWIND.**
12 ELISHA SAW THIS and cried out, "My father! My father! The chariots and horsemen of Israel!" And Elisha saw him no

more. (***Pay attention to this too...the BIBLE is revealing a lot here!***)
13 Elisha then picked up Elijah's cloak that had fallen from him and went back and stood on the bank of the Jordan.
14 He took the cloak that had fallen from Elijah and STRUCK THE WATER WITH IT. "WHERE NOW IS THE LORD, THE GOD OF ELIJAH?" he asked. When he struck the water, it divided to the right and to the left, and he crossed over.
15 The company of the prophets from Jericho who were watching said, **"THE 'SPIRIT OF ELIJAH' IS RESTING ON ELISHA." AND THEY WENT TO MEET HIM AND BOWED TO THE GROUND BEFORE HIM.**

(And the water has remained pure to this day, according to the word **Elisha** had spoken.)
I now repeat this verse... BUT WITH A NEW TESTAMENT TWIST ADDED

Malachi 4:5

REINCARNATION

"**BEHOLD, I WILL SEND YOU ELIJAH the prophet** before the coming of the great and dreadful day of the LORD:" Malachi 4:5 (KJV) Remember, BOTH, Elijah and Elisha had been prophets in the Bible's Old Testament <u>ELIJAH was a prophet who RANKED WITH MOSES in saving the religion of Yahweh from being corrupted by the nature worship of Baal. ELISHA was also a prophet and miracle worker who learned from ELIJAH and "succeeded him" after his ascension to heaven.</u>

(Add now, the New Testament)
HERE IS THE ANSWER <u>TO "I SHOW YOU A MYSTERY</u>".
Elijah <u>did come</u> but **only with** 'slight' **spirit, but <u>instead</u> ELISHA WAS 'REINCARNATED AS JOHN'**. **(ELISHA GOT 'DOUBLE' ELIJAH'S POWER WHEN 'ELIJAH DIED'**, so **WITH <u>his own power too</u>** ,he **came as ELISHA WHO THEN, WAS THE REINCARNATION TO JOHN THE Baptist**....(not Elijah). **ELISHA had 'double'** Elijah's **power given to him, so 'Elijah's ONE part wasn't as**

strong as ELISHA'S TWO PARTS ...MAKING him OVER HALF!

1The BIBLE SAYS THERE IS NOTHING NEW UNDER THE SUN. What is has been and will be is all figured in the Bible. It is as if there is a blueprint for the world that was made at creation and we are just following it, no matter if we think we are in control or not.

Therefore, the coming of Eli**sha** was already in the plan and is proved by the new scripture that says 'will' come in the **'SPIRIT' of** Elijah. (Instead of the original, **Elijah will** come.

Luke 1:17
"And he shall **go before him in the 'spirit' and 'power of' Elias,** to turn the hearts of the fathers to the children, and the disobedient to the wisdom of the just; to make ready a people prepared for the Lord." (Notice here it is saying in the 'spirit' of... Elias (Elijah).

In Malachi 3:1 of King James Version, it also doesn't say Elijah, but merely a 'messenger'.) "Behold, I will send my messenger, and he shall prepare the way

REINCARNATION

before me: and the Lord, whom ye seek, shall suddenly come to his temple, even the messenger of the covenant, whom ye delight in: behold, he shall come, saith the LORD of hosts."

In 'both cases' it covers the fact that because **ELISHA got double the power of Elijah after he died, ELISHA was the one who become John the Baptist reincarnated. (NOT ELIJAH)** ELIJAH AND ELISHA'S **'JOINED' LEGACY** PROCEEDED TO HELP ISRAEL EVEN **AFTER THEIR LIVES.... AS... John the Baptist...** because it was a **'joint' effor**t.) **Elijah himself would remain who and where he was because after Elisha died, the 'double' power of Elijah he had would have been used up and be gone, leaving Elijah back to his position.**
(*I DON'T NEED TO GIVE THE NAMES OF any people who have <u>articles out for DISPUTING that John the Baptist is Elijah</u>, because I haven't used any of their sites. However, I 'will mention' their 'collective' thoughts and beliefs as to WHY THEY THINK THE WAY THEY DO.) First of all IS

THEY DON'T BELIEVE IN REINCARNATION. Because they say the Bible doesn't say there is. (***I've answered that one already. Because it was <u>removed</u> by many people in a variety of ways. (Just because it isn't there 'in so many words' saying there is, doesn't mean there wasn't something there before, revealing the truth. It got 'taken out' because of 'high ranking persons who don't want to believe in it, so they got rid of it. (That doesn't mean it didn't exist!) Those that say Elijah <u>COULDN'T BE John the Baptist</u> BECAUSE they say that <u>John himself declared that he was NOT ELIJAH</u>, and he should know! Reincarnated people don't remember past lives.... (in fact, many people I know 'these days' don't even remember what they did last week!)
The person they 'were' in a different lifetime before is gone, and this is a brand-new body (not soul) incarnation. The knowledge is not remembered by the new physical body but IS connected within their 'spirit and soul' so that the new incarnation can work to 'better' themselves.

REINCARNATION

The 'icing on the cake' for '<u>those people</u>' <u>WHO SAY JOHN THE BAPTIST COULD NOT BE ELIJAH</u> IS THAT ELIJAH HIMSELF <u>IS SEEN LATER IN TIME</u>. (I JUST EXPLAINED THAT! ...Because it was **ELISHA IN the 'SPIRIT OF'**... Eli<u>jah</u>!)

SO THIS IS THE ANSWER TO THE MYSTERY. <u>ELISHA </u>WAS JOHN THE BAPTIST!

***HERE IS ANOTHER THING TO PONDER. John the Baptist was A '<u>JOINT EFFORT</u> 'with Elisha having the '<u>double power</u> ' Of Elijah. However, Elijah <u>never saw death</u> and was 'taken up'.

There will be '<u>another</u>' '<u>joint effort</u>' mentioned soon. That of MELCHIZEDEK WHO WAS 'PERFECTED' SO <u>NEVER DIED</u> AND SITS AT <u>THE 'RIGHT HAND 'OF GOD ALMIGHTY'</u>. THEN AFTER DYING FOR OUR SINS, JESUS Joined HIM THERE. The 'two' are one'.

NOW AS FOR <u>John</u> 1:23

[20](And he confessed, and <u>denied not;</u> but confessed, <u>I AM 'NOT' THE CHRIST</u>. (RIGHT) And they asked him, What then? ART <u>THOU ELIAS</u>? (Here we go again with another 'close' name to Elisha and Elijah) **And HE SAITH, I AM NOT. (RIGHT) ARE THOU <u>THAT</u> PROPHET? AND HE answered, No.** (<u>Isaiah, also known as Isaias or Esaias, was the 8th-century BC Israelite prophet after whom the Book of Isaiah is named. Within the text of the Book of Isaiah, Isaiah is referred to as 'that' prophet, ...</u>So when John was asked if he was 'THAT' prophet, he said NO.)
I found ESAIAS IS A <u>NAME</u> USED FOR <u>TWO</u> <u>'DIFFERENT'</u> PROPHETS IN THE BIBLE. (These 'biblical' names are so close to one another; it is very confusing and no wonder why people can't understand the Bible.) **ESAIAS and ISAIAH are the same word <u>AND</u>** ('SAME') **PERSON. ONE …WAS <u>ISAIAH</u> WHO PROPHESIED IN JUDAH AND WAS MARTYRED BY KING MANASSES.**

THE 'REST OF THE STORY'

ELIJAH AND ELISHA'S **JOINED LEGACY** PROCEEDED TO HELP ISRAEL **EVEN AFTER**

**THEIR LIVES. THE NEW TESTAMENT TALKS OF THE ANTICIPATED RETURN OF ELIJAH, a role answered by <u>JOHN THE BAPTIST</u>.
2 Kings 2**

Elisha had great powers on his own and was at a point of doing even more and greater things than Elijah, but after asking Elijah for double his power after he died, Elisha could do even greater things.
Elisha dedicated his ministry <u>to finishing what Elijah had started</u>; <u>to get rid of the worship of Baal. 2 Kings 10:28</u>

**THE <u>OTHER</u> WAS AN '<u>ANCIENT</u>' PROPHET WHO 'LIVED' IN <u>THE 'TIME OF ABRAHAM' WHO 'RECEIVED HIS BLESSING.'</u>
(THIS WAS MELCHIZEDEK!!!)... THIS IS SHOWING A 'SECRET' EVEN HERE.)** If 'BOTH' are the same person but merely used a different spelling according to <u>where</u> in the Bible THEY NOW LIVE, it is used. They have 'different' names... and 'bodies'... but 'ARE 'ALIVE' <u>AGAIN</u> in A 'TOTALLY <u>DIFFERENT</u> LIFETIME'! (SO THEN, we have a 'REINCARNATION' of ONE 'SOUL' 'being' two

different 'persons' yet ALTHOUGH THE 'SAME person' ('SOUL' WISE)... One AS ISAIAH AND the other as MELCIZEDEK! However, we add yet <u>'another' one</u> of their lives... JOHN THE BAPTIST. ISAIAH is the one who is revealing the crying of the voice in the wilderness in Matthew 3:4 and in Matthew 13:14. It says, And in them is fulfilled the prophecy of Esaias (ISAIAH) which saith, **"BY HEARING YE SHALL HEAR, AND SHALL NOT UNDERSTAND; AND SEEING YE SHALL SEE, AND SHALL NOT PERCEIVE."**

"THE VOICE OF ONE CRYING IN THE WILDERNESS, MAKE STRAIGHT THE WAY OF THE LORD," AS SAID THE PROPHET ESAIAS. JOHN 1:23
<u>ISAIAH PROPHESIZED THE COMING OF THE MESSIAH JESUS CHRIST.</u>
<u>ISAIAH LIVED ABOUT 700 YEARS BEFORE JESUS CHRIST</u> and is known<u> for his book in the Bible with his name.</u>
<u>**ISAIAH WAS ALSO KNOWN FOR PREDICTING THE COMING OF JESUS CHRIST TO SALVAGE MANKIND FROM**</u>

SIN [1]. **HE BROUGHT THE MESSAGE OF CONDEMNATION AS WELL AS A MESSAGE OF HOPE AND SALVATION THROUGH THE COMING OF THE MESSIAH, JESUS CHRIST.**

Luke 3:4
The **WORD OF GOD came UNTO JOHN** the son of Zacharias in the wilderness. And he came into all the country about Jordan **PREACHING THE BAPTISM OF REPENTANCE FOR THE REMISSION OF SINS; EVERY VALLEY SHALL BE FILLED, AND EVERY MOUNTAIN AND HILL SHALL BE BROUGHT LOW; AND THE CROOKED SHALL BE MADE STRAIGHT, AND THE ROUGH WAYS *SHALL BE* MADE SMOOTH;** [6]**AND ALL FLESH SHALL SEE THE SALVATION OF GOD.** [7]**THEN SAID HE TO THE MULTITUDE**

THAT CAME FORTH TO BE BAPTIZED OF HIM, "O GENERATION OF VIPERS, WHO HATH WARNED YOU TO FLEE FROM THE WRATH TO COME." AND THE SAME JOHN HAD HIS RAIMENT OF CAMEL'S HAIR, AND A LEATHERN GIRDLE ABOUT HIS LOINS; AND HIS MEAT WAS LOCUSTS AND WILD HONEY."

Repeat:
ELISHA and JOHN THE BAPTIST were also similar in many ways. Both were prophets who lived life with the spirit of God within them and bravely spoke for His good while fighting the evil against him.
They believed both religiously but also with a strange seemingly mystical knowledge, seemingly to know that something in the future would happen.

The mysterious Angel of Yahweh in the Hebrew Bible would appear numerous times from out of nowhere and in unexpected settings. This unique Angel would appear as a <u>divine visitor</u> to Abraham, comfort to Hagar, wrestling opponent to Jacob, saved Isaac from being sacrificed, and spoke in a burning bush with Moses. **THIS ANGEL WAS GOD IN THE FORM OF MAN, THE PRE-INCARNATE CHRIST. THIS** special Angel appeared in many other settings in the Old Testament and every situation is distinct and unique. **GOD CANNOT BE SEEN BECAUSE HE IS SPIRIT** and is comprised of a substance of light so pure THAT He cannot be experienced face-to-face by any human. God sent Jesus as His unique representative to speak and do His will on earth. God, as an angel, took roles of deliverer, judge, and revealer. Through the incarnations of Jesus we see his works for lessons and through reprimands, to better oneself for final judgement.

Pauline E. Petsel

God is Love

GOD IS LOVE … GOD **IS** LOVE … GOD IS **LOVE!**
Three words, and no matter how you pronounce them, they are ALL right!
There is nothing new saying 'GOD IS LOVE' because people in church have heard it said over and over again, and those who don't go to church may even have heard it, but the way they live their lives with so many issues and problems, are quick to point out that if 'this' is love, it's a bunch of baloney and this is exactly why 'they know' there IS NO GOD!
Therefore, 'anything else' they hear about GOD and 'judgement' is also a bunch of 'hogwash'! Those kinds of people feel that 'love' is 'whatever **you** do' to make yourself 'happy!' Get drunk or have meaningless sex, but as many things as you can do that make you happy and if you don't have enough, you steal it. If lying **benefits you**, and cheating others, or even in some cases fighting or beating someone up because they have something you want, it is fine!?!?! 'Most' <u>do</u> draw the line with murder or rape, BUT 'some' are even willing to do those, if

it would get them what they want, and THAT would make them happy!

Now 'church goers' merely feel those 'words' mean that God loves them. The Bible is <u>clear</u> about 'those words' and what they mean, but many 'supposed' Bible interpreters of scripture give meaning to many scriptures <u>by their own</u> belief system, and 'believed' educational background. I have neither of those so am merely taking the **Bible itself** for what IT IS SAYING. **Think of this and how <u>those three simple words</u> can be emphasized three different ways, and no matter which you use, it is revealing GOD. GOD is love. God IS love. ...or God is <u>LOVE</u>!**

Love's dictionary definition is:

1. **an intense feeling of deep affection**
2. **a great interest and pleasure in something**
3. **a person or thing that one loves,**
   feel deep affection for (someone),
   like or enjoy very much

In the Bible, love conquers all things, and the word 'love' is found in many, many places throughout the Bible.

While growing up, the definition I remember having of love was, "Love is a feeling that you feel when the feeling you feel is felt without ever feeling it before." Now with my aging years, where I don't remember a 'lot of things' 'where' I came up with it is 'beyond me, but yet those words themselves remain strong and clear!

But I have no idea where I got it or who said it, yet in my aging years when you don't remember things a lot, **those words** are still there! Remember, Jesus spoke in parables and not everyone actually understood his messages' depths. Some did at first but then easily lost or forgot them. (I've had times where I've gone into a room to get something and forgot what it was by the time I got there... AND it wasn't 'someone else' telling me to do it... it was ME!')

Some remembered Jesus words for a while but then life's demands take over and they can only do one thing at a time, so they let their own priorities take over.

'HERE' we have the 'Bible's explanation' for the aspect of LOVE. Three words twisted around and every way, it is telling you what God is.

(There are many places in the Bible where the words of 'God is love' or love is Indicated but let's look at love the way God means it. If we use these facts, you will be living and reaping love in your life and will be one with

God! Think of your life you live now. Where do YOU fall short?

LOVE IS PATIENT, LOVE IS KIND, IT DOES NOT ENVY, IT DOES NOT BOAST, IT IS NOT PROUD, IT DOES NOT DISHONOR OTHERS, IT IS NOT SELF-SEEKING, IT IS NOT EASILY ANGERED, IT KEEPS NO RECORD OF WRONGS. LOVE DOES NOT DELIGHT IN EVIL BUT REJOICES WITH THE TRUTH. IT ALWAYS PROTECTS, ALWAYS TRUSTS, ALWAYS HOPES, ALWAYS PERSEVERES. LOVE NEVER FAILS.

But where there are prophecies?... They will 'cease' and where are tongues, they will be' stilled'. Where knowledge was, it will pass away.

Look at life around us. What do people argue about? Politics, religion, race, color of skin or colors of anything, money, bills, abortion, when life starts, reincarnation, clothes, how they wear their hair, designs, best cars, tattoos, prices, animals, cars, relatives, celebrations, boats, vacations, music, entertainment, and so much more. Somehow 'someone' seems to find absolutely anything to argue about. At times, these are just conversations or discussions, but how many times do they end up with 'verbal or heated' arguments, to the point of yelling, screaming, verbal abuse, and even times of violence or going off mad and never speaking to each other again? These lives do not feel the love available for their lives and live in a frustrating unkind world not worth living in. Look again at the highlighted massively large paragraph above, for in this paragraph lies the answer to the inner peace you seek. It's for everyone …not just for 'religious' people!

"*God is love*" isn't just one of God's characteristics or activities. It is God's very essence. Even when he teaches or chastises or disciplines, it is through love to help you become better and thereby reap a happier, more loving life to live. A parent doesn't correct or punish their child when they do something wrong because they are mean, but through their punishment they are making the child a better person and help them be able to find happiness in their future because of the lessons they learned. There are people out there who never punish their child for 'anything' and feel they are being 'great, loving' parents. The opposite is

true. Through discipline, reprimands, and direction, the child is put on a straight path to experience LOVE in their life by the way they live.

How many times have you 'religious people' said this prayer? How many times has it been simply become 'repeated words' like a ritual, but has lost its **'real'** meaning in your thoughts? Think of it <u>NOW</u>! What are you really saying?

"Our Father, who art in heaven, 'hallowed' be thy name. THY **'<u>KINGDOM</u> COME'** … THY **'<u>WILL</u> BE DONE'**.. **<u>ON</u> 'EARTH'** …**('AS IT IS'** … in, **'HEAVEN'**…**)** GIVE US THIS DAY our daily bread and **FORGIVE 'US'**… **<u>'OUR' 'TRESPASSES'</u>**… **'AS' 'WE'**…**'<u>FORGIVE</u>' THOSE** …WHO <u>TRESPASS</u> **'AGAINST 'US'**…and **lead us not into temptation,** but **deliver us from evil, for THINE is the kingdom and the power forever. Amen.**
Do **WE <u>follow</u>** what **WE** say? **(Realizing what you are saying in that prayer may have you thinking more about how you live your life with others!) It is saying to 'forgive <u>US</u>'** our

trespasses AS WE 'OURSELVES' forgive others who do the same to us! (DO YOU?) We become our 'own judge as to what 'we' think is right or wrong! We always interpret things from 'inside' us, as our '**minds**' decided what '**we**' think or say is right, wrong, correct or incorrect, smart or stupid, true or false, what to believe or not believe! (Each one of you reading 'this' book (if there are any of you left) are doing that very thing.

Love and Peace be with you!
I hope you enjoyed the book and that **'SPIRIT'** has touched you in a special way' meant' **JUST FOR 'you'. I hope you learned things you never knew before and that it has helped you to find 'meaning' and/or direction to help you on that 'path' that leads to being one with God in Heaven or living your life with the thoughts of 'what' you do 'today' effects 'what' you reap 'tomorrow' (even a different lifetime away.)**

Because all of us fall short of being what we 'should be' I leave you with a list of things where people fall short, and where in the Bible you can look them up on you own if you need or wish!

Adultery- Matthew 5:27-28, 32; 19:9, 18; Mark 10:11-12; Luke 16:18; Hebrews 13:4; 1 Corinthians 6:9-10; Mark 7:21; John 8:1-11
Anger- Galatians 5:20; Ephesians 4:26, 31; 6:4; Colossians 3:8; James 1:19-20
Bitterness- Ephesians 4:31; Hebrews 12:15; Romans 2:24; 3:14; Acts 8:23; James 2:7
Brutality- 2 Timothy 3:3
Coveting- Mark 7:22; Ephesians 5:5; Acts 20:33; Romans 13:9; 1 Corinthians 5:10-11; 6:1
Deceit- Mark 7:22; Acts 13:10; Romans 1:29; 1 Peter 3:10
Disobedience to parents- Romans 1:30; 2 Timothy 3:2; Titus 3:3
Divorce- Matthew 5:32; 19:9; Mark 10:11-12; Luke 16:18
Drunkenness- Romans 13:13; 15: 13; Ephesians 5:18; 1 Corinthians 5:11; 6:10; Colossians 3:13; 1 Peter 4:3
Envy- Mark 7:22; Galatians 5:26; Titus 3: **Greed-** Ephesians 4:19; 5:3; 2 Peter 2:14
Hatred- 2 Timothy 3:3; Titus 3:3
Homosexuality- 1 Corinthians 6:9; 1 Timothy 1:10; Romans 1:26-27
Idolatry- 1 Corinthians 5:11; 6:9; Galatians 5:20; Revelations 21:8; Ephesians 5:5

Jealousy- Galatians 5:20; 1 Corinthians 3:3; 2 Corinthians 12:20; James 3:16
Judging- Matthew 7:1-5; Romans 2:1; 14:13; Luke 6:37 James 4:11
Lying- Revelation 21:8, 27; 22:15; Ephesians 4:25; Romans 9:1; 2 Corinthians 11:31; Galatians 1:20; 2 Timothy 2:7
Stealing- Ephesians 4:28; 13:9; Matthew 19:18; Mark 10:19; Luke 18:20; Romans 2:21; 13:9
Strife, quarreling- Galatians 5:20; Romans 1:29; 13:13; 1 Corinthians 3:3; 2 Corinthians 12:20; 1 Timothy
Unforgiveness—Matthew 6:14-15; Mark 11:25-26
(copied off internet resources)

Golden Age and Ages

The term **Golden Age** comes from **Greek mythology, particularly the *Works and Days* of Hesiod, and is part of the description of temporal decline of the state of peoples through five Ages.**
Plato **in *Cratylus*** (397 e) recounts the golden race of humans who came first. He clarifies that Hesiod did not mean literally made of gold, **but good and noble.**
In classical Greek mythology, **THE GOLDEN AGE was presided over by the leading Titan Cronus.** In some versions of the myth, Astraea also ruled. **She lived with men until the end of the Silver Age. But in the Bronze Age, when men became violent and greedy, she fled to the stars where she appears as the constellation Virgo, holding the scales of Justice, or Libra.**
European pastoral literary tradition often depicted nymphs and shepherds as living a life of rustic innocence and peace. (I give the sources so 'you' can look it up in THEIR 'entirety', but I will be giving only a small bit to familiarize you with them.)
https://www.history.com/news/bronze-age-collapse-causes

(BY: **DAVE ROOS** UPDATED: JUNE 29, 2023 | ORIGINAL: JULY 28, 2021)

The fivefold division of Ages of Man, according to Hesiod, are[1]:
- Golden Age: 1710 to 1674 BC
- Silver Age: 1674 to 1628 BC
- Bronze Age: 1628 to 1472 BC
- Heroic Age: 1460 to 1103 BC
- Iron Age: 1103 BC, still going on.

Learn more:
1. wikipedia.org 2. tf.uni-kiel.de

Gold, being the first and the one during which the Golden Race of humanity began. "**GOLDEN AGE**" WAS THE FIRST PERIOD WITH **PEACE, HARMONY, STABILITY, AND PROSPERITY.** PEOPLE DID NOT HAVE TO WORK TO FEED THEMSELVES because the earth provided food in abundance. THEY LIVED TO A VERY OLD AGE WITH A YOUTHFUL APPEARANCE, AND WHEN THEY DIED, it was peacefully, with spirits living on as "guardians".

3,200 YEARS AGO, THE MEDITERRANEAN AND NEAR EAST WERE HOME TO the **BRONZE AGE CIVILIZATION.** The Bronze Age was the first time humans started to work with metal. Bronze tools and weapons replaced earlier stone versions. TECHNOLOGICAL CAPABILITIES TO BUILD MONUMENTAL PALACES AND SCRIBES TO KEEP RECORDS OF THEIR FINANCES AND MILITARY endeavors came into play. However, in matter of decades, their thriving culture went through a quick and near-total collapse. Survivors of this Bronze Age collapse plunged into a centuries-long "Dark Ages" that saw the disappearance of some written languages and collapsed once-mighty kingdoms.

"SILVER AGE" WAS THOUGHT OF AS NOTABLE BUT INFERIOR TO A GOLDEN AGE." IT WAS secondary to THE golden age. (According to the Oxford Dictionary) Things 'sort of matched' abilities of the Golden age, yet didn't measure up to their abilities. When the golden age had ended, the golden race still existed AND roamed the earth as kindly spirits. **The** silver race was <u>inferior to the golden race and</u> **were immature, needing a hundred years to grow up but when they did, they lived short lives because of their**

foolishness to keep sinning and not listening and honoring the gods who were losing patience.

BRONZE AGE
Beings of silver age were sent to the underworld and became known as the blessed spirits **OF HADES.** A third generation, was formed called the brazen race of men. The men were strong and warlike and had weapons and armor of bronze and even houses of bronze. They worshipped the destructive works and instead of bread, ate hearts of fellow men. IN THE END, THEY WERE CONSUMED BY THEIR OWN RAGE, DESTROYING EACH OTHER, AND WERE SENT TO THE UNDERWORLD FOR ETERNITY, NEVER TO SEE THE LIGHT AGAIN.
According to THEOGONY OF
THE APOLLODORUS' BIBLIOTHECA, the BRONZE AGE **WAS ENDED BY THE DELUGE OR THE GREAT FLOOD,** set up by **Zeus** for being disappointed and outraged by the aggressive and cannibalistic **behavior** of the bronze race.
AGE OF HEROES came next. After the bronze age, Zeus created another race: an honorable race of heroes who were noble and respected the gods. Among them were also individuals with divine qualities, called demi-gods. Most of

them died in wars such as the Trojan war and Seven against Thebes. The souls of those who passed away went to a special place called the Elysian Fields or the Islands of the Blessed, somewhere in the Underworld, surrounded by deep-swirling <u>Oceanus</u>. **It was a place where the souls would remain forever and live a blessed and happy life in the same role they had enjoyed in life. It is also said that Zeus eventually promoted his father Cronus, from the depths of Tartarus, to become a ruler of the souls of these righteous and significant people.**

IRON AGE
And finally, **Zeus created the last race of man**, called the **IRON RACE**, where HESIOD PUTS HIMSELF IN. **It is a time of CONSTANT STRESS AND LABOUR. MORALITY IS GONE AND MEN ARE CONSTANTLY OPPOSING EACH OTHER, LYING AND SEEDING MISTRUST. IT IS A TIME WHERE HUMANS GROW OLD QUICKLY AND ARE CONSTANTLY BESET BY TROUBLES AND PRESSURES. AT THE PEAK OF THIS AGE, PEOPLE WILL NO LONGER FEEL SHAME OR REGRET AT WRONGDOING AND THERE WILL BE NO HELP AGAINST EVIL. MANKIND WILL BE FORSAKEN BY THE GODS AND**

GODDESSES AND ZEUS IS SET TO RETURN ONE DAY TO DESTROY THIS RACE, JUST LIKE HE HAD DONE IT IN THE PAST.
(I think THIS is what drew my attention to 'perhaps' all the other AGES' information mentioned and might just be true, because we SURE ARE GOING THROUGH WHAT IS MENTIONED FOR THIS IRON AGE.
The name <u>Zeus</u> just caught my eye ... Zeus/JESUS?! Is all this information about the different 'ages' revealing GOD/JESUS? Going back over the information, I see similarities being revealed that can be pertaining to God's creation and events. It would be connecting to 'there is nothing new under the sun' but through a different way.
The golden era was the world 'before' Adam and Eve, when all things were created and placed on the earth for us to enjoy. Being made in God's image, male and female, was the 'spiritual realm' we first existed in, in heaven. The description of that 'Golden age' is the goal we want to once again reach but can only do so at the 'final judgement' and can only be done by the way we live our lives at the 'final' call.
FOLKS... **'THIS IS THE FINAL CALL!'**

REINCARNATION

Jesus spoke to the people with parables and this, 'HESIOD'S WORKS AND DAYS, TRANSLATED BY HUGH G. EVELYN-WHITE' IS EXACTLY THAT.

When you put JESUS and GOD behind each story, our lives are laid out as things 'were', 'are', and 'will be'. (Thus, "There is nothing new under the sun.")

According to the Christian faith, God created Satan as an angel in heaven to serve Him [1]. Lucifer, also known as Satan, was initially created "blameless" with wisdom and perfect beauty [1]. However, he became consumed with pride over his splendor and desired to be higher than God [1]. Lucifer's rebellion against God, which ultimately led God to cast him out of heaven, was a path of Lucifer's own choosing [1].

As for other gods, the Christian faith believes in one God who created everything in the physical and spiritual realm, including angels and humans [1]. The Bible states that there is only one true God and that all other gods are false idols [1].

As God's creation, we know that Lucifer was created good. In fact, we're told that Satan was initially created "blameless"

with wisdom and perfect beauty. Lucifer became consumed with pride over his splendor, desiring to be higher than God.

https://www.christianity.com/

doloressmyth.crosswalk.com

(Remember the source I use for all my Biblical references is the KING JAMES AUTHORIZED online Bible with using the 1611 or standard versions. There have been times where I also actually copied from 'my own' King James version Bible copyrighted by The Methodist Publishing House in 1963 and manufactured in the United States of America.)

"Hidden, spurious, the name given to certain ancient books which" found a place in the LXX and Latin Vulgate versions of the Old Testament and were appended to all the great translations made from them in the sixteenth century, but which have no claim to be regarded as in any sense parts of the inspired Word.(1) They are not once quoted by the New Testament writers, who frequently quote from the LXX. Our

Lord and his apostles "confirmed by their authority the ordinary Jewish canon" which was the same in all respects as we now have it. (2) These books were written not in Hebrew but in Greek, and "during the" period of silence, from the time of Malachi, after which oracles and direct revelations from God ceased till the Christian era. (3) The contents of the books themselves show that they were no part of Scripture.

The Old Testament Apocrypha consists of fourteen books, the chief of which are the Books of the Maccabees (q.v.), the Books of Esdras, the Book of Wisdom, the Book of Baruch, the Book of Esther, Ecclesiasticus, Tobit, Judith, etc. The New Testament Apocrypha consists of a very extensive "literature, which bears distinct evidences of its non-apostolic" "origin and is utterly unworthy of regard."

Apocrypha

The apocrypha is a selection of books which were published in the original 1611 King James Bible. These

Apocryphal books were positioned between the Old and New Testament. (It also contained maps and genealogies). The Apocrypha was a part of the KJV for 274 years until being removed in 1885 A.D. A portion of these books were called deuterocanonical books by some entities such as the Catholic church.

Many claim the Apocrypha should never have been included in the first place, raising doubt about its validity and believing it was not God-inspired (for instance, a reference about magic seems inconsistent with the rest of the Bible: **Tobit chapter 6, verses 5-8**). Others believe it is valid and that it should never have been removed and that it was considered part of the Bible for nearly 2,000 years before it was recently removed a little more than 100 years ago. Some say it was removed because of not finding the books in the original Hebrew manuscripts. Others claim it wasn't removed by the church, but by printers to cut costs in distributing Bibles in the United States.

Both sides tend to cite the same verses that warn against adding or subtracting from the Bible: **Revelation 22:18.** The word '**Apocrypha**' means 'hidden'. Fragments of Dead Sea Scrolls dating back to before 70 A.D. contained parts of the Apocrypha books in Hebrew, including Sirach and Tobit. *(wikipedia.org/wiki)* [source]

Luther said, "Apocrypha--that is, books which are not regarded as equal to the holy Scriptures, and yet are profitable and good to read." (*King James Version Defended* page 98.)

"For I testify unto every man that heareth the words of the prophecy of this book, if any man shall add unto these things, God shall add unto him the plagues that are written in this book." Revelation 22:18 (KJV)

This is hard to understand in the way it is written. Just the people who gathered together to decide which books to use for the Bible are in fact adding or taking away books written material in existence. One group of people deciding what all people would be able to use goes against these very words. You can take scriptures from the Bible we do

have, and have fifteen ministers, or people, read them and you will get fifteen different answers as to what it says. How are we to know that books not accepted are books we should have?

Now we come to the point of 'Melchizedek' being without mother and father as the Bible says. With all of this being given as background, Bryne, (who is included in the 'dedication of this book', brought my attention to it.) He was close to having become a MONK and so with all the studying and research he did, he has this bit of information to add from sources.) He said there was a book of Enoch and while Enoch was mentioned here and in the Bible, there is no mention of there ever being a 'BOOK' of Enoch! In it gives the parents of Melchizedek and an awesome story behind it. Book of Enoch (aka 1 Enoch), composed in **Hebrew** or Aramaic and preserved in Ge'ez, first brought to Europe by James Bruce from Ethiopia and translated into English by August Dillmann and Reverend Schoode – recognized by the Orthodox Tewa Hedo churches and usually dated between the third century BC and the first century AD.
en.wikipedia.org/wiki/Enoc

The Book of Enoch is an ancient Hebrew Apocalyptic religious text ascribed by tradition to the patriarch Enoch who was the father of Methuselah and the great-grandfather of Noah[1]. The book contains unique material on the origins of demons and Nephilim, why some angels fell from heaven, an explanation of why the Genesis flood was morally necessary, and a prophetic exposition of the thousand-year reign of the Messiah[1]. Three books are traditionally attributed to Enoch, including the distinct works 2 Enoch and 3 Enoch[1]. None of the three books are considered to be canonical scripture by the majority of Jewish or Christian church bodies[1]. The older sections of 1 Enoch (mainly in the Book of the Watchers) of the text are estimated to date from about 300–200 BC, and the latest part (Book of Parables) is probably to 100 BC[1]. Modern scholars believe that Enoch was originally written in either Aramaic or Hebrew, the languages first used for Jewish texts[1]. Various Aramaic fragments found in the Dead Sea Scrolls, as well as Koine Greek and Latin fragments, are proof that the Book of Enoch was known by Jews and early Near Eastern Christians[1]. This book was also quoted by some 1st and 2nd century authors as in the Testaments of the Twelve Patriarchs[1]. Authors of the New Testament were also familiar with

some content of the story[1]. A short section of 1 Enoch (1:9) is cited in the New Testament Epistle of Jude, Jude 1:14–15, and is attributed there to "Enoch the Seventh from Adam." (1 Enoch 60:8), although this section of 1 Enoch is a midrash on Deuteronomy 33:2[1].
Learn more
1. **en.wikipedia.org**   2. **archive.org**
3. **christianity.com**   4. **thecollector.com**

All this is NEW even to ME, but I am being 'led' to a lot of places that I don't know about yet seem I am to share. Because of this, I am using many sources from the internet, Bible authorized dictionaries, encyclopedias, Wikipedia and so many more. This is why I chose from the beginning of the book to put 'my sources' right where I am using them. Most books give a list of materials used at the end of the book, but people mostly don't ever read it. By me putting where to find it WHEN I use it, people have a source to 'go to right then' to find more information should they wish or go back later to that topic area that held an interest of some sort and can then look it up.

As he prays, the altar is shaken and the knife leaps into his hand. From that time on he is honored as a prophet. Methusaleh remained at the altar of the Lord for ten years, during which time not a single person "turned away from vanity." (chapter 71) Methusaleh's son Lamech has two sons, Nir and Noe. After Methusaleh is given a disturbing vision of the coming flood, Nir is made a priest.

Methusaleh dies and people continue to turn away from the Lord. The devil, we are told, came to rule a third time (70:24-25).

Nir's wife Sopanim becomes pregnant in her old age, having been sterile (chapter 71). This is described as a "virgin" birth. While this story has elements similar to Matthew 2 and Luke 2, the differences are fantastic and legendary. She is embarrassed by this pregnancy and hides herself until the child is due. When Nir discovers she is pregnant, he rebukes her and intends to send her away because she has disgraced him, but instead she falls dead at his feet. Noe discovers this and tells Nir that the Lord has "covered up our scandal." They bury Sopanim in a black shroud in a secret grave.

The child, however, was not dead and came out of the dead mother as a fully developed child. This terrifies Nir and Noe, but since the child is "glorious in appearance" they realize the Lord is renewing the priesthood in their bloodline. They name the child Melchizedek. We are told that Melchizedek will be the head of "thirteen priests who existed before" and later there will be another Melchizedek who will be the head over twelve priests as an archpriest. Melchizedek is only with Nir for forty days, then the Lord instructs Michael to go and take the boy up to Enoch. The Lord calls him "my child Melchizedek". (72:1-2) The child is to be placed in Paradise forever. Nir is so grieved by the loss of his son, he also dies leaving no more priests in the world, allowing the world to become even more evil. Noe is therefore instructed to build the ark in chapter 73.

This strange miraculous birth story for Melchizedek is part of an interest in the King of Salem first mentioned in the Bible in Genesis 14:18. Psalm 110:4 describes the king/Messiah as a priest forever, in the order of Melchizedek. This text is cited twice in Hebrews 5:6-10 and 7:1-17 and applied to Jesus. The writer of Hebrews is likely tapping into a common image of a true priesthood which runs outside of the line of the Levites and Aaron. In the case of *2 Enoch*, the "legendary" elements of Melchizedek's story pre-date the flood. This could be used to argue for an early date for this section as well, since the Melchizedek legend was popular in the first century. It is possible a medieval writer created a pre-flood Melchizedek birth story, but it is more likely 2 Enoch is reflecting a first century or earlier tradition.

Melchizedek was an important figure for the Qumran community. *11QMelch* is a poorly preserved but important fragment in which the character Melchizedek is tied to Old Testament texts on the Jubilee and describes him as returning to proclaim liberty, probably based on Isaiah 61:1. There are no real parallels between this Melchizedek legend and anything in the first 16 thoughts on "Enoch and the Birth of Melchizedek Enoch 2: 64-73."

Pauline E. Petsel

It's time to put the book to bed

It's time to put this book to bed and allow you to keep anything you reaped from it to penetrate deep within you and allow your 'soul' to <u>find the truth within</u>. The book may have been different for everyone. It may have been a mystery, adventure, enlightenment or awakening, a fantasy or fairytale, brain teaser, puzzle to conquer, or a book of information to ponder over and test your logic or beyond. For some, it is trash and brings out pure negative emotions of ridiculousness and was a waste of money and time. This book was again continuing to drive me nuts. With things seeming to 'come to me' which I had no knowledge of, so had to research the Bible dictionary, dictionaries, 'authorized' King James Bible standard edition online, and numerous 'online' computer sources. I had had it and once more was ready to trash the whole thing. This book was way off from what the original book was 'planned' to be. This time our minister became involved, without his being aware of it. Several times he would say, "I don't know why, but for some reason I've changed my sermon from what I originally had planned it to be." Each of those times his 'new

REINCARNATION

message' seemed to be directed at me. It either gave me words to tell me not to give up, or at times he even used the book of the Bible and verses I needed to find my answers for where I was writing. One time something happened and I laughed to myself.

"Ya, let's see if he covers this one!" Two days later at church...'he did'!

So, when I get 'tarred and feathered' and 'kicked out of the church' when my book comes out about reincarnation, 'He' will have 'unknowingly' been a 'part' for it getting published!

The body has 'inner abilities' to help get us through life. **Emotions can be positive or negative and can lead us to peace and progress or to dissention and anger actions. It can make us believe or disbelieve.**

The 'mind' can help us by using the two parts of our brain to make decisions. However, if the right side of creativity is used, we could create ourselves into a wrong direction but the left side of rationalization can also give us the wrong conclusion. We can say, "The scientists, investigators, and highly educated specialized experts should 'know', so we need to believe them". Yet someone else can look at pictures and remember the saying that 'pictures are worth a thousand words' and with no one having the answers after all these years of investigations, maybe the 'pictures' are revealing the true fact.

There is still one more thing we are gifted with. **"GUT FEELING"**! The 'gut feeling' can't be weighed for decision of yes or no, or 'no emotions' tied with a decision. The 'gut' is just that. Not changeable. You can go **'against'** <u>what you feel</u> (in the 'gut'), but then 'that' weighs on your mind because you feel the clashing within. Your 'mind' by itself can't always be reliable because we tend to try to sway it to the 'way we **want** it to be', yet when it matches the 'gut feeling' it is a winner!

 So, what does your 'gut' tell you about the book, information in the book, or 'pictures shown' in the book? If there is no strong 'gut feeling', you are still 'waiting' to <u>get more information before deciding for sure,</u> so are not 'accepting or denying' the information for sure yet.

I hope that at least 'somewhere' in the 'book' it has given you 'something' in a POSITIVE WAY that will cause you to retain the information, thought, feeling, emotion, memory, or interest, so it might act as a 'seed' with which to grow.

REINCARNATION

I wish you 'LOVE, Good Health, and Inner Peace.'
PAULINE E. PETSEL

The Prayer everyone knows and says all the time may be different as to how 'you' <u>say it</u> and what is meant. Again, 'punctuation' comes into place or this case where you end your 'voice' for a second.
"Our father...who art in heaven...Hallowed be Thy name... Thy kingdom come....Thy will be done...on earth as it is...in heaven...Give us this day...our daily bread...and lead us not into temptation...but deliver us from evil...for thine is the kingdom...and the power...and the glory forever...Amen.
NOW look at what you are saying: Our Father who art in heaven. Hallowed be Thy name...Thy 'kingdom come,' thy 'will' be done on <u>EARTH</u> **'AS IT IS'** in HEAVEN...Give us this day our daily bread and lead us not into temptation but deliver us from evil... for thine is the 'kingdom' <u>and the 'power' and the 'glory forever' ... Amen.</u>
<u>And...It IS (the book) now finished!</u>

Pauline E. Petsel

Acknowledgments

I want to add a big 'THANK YOU' to TWO people, who if it were not for them in the final stages, the book would never have gotten done. My great neighbor, Rebecca B., who has come over so many times to get my computer working and after the storms, we've had to get me back to a working condition. (Her husband Tony has helped me since my husband passed away with doing yard and maintenance work and giving me directions for other things I am at a loss of knowing.)

My daughter, Kristie, has worked with me to learn how to find things I screwed up myself on the computer (which I know nothing about). God puts people in places of needs if we are lucky enough to be aware of it.

Pauline E. Petsel

www.ingramcontent.com/pod-product-compliance
Lightning Source LLC
Chambersburg PA
CBHW050119170426
43197CB00011B/1639